FRENCH ALL AROUND US

French Language and Francophone Culture
in the United States.

Kathleen Stein-Smith & Fabrice Jaumont (editors)

TBR Books
New York - Paris

TBR Books is a program of the Center for the Advancement of Languages, Education, and Communities. We publish researchers and practitioners who seek to engage diverse communities on topics related to education, languages, cultural history, and social initiatives.

CALEC - TBR Books
750 Lexington Avenue, 9th floor
New York, NY 10022
USA
www.calec.org | contact@calec.org
www.tbr-books.org | contact@tbr-books.org

ISBN 978-1-63607-208-1 (paperback)
ISBN 978-1-63607-244-9 (hardcover)
ISBN 978-1-63607-245-6 (ebook)

Library of Congress Control Number: 2021953265

Foreword

From the streets of Wall Street to the beaches of California, listen, and you will hear this dulcet language, sometimes even monotonous, so particular and yet so resounding as it embodies such a large chunk of French-speaking cultures: The French language. Often categorized as an official diplomatic language, it is much more – I am deeply convinced of that. As you read *French All Around Us: French Language and Francophone Culture in the United States of America*, you will discover the driving force of culture that is the French language. A fundamental tool for the socio-historical construction of a culture, it seems to me necessary to recall the fundamental place that language occupies in our interpersonal relationships and in our plural identities.

Often, when the exchanges are recurrent and take a preponderant place, internalized language and culture mingle with the adopted culture, creating multilingual and multicultural individuals and an adaptive subculture which, depending on the environment, will highlight different aspects of their multicultural identity. A true standard of Francophone cultures internationally, the French language has achieved the feat of bringing together individuals from diverse backgrounds around the world-- bringing together 300 million Francophones in more than 80 countries. The following volume retraces the history of the French language and French-speaking culture in the United States in all its complexity and beauty.

From the implementation of the first French-American and French dual-language immersion programs in urban centers to the reappropriation of French culture by the French-speaking descendants of Louisiana or New England, the contributors, whether researchers or practitioners, tell the story of an atypical and fascinating cultural amalgamation.

In a globalized world where intercultural relations, although numerous, are sometimes delicate, cultivating a common history seems to be a necessity. From the building of the United States of America to the present day, Francophone cultures have always, in one way or another, existed on American soil, both inside and outside the North American borders.

Whatever the prism of the study, whether it is an institutional question - especially within international organizations like the United Nations - historical, cultural, or migratory, the conclusion is always similar.

Francophone culture, like its North American Anglophone counterpart, has a strong identity — a phenomenon which, far from creating a force of opposition, has on the contrary created a mechanism of attraction and reciprocal fascination. Many intellectuals such as Tocqueville have thus crossed the ocean from one land to another to observe the functioning mechanisms and the cultural particularities of this Other, so different and attractive. Close links were thus built between these two apparently diametrically opposed cultures, one originating from old Europe, from its former colonies and former protectorates, for the other of the New World.

This corpus of texts thus sits between the essay, the textbook, and the sharing of experiences to allow the reader to immerse themselves in this multicultural world apart. From page to page, myriad politico-linguistic issues, sociological discussions, and personal feelings mingle to sketch out the reality of French and Francophone cultures in the United States.

—Philippe Etienne
Ambassador of France to the United States.
Washington, DC – January 2022

Praises

French language and Francophone Culture in the United States is a fascinating travel, deep into American culture and the many Francophone components of the country. I should like to highlight the contribution of the Association for the Advancement of French Language and Francophone Culture in the United States book project to a better understanding of the vitality of the Francophonie, its diversity and its presence in the daily life of so many people living in the United States.

In 2018, for the first time, a US State, Louisiana, joined the International Organization of La Francophonie (OIF). The OIF, which celebrated its fiftieth anniversary in 2020, was born in Niger (Africa). From 21 founding Member States, the Organization grew to one of the largest intergovernmental Organizations with 88 Member States and Governments, on five continents. The adhesion of Louisiana represents a milestone, which raises our awareness on the longstanding practice of French in Louisiana, its current challenges and opportunities. The vitality of French Language and Francophone Cultures in so many other US States is heartwarming. It is fragile though, and we feel responsible for this unique heritage.

Education is critical for the future of the Francophonie as emphasized in many contributions, all brilliant in the scope of insights and perspectives provided. I am humbled by the amount of work and passion, at all levels – parents, students, educators, authorities -, that make bilingual education in French a reality in American public schools in 2022. I express my warmest congratulations to all contributors and sincerely thank them for this very inspiring endeavor. Your call to action is heard. We will fully play our role.

—Ambassador Ifigeneia Kontoleontos
Permanent Observer for the International Organization of
La Francophonie (OIF) to the United Nations

Through this collection of essays, I understand my own family's story more clearly. In the 1960s, my mémère, pépère, and my dad moved from a rural town in Québec to Maine to work in Biddeford's textile mills. They were French-speaking immigrants who felt pressure to keep the French language from the next generation. My grandparents believed success could not be realized for their kids and grandkids unless they sounded more like those of English descendants.

As a child, I did not learn French at home. However, as an adult, I've gained a deep appreciation for my Franco heritage. Becoming Maine's Speaker of the House has given me a new perspective. I am only the second Franco speaker in Maine's history. I now believe we have the opportunity to help a new generation of French-speaking immigrants recognize the importance of protecting language and culture—and treasuring it. This text is a testament to the resilience of those who have preserved the language and traditions that are at the heart of who we are.

—Representative Ryan Michael Fecteau,
Speaker of the House of Representatives, The State of Maine.

Acknowledgements

The authors would like to express their appreciation to everyone who has encouraged and participated in this Association for the Advancement of the French Language and Francophone Culture in the United States (AAFLFC) book project and to all supporters of French language and Francophone culture in the United States and beyond. This project has been a wonderful experience from the very beginning, bringing together many voices, each with a unique story and perspective, and inspired by interesting and enlightening conversations with many of the chapter authors.

Special thanks to French Ambassador to the United States Philippe Étienne for his willingness to author the Preface, and to Ambassador Ifigeneia Kontoleontos, Permanent Observer for the International Organization of La Francophonie (OIF) to the United Nations and Representative Ryan Michael Fecteau, Speaker of the House of Representatives, The State of Maine, for their support. Heartfelt thanks to French Consul General in New York, Jérémie Robert, for his gracious interest and encouragement, and to the French cultural andeducational team at the Embassy of France for all that they do topromote multilingualism and bilingual learning in the United States.

Heartfelt thanks to all the chapter authors for sharing their stories, perspectives, and experiences – Mélissa Baril, Timothy Beaulieu, Elizabeth Blood, David Cheramie, Melody Desjardins, Anthony DesRois, Joseph Dunn, Georgie Ferguson, Katharine Harrington, Marine Havel, Marguerite Justus, Emmanuel Kayembe, Étienne Kouakou, Mark Labine, Ben Levine and Julia Schulz, Jesse Martineau and Monique Cairns, Jean Mirvil, Jerry Parker, Robert Perreault, Scott Tilton, Agnès Ndiaye Tounkara, and David Vermette.

We would also like to thank the members of the AAFLFC Advisory Board for all that they do and for their support of this project, especially Timothy Beaulieu, Joseph Dunn, Jesse Martineau, Julia Schulz, and Scott Tilton, who are among the authors.

Thank you to TBR Books, the publishing division of The Center for the Advancement of Languages, Education, and Communities, and to CALEC's board of directors, advisory council, and global supporters for their belief in this project. Lastly, a thank you to all French language supporters in the United States and beyond.

—Kathleen Stein-Smith and Fabrice Jaumont

Table of Contents

Introduction
Kathleen Stein-Smith & Fabrice Jaumont

The significance of the French language and Francophone culture in France and around the world is widely known and respected, and its impact on the United States – including the role of French ideas and of French aid and military support during the American Revolution – is common knowledge. French culture – including not only literature and the arts, but also entertainment, media, fashion, and cuisine – is more popular than ever before among Americans, and Americans generally have a positive attitude toward France. French is also the second most widely studied foreign language in the United States, as it is around the world. It places second in the list of the most common languages of which the teaching is offered in primary, middle and high schools, after Spanish, and before Latin, German and Chinese.

The vitality of the French language in the United States is a particularly interesting case, because native Francophones are represented by several communities, each with distinct geographical and historical circumstances, which also include both recent immigrants and descendants of centuries-old settlements. Paradoxically, French heritage language speakers in the United States encounter many obstacles to maintain the language that was passed on to them by their ancestors. Franco-Americans, Acadians in Maine, and Cajuns and Creoles in Louisiana testify to efforts to protect and revitalize French as a heritage language. In large urban centers, French expatriate communities and recent Francophone immigrants have collaborated to ensure the French language is maintained. It is not only a question of maintaining a cultural identity, but also of charting a path towards academic success and financial security. In the historic regions of Maine and Louisiana, while the study of French is promoted for Anglophones in public schools, Francophones by family or country of origin have ironically encountered significant obstacles to continue to use their language. In New York, socio-economic factors and the essential need to learn English discourage French-speaking immigrant community members from maintaining and developing their level of French.

In this book, we highlight the efforts made by these various French language communities in the United States to preserve the use of French in families, schools and larger communities. These efforts include the establishment of formal educational initiatives adapted to those who identify as Francophones by family or country of origin, as well as by public policies that have revitalized and encouraged the maintaining of French in various social and economic contexts. These include long-standing Franco-American and Acadian communities in Maine and the Houmas and Cajuns in Louisiana, who seek to stimulate the use of French after years of neglect and persecution in their local communities. In addition, we take a closer look at the situation of expatriates and Francophone immigrants in New York who have succeeded in creating bilingual programs in public schools so that their children have the opportunity to maintain and develop their fluency in French.

The presence of large Francophone communities in the United States is not surprising. French is the seventh most commonly spoken language in the country after English, Spanish, Chinese, Tagalog, Vietnamese, and Arabic (United States Census Bureau, 2019). It is very likely that the real number of Francophones residing in the United States is much higher than official estimates, especially if we take into account the large number of illegal immigrants. Some Francophones also speak several languages fluently. According to his research on Haitian Americans, Flore Zéphir (2004) estimates that 20% of them also speak French, in addition to Creole and English. It is the same for people who choose to declare Arabic, Wolof or any other language, during censuses, and who could just as easily declare themselves as Francophones. Finally, the growth of the population of French-speaking countries, in Africa in particular, suggests that the number of French-speaking people in large American cities will continue to grow, in part thanks to immigration.

The French language is particularly common in historically French-speaking regions such as Louisiana and Maine, but also in urban centers where there has been an increase in French-speaking immigrants. Acadians and other French-speaking Canadians settled in the north of New England and in New York State in the 18th and 19th century, while Louisiana was originally a French colony. These historically French-speaking regions have been able to preserve the local dialects despite persecution and limited opportunities for using any language other than English. This courageous act of preservation is due to the inhabitants who continued to use the variations of the French language within families and within their communities. Thus, French is an interesting example of the vitality of a heritage language, not only because of the geographic and historical diversity of its speakers, but also because of its vernacular varieties that continue to be recognized under the great umbrella of "Francophonie", as the chapters of this book clearly demonstrate. The authors' various perspectives on language preservation and language development strategies will help readers understand the level of vitality of the United States' French speakers. From personal accounts to professional and scholarly inquiry, our authors have examined how language transmission occurs through formal and informal communication in communities of French heritage language speakers. Our authors also explore the use of the language and the opportunities created by distinct groups such as the Franco-Americans and Acadians of Maine; the Cajuns, Creoles, and Houmas of Louisiana; the Haitians, West Africans and French in New York, Miami, or Los Angeles (Chik, 2022; Jaumont & Ross, 2016; Garcia et. al., 2012). What has emerged is a landscape rich in opportunities for Francophones who seek to maintain and transmit their linguistic heritage to other French speakers, heritage language learners, and those who identify as culturally Francophone in the United States.

This book tells the story of French language and Francophone culture in the United States from the perspectives of Franco-Americans, including both academic and historical accounts. These stories are written from a variety of disciplinary and regional perspectives, and feature deeply personal and moving family narratives of language and culture as part of the authors' cultural identity. They tell the compelling stories of Francophone individuals, communities, and organizations, who have figured prominently among those who have built the United States, and who provide inspiration for the present and future. Driven in part by impact of the COVID-19 pandemic on all aspects of American life and the lack of information on and awareness of the full breadth and depth of the Francophone experience in the United States, this book project began in early 2021 with a call for proposals from the Advisory Board of the

Association for the Advancement of the French Language and Francophone Culture in the United States (AAFLFC). Interested authors were invited to submit a proposal for a book chapter on the impact of French language and Francophone culture on their lives, any efforts of theirs to advance the cause in the United States, and their thoughts on the future of French in the US. The proposal, or research question, was deliberately phrased in general terms in order to encourage the widest range of potential authors, reflecting the true scope of the Francophone experience in the US. The response was overwhelming, as demonstrated by the diversity and number of authors and stories. In an often-quantitative world, the depth of feeling and affection toward the French language and Francophone cultures expressed by the authors is the unifying theme in diverse accounts spanning time and geography, and reflecting academic, historical, contemporary, and family interests and experiences.

The organization of the book has been driven by the nature of the story. Rather than reflecting the development of a single story, the chapters are very different, each reflecting the experience and insights of one or two individuals, so an alphabetical and regional sequence was indicated, and in no way implies any difference in value or importance. The chapters highlight the geographic distribution of Francophones spanning the nation. The order of the chapters may appear arbitrary at first glance, but this order is also alphabetical, and is in no way intended to prioritize any one particular part of the country. Within each section, the authors are listed in alphabetical order by last name. The Francophonie in the United States reflects the diversity of the Francophone world globally, in terms of where Francophones are currently located (basically, everywhere, across the country), but also in terms of their countries and cultures of origin. In light of this diversity, it seemed appropriate to begin the story with global voices, and the first four chapters, written by Marine Havel, Emmanuel Kayembe, Étienne Kouakou, and Agnès Ndiaye Tounkara, reflect not only the diversity of the Francophone world but also represent the very real and present challenges facing new American families wishing to maintain their heritage language.

The subsequent sections include authors of Francophone heritage residing in various regions of the country, beginning with Louisiana, followed by the Midwest, the Northeast, and the South. In the section on Louisiana, David Cheramie, Joseph Dunn, Marguerite Justus,

Jerry L. Parker, Georgie Ferguson, and Scott Tilton tell the story of the Francophonie in Louisiana from historical, contemporary, community and educational perspectives. In the section on the Midwest, Mélissa Baril and Mark Labine highlight the power of the written word and of language in general, as well as the depth of our shared French and American historical experience. In the section on the Northeast, Timothy Beaulieu, Elizabeth Blood, Melody Desjardins, Katharine Harrington, Ben Levine, Julia Schulz, Jesse Martineau, Monique Cairns, Jean Mirvil, Robert Perreault, and David Vermette tell the story of French language and Francophone culture in the Northeastern United States from the earliest times to contemporary global and diverse Francophone communities. In the final regional section, on the South, Anthony DesRois skillfully weaves together the impact of the French language and Francophone culture on the past, present, and future, establishing the linkages between his French-Canadian heritage, his personal journey, and what the future may hold for the next generations.

These stories reflect the experiences and insights of the descendants of early settlers in North America from France and the Caribbean. They are also stories of the French Canadians, Québécois, and Acadians who came to the United States at the time of the *Grand Dérangement*, the rise of the textile industry in New England, and at other times throughout our history. For this reason, many Americans of French heritage are among the many Americans who no longer speak their heritage language. Notwithstanding language loss, this remains their story, too. Indeed, the challenges are legion and the maintaining of French as a "living" language in the United States is not without difficulty. We cannot forget the harmful effects of past repressions, especially in French-speaking areas (Maine, Louisiana) where anti-French language laws, accompanied by brutality and criminal acts, forced Francophones to go into hiding for much of the early 20th century. More recent laws, particularly those ratified in Louisiana in 1968, and in Maine more recently, create more reassuring and favorable conditions to the sustainable development of the country's French-speaking heritage. These institutional supports attempt to increase the possibilities of education and of passing on the language to the next generation. This is the case for initiatives that support dual-language immersion, where learning French complements the acquisition of the English language, not threatening it in any way.

These stories are sure to inspire all of us – those who speak French, those who do not, and those who aspire to do so. However, it is not just a question of French, but of the learning and use of additional languages, whether they are heritage or new languages. Learning a language offers a wonderful window into another culture, whether it is the culture of our family or the language of another culture that interests and fascinates us for any number of reasons. Our world includes many languages and many cultures, as does the United States. Knowledge of other languages and cultures in an essential skill, and tool, for global citizens. However, this story – while part of United States history – is still being written by Francophones from France, the Caribbean, Africa and from around the world who continue to arrive on United States shores, making America and the United States their home. The present and future mosaic of United States culture and identity is multilingual, as has been its history, and this mosaic includes French. For those who believe in a multilingual United States and society, the advantages are clear – cultural, cognitive, and professional value for the individual; social and economic benefits to our society; and, most importantly, the recognition of our diversity as a core United States value.

In the United States, speakers of a language other than English undergo constant assimilation pressures, in the midst of a sea of English and dominant monolingualism and linguistic hegemony around the world (Salomone, 2021). Francophones in this country are no exception to this rule and strive as best they can to maintain the use of French at home, at school and in their communities, thanks to transmission and appropriate forms of teaching, as well as solidarity between speakers of multiple origins. The population of Franco-Americans long established in the United States provides proof, for their part, of a strong desire to maintain, even revitalize "their French", after a long decline often linked to forms of more or less violent discrimination.

The challenges are many, as are the rewards, and the challenges include a historical tendency toward assimilation and language loss in the United States. Just as Francophones and Francophone culture form part of the fabric of the United States, past and present, so too does the process of ensuring the future of French in the US. Children and young people are our present and future, and it is essential that all our children and students have the opportunity to learn heritage and additional languages, including French, from the earliest age. Increasing awareness of the benefits of language learning and the use of additional languages and increasing access to language learning are essential in safeguarding the multilingual and Francophone future of the US. Beyond the classroom, it is important to provide opportunities to use French in meaningful and authentic situations in the workplace and in daily life. French language supporters, advocates, and stakeholders can play an important role in strengthening French language and Francophone culture in the United States by supporting the development of French language programs in the earliest grade levels in our public schools and online. This support is especially important for immersion programs, and in developing funding for after-school, weekend, summer, and study abroad programs, so that all interested students have the opportunity to attend. Access and affordability are key advocacy goals.

The solution is to work together. As we know, *l'union fait la force*. We can all play a role in increasing awareness of the benefits of language learning and language use among our families, communities, and in our educational, social, and public institutions. The more creative among us can make French and Francophone culture a vibrant, living force that transcends history. The resurgence of French includes not only those who speak French and those in the United States of French ancestry, but also all those who love and respect the French language and Francophone culture in France and beyond.

The lives of French-speaking peoples or people who identify with French-speaking cultures in the United States are incredibly diverse and nuanced. Francophones in this country define themselves by historical, geographical, cultural or socio-economic criteria that are all in constant mutation. Some Francophones, descendants of first settlers, succeeded in transmitting their language over several generations, even several centuries. Starting with refugees from Europe and Canada, the 17th and 18th century, settled in the states of New England, the Midwest and the great South. Other Francophones, more recently established, get rid of their French after a few years, failing to find a favorable context to maintain it. Generally speaking, French speakers in the United States who are very quick to organize and mobilize, educationally and culturally, do not lose their French and encourage the transmission of their inheritance to their children. These French speakers increase the economic potential of their family or community network and guarantee the vitality and sustainability of French in their new environment (Ross and Jaumont, 2014).

Maintaining French, or any other language besides English, in the United States has usually been a difficult task, met with internal and external forces of resistance. Throughout the much controversial history of learning foreign or heritage languages in the United States, the French language has long enjoyed a privileged status. It continues to be the second most studied foreign language in schools and universities, after Spanish (American Councils, 2017). As a result, the community of Francophones stands out from other immigrant communities by the significant place occupied by the French taught as foreign language in the United States (Rhodes and Pufahl, 2010).With more than a million pupils learning French, it is obvious that the linguistic self-defense of Francophones is not the same as that ofother immigrant communities.

However, the emphasis placed on the teaching of 'Parisian French' had the consequence of slowing down the use of other types of French outside of family contexts. Therefore, and not without irony, the historic regions, endowed with a strong presence of Francophones, are those who probably most encountered the phenomenon of stigmatization in formal educational settings for speaking "French at home" within the Franco-American communities, rather than the use of "noble" French, "good French". Access to these classes is often difficult for native French speakers, but initiatives such as those carried out by the Council for the Development of French in Louisiana (CODOFIL), those of the French Heritage Language Program (New York, Maine, Florida, Massachusetts), or the actions taken by parents' associations such as Education in French (in New York, San Francisco, Houston, Atlanta, among others) offer innovative solutions that allow for French to be passed on through schools, while encouraging the development of a dynamic linguistic community.

In large urban centers, socio-economic factors, associated with the virtual obligation to master English for societal success in the United States, tend to discourage members of Francophone immigrant communities in their maintaining or transmission of French. It is clear that the new immigrants from Africa, the Caribbean and the Middle East encourage the practice of English in the home, while privileging that of the dialect language, rather than French, which becomes the third language spoken in the homes. Some counterexamples can be found, like that of the Malian community of the Bronx which, deeply attached to the French language, strives to teach French as well as Bambara, during classes for younger ones organized on Saturdays.

In addition, Francophone immigrant communities from West Africa and Haiti play a decisive role in the dissemination of French at cultural centers, places of worship and through community media, thereby enabling families to maintain a link, albeit fragile, to the French language. As to communities of expatriates, such as European and Canadian families, they have succeeded in creating bilingual programs and extracurricular education in French in public schools. These developments are most easily seen in large urban centers, such as New York, Miami, Los Angeles, particularly among those who cannot afford to pay the high costs of tuition that private bilingual schools require. (Leveen, 2021; Ross, 2020; Jaumont, 2017).

Some basic tenets for helping families and community groups to keep up their heritage language have occurred to us. To promote the learning of a heritage language among the younger people, communities must insert them into local educational institutions, consequently becoming more valuable as organizations and as people, especially when we measure the impact of a good school on a district or a city. This principle has been particularly well illustrated within the Francophone communities in large American cities where parents from very different backgrounds have become builders of educational opportunities for their children. It is thanks to the ethnic and socio-cultural diversity of this great linguistic and cultural family that is the Francophonie, that the French language is regaining ground in the United States. In addition, the collaboration between multiple community partners with varied profiles, from government agencies to parent associations, fosters and encourages the promotion of multilingualism in educational institutions of a country often criticized for its lack of interest in the learning of world languages.

1. FLAM Kids: a network of US-French bilingual ambassadors for the future.
Marine Havel

Parenting a child in a different country is a unique experience, forcing us to think about our connections with our own families, our native language, our homeland, as well as our newly adopted country. On February 21, 1999, UNESCO announced the inception of the annual International Mother Language Day, to commemorate and honor the world's linguistic diversity and multilingualism, by celebrating the power of languages to build peace and sustainability. Language is a passport to discovering the world, a key to opening doors, understanding other cultures, and building bridges between them, which strengthens our collective relationships, and our kindness towards people's differences, benefits which can be especially rewarding in the United States.

There are many ways to educate à child in a bilingual environment: tutoring, private school, immersive summer camps, or a dedicated afterschool program for native speakers. This last example has several iterations across world languages, such as *Agrupación de Lengua y Cultura españolas* (ALCE) for Spanish speakers around the world; or the German Saturday school network; or FLAM - *Français Langue maternelle* (French as a native language) - for the French-speaking children. This program is supported by the French government, through the agency in charge of education of French language abroad (the AEFE). Our FLAM mission is simple: to make sure that no child will lose her/his/their language, their cultural heritage, their identity as global citizens, their link to their family and to the Francophone world. An exemplary training ground for bilingualism, the FLAM community prepares us to welcome children of the Francophone local community coming from all over the world, and to begin to understand the diversity of lives abroad, including those of expatriates and immigrants.

There are now more than twenty FLAM organizations in the United States, offering lessons to more than 3,500 students. This is thanks to the devotion of 300 teachers, coordinators, directors and volunteers. In 2017, we launched with all these directors, the

Federation FLAM USA, to share information, best practices, resources; to expand our mission objectives, offer more to our students, collectively and individually; and, lastly, to demystify multilingualism by imagining a "FLAM 2.0". As a result, at the outbreak of the COVID-19 pandemic, we were ready to support all FLAM teachers in the United States, to be sure that all FLAM students could continue to receive an education in French. Education is the most powerful tool for a nation and its peoples. France understands this well. Its soft diplomacy has helped maintain French as a major world language in spite of English predominance around the globe

What is a maternal language? Paternal too!

I have lived in Philadelphia since 2005. Since those early days, I was in love with the city and Philadelphians, who were always enthusiastically trying to speak French with our family. My oldest child was a baby when we moved to Philadelphia, and my son was born here, the most Francophile city on this side of the Atlantic. Lafayette was commemorated all summer long at Valley Forge with military reenactments. Bastille Day is celebrated each year downtown. Even recently, when the beautiful Museum of the American Revolution was created, historical guides have systematically referred to the strong friendship between our two countries.

Americans, in general, love the French language and culture. Even during the "freedom fries" diplomatic crisis of the early 2000s, my husband, who was traveling in Nashville, Tennessee at the time, still remembers the heartwarming welcome of so many people who smiled when they heard talk of Paris and dreamed of visiting France one day. On Netflix, *Emily in Paris* is a hit (despite all the clichés). French is sexy! Everybody is in love with Timothée Chalamet and his Frenchy "*je ne sais quoi*"!

French abroad: parenting bilingual kids

Timothée is what we call "*un français de l'étranger,*" or a "French person abroad," in the French community within the United States. His father is French and made sure he would continue to speak

French. What I did not realize when we moved to the United States is that it would be so difficult to carry this out. As expatriates and immigrants facing multiple challenges professionally and personally, we have had to make important decisions regarding our children without a lot of support and without having all the knowledge ourselves. Concerning their education, their language: Which system should we choose? French? US? International? Public? International Baccalaureate? Which is the better choice for our children: Should we immerse them entirely in the American education system or should we continue to speak French at home even when it is so difficult after a long day at work. In addition, how can we support our teenage children who are going through intense questions about cultural and linguistic identity?

I will always remember the despair in the eyes of a friend, whose five-year-old son told her abruptly one day: "Stop talking to me in French, I do not want to be different". We had to act. We had to show them that speaking another language, speaking French is important; that the rest of the world is bilingual, even multilingual. We had to share ourselves, our values with them, through our language, which is ultimately, according to Albert Camus, our homeland, so far away from our birth country.

That is why it was necessary to create PhilaFLAM back in 2012. For my friend's children, and for mine too, of course, with whom I wanted to share this amazing opportunity of being a global citizen-- multicultural and bilingual-- We can then share this with all the countries where we will live, with all the people with whom we will cross paths one day. As an army brat, I know how rich this act of sharing is for oneself and for our society, when a whole generation brings forth the best from each of their respective worlds. Let us share. Let us exchange ideas and bring together the best of both worlds, the United States and France.

Our primary language, our homeland

The primary language of a child is first and foremost the language of personal identity, but this identity can be rejected when the child grows up. A few months after we moved to the United States, I was shocked to see so many Francophone families with children who stopped talking or even understanding French. We take for granted that our children will speak to us in our language. It is a constant, daily effort because every day they spend hours playing and studying in English. Between siblings, the language used at home quickly becomes the one used at school, at daycare, on the playground. So many times, we say, with a huge smile when they are home, "*en français!*" ("in French please!"), each day with less and less impact. Many parents stopped trying, choosing their battles, prioritizing for the sake of their family. They need support. Children need to see that others are bilingual like them. They need structure, a school where bilingualism "happens." It is much easier than it seems to create a FLAM school in the community that needs it. Ten years after I launched PhilaFLAM, my husband still tells the story of the day I informed him "I am creating a French Saturday School!" He tells of how he believed it would take years to create the infrastructure, find a location, recruit teachers and how stunned he was when everything was done in mere weeks! When PhilaFLAM was created, we helped twenty-five students near Philadelphia, and after only a few years, we answered the French-speaking community's calls to rapidly create five other heritage schools: in Exton PA, Princeton NJ, Allentown PA, Newtown PA, and in Hoboken, NJ. We counted close to 250 students in all in September 2021 in the middle of the pandemic. In less than ten years, we were able to help ten times more students. Our students have a 100% success rate with major international exams like DELF B2, and the French International Baccalaureate exam. Our secret: find the best teachers, those who are passionate about their work and do everything they need to do to support their students.

> If only we, as a society, invested more in education, and especially in language lessons.

France has an entire worldwide system for French people abroad, including elected representatives to represent these 2.5 million French citizens who live outside of the Hexagon. They are immigrants, expatriates, employees, or entrepreneurs, working in French Tech and other successful French companies; "*détachés*" in our embassies and consulates or in one of the French International Private Schools which form the well-known network of French Education Abroad institutions. Budgets, which together represent several billion euros, are voted on each year to support the cultural and linguistic development of French through these schools, the French Alliances network, and many other cultural initiatives.

During the Olympic Games in Tokyo, we learned that another French Person Abroad, Romain Cannone, had spent most of his youth abroad in Brazil and the USA: we were all so proud! But what if he had lost his French? What if he had lost his link and love of his birth country? There are a hundred times more celebrities of French descent who do not speak or understand French today: Beyoncé Knowles, Angelina Jolie, Jessica Alba, Charlize Theron... How many other children do not speak their maternal or paternal language anymore? Millions.

According to the French Ministry of Foreign Affairs, up until a few years ago, three out of four French children abroad did not have access to an education in French, and inevitably they stopped being Francophone very quickly. How many times at the French elections polling place, in our very own French International school of Philadelphia, do we see eighteen-year-old French citizens, pushed by their parents to participate, and vote in these French Abroad elections? They, sadly, cannot understand anything we are telling them in French. And how many are not even coming out to vote, because they do not feel any attachment to their birth country or their cultural heritage? We have failed them. Collectively.

Why are we spending billions to teach *Français Langue Etrangère* (FLE) to non-native speakers, while we are not able to keep millions of children fluent in French? That is why in 2018, the Federation FLAM USA has been invited to participate in the French Assemblée Nationale, to the first major conference that includes all the stakeholders in French Education Abroad (EFE). This conference was organized by Samantha Cazebonne, *Députée des Français de l'Étranger*, whose very important work once again put the FLAM organizations in the spotlight, promoting the need to develop alternative solutions for providing an education to the Francophone children without access to the French International schools' network.

The recognition of the educational needs of all FLAM children

Many French abroad Representatives and Senators already recognized the work from the French abroad community who started to organize themselves and provide activities for the children in many countries. The FLAM program is not new: it was created in 2001 and developed rapidly in the United States in the past ten years. It is now a global network of 170 organizations that gives an education in French for all the kids who did not have access to the French private schools for geographic, economic, and many other practical reasons, keeping them in a Francophone learning environment.

Many FLAM leaders, after two decades of experience, know that we have to approach each student differently because, in practice, there are many ways to be FLAM, and it is important to understand that it is not that always easy to tell a child's what a "maternal" language. First of all, it can be a paternal language! I see year after year, many dads eager to transmit their language to their kids. The new generation is very involved in making sure their children receive a proper education in both languages. After all, we also use the words, father and fatherland in English. Every child is different, and each of their stories in this French path is beautiful. Some kids were born in a French-speaking country with French speaking parents. Others were born here but both parents continue to read to them in French. It is both their maternal and paternal language. But what about the FLAM children who learn two or three languages at birth in a multicultural and multilingual family? Which one is their primary language? And what about after a few years, when they start daycare or preschool, when the language in which they were born is becoming a second language, breaking its bond to them, because of the complete immersion in the United States school system? It takes a tremendous amount of effort for parents to maintain that linguistic umbilical cord to their children, transmitting more than words: an identity, a cultural heritage, an attachment to their ancestors.

We welcome kids from pre-K, but sometimes older students as well. A teenager who would have seen his relationship to the French language, and to his own family story, weaken, may ask to learn it again, sometimes with success, regarding improvement or acquisition of the accent and fluency. This latter example is, unfortunately, much too rare, and much more difficult, reinforcing the necessity to never let them go too long without an education in their birth language. I have never heard anyone say that they regretted that their parents forced them to learn their family language. But I have seen hundreds regretting that their parents did not push them to do so! A maternal/paternal language is therefore one that we designate as such. FLAM associations, as Heritage "Saturday schools" will help keep these children Francophone: French fluent speakers with a Francophone mind and connection to the French-speaking world.

By continuing to use their language, even though they no longer speak it at school, or even regularly, or even if English becomes the primary language at home, this new generation understands that the world is not intended to be expressed in only one language; French reminds them that there is another point of view, another way to see and feel the world. It can not only be told in two or more languages, but it can also be viewed differently accordingly to a set of principles and values that are transmitted by a very subtle choice of words. Or expressed very frankly through our education (*laicité, liberté, égalité, adelphité!*). That is why I always say that FLAM students will be our best ambassadors for both of our countries as Global Citizens! I already see it each year when our students leave their home to study in a different country. Canada has the benefit of many of these students: it is a beautiful mix of both countries, historically; it is also a country where they feel their dual languages and cultures are well accepted and appreciated as an asset!

Beyond a program aimed at consolidating the Francophonie, while a child integrates himself deeply into the host country and its core values, FLAM is a program that allows for the promotion and enhancement of multilingualism, without giving up one of the essential components of one's identity. The "mother" tongue is the language that places you in a lineage, it is the language that gives you access to memory; it is not always the first language learned, nor even the language of the country you were born in. It is the language of a country with which one decides to have a primordial link. Yes, we can definitely say that FLAM Heritage Schools give, through language, the gift of a homeland.

The latest solution in the *Enseignement Français à l'Étranger* for the Francophone community in the United States

There is a fantastic network of private French international schools around the world, some of them directly managed by the French agency *Agence pour l'enseignement français à l'étranger* (AEFE), including some here in the United States. So why is FLAM necessary? System of education is the second question asked by future expatriates who parents are, after the type of work visa. Where can my children engage in an education in French? This is because, around the world currently, we still have two French children out of three who have no access to an education in French. We are still failing them. And we are losing them. To all the parents who are choosing a bilingual or multilingual education for their children, and to all the migrant or expatriate families who are bringing up children in a different language - their heritage language - and are faced with the difficulties of living and going to school in another language; to those who are confronted with cultural integration: We accompany you, we support you, we advise you in your choices, wherever you are. Even in small cities.

FLAM associations were created themselves, alone, for many years, to answer the need of a growing French speaking community in many cities. The abrupt rise of French schools' tuition (+35% in five years in the United States) left out even more Francophone families. Our associations, deprived of adequate access to the training and educational resources of EFE or financial support from the French government (or other Francophone governments, companies, organizations) showed an exceptional educational creativity in response, a creativity that is one of the strengths of the FLAM program. Several congresses have brought together FLAM directors and coordinators, concerned by the development the FLAM Saturday schools. The French government, their representatives, elected Senators, all believe in the growing strength of these programs, but they also understand the needs of FLAM programs around the world. It is a laboratory of educational practice that encourages bilingualism and demystifies ideas around it.

Through the Federation that we created in our personal time, on top of the many responsibilities of our own local associations, we developed a common reflection on programs, objectives, tools, resources, and training. We hired a United States coordinator in 2019, Emilie Nolf, who helped each FLAM teacher and association. For her work and support to the FLAM network during the pandemic, she just received the *Palmes Académiques*. This United States coordination helps us improve our practices, creating a link between teachers to share their ideas, curricula, and lesson plans. We organize monthly meetings between coordinators, and amongst directors, discussing strategies, development, creating a better approach to better assist more students. Annual conferences and training are an important component of each school, and we were able to organize one ourselves. *Plus vite, plus haut, plus fort, ensemble!* Together, we are going higher, faster, stronger! We also helped with the creation of new FLAM associations.

When the pandemic hit, and affected every school in the United States, most of our associations were banned from the schools where we used to rent classrooms. Thanks to our Federation, all our teachers received the support and training necessary to transition and stay online as early as the beginning of the pandemic. Our ambassadors: educated in both systems. This is a win-win for the United States and France. French President Emmanuel Macron, in a speech delivered at the French Academy in March 2018, expressed his ambition for the development of French education abroad, with an objective of doubling the number of students by 2025, one of France's commitments to the Francophonie.

French educational "soft power" relies on many private schools, alliances, dual-language programs in public, charter, or private schools, and now FLAM associations, and each one, in its own way, is growing the influence of French education. We are all convinced of the importance of bilingualism, and frankly we are proud that French is still a very important language, especially in international organizations and diplomacy. In the competition between the Anglo-Saxon and French models in education, FLAM students win by being representatives of both.

Universities and *"Grandes Écoles"* alike, are very interested in their bilingual profile, but more than that, their complete cultural fluency as well. They have the confidence of the United States students, who were taught at a very early age to speak in public, to debate. I am still ecstatic about the many choices for my teenagers in terms of studies in high school here: they can study business, criminal justice, psychology, ethics, environmental science, computer science, genetics, astronomy, forensic science and much more! They can be editors for a high-quality newspaper, preparing them de facto to become journalists. They are also encouraged to express their creativity: art, music, sports, are highly valued early on. *Mens sana in corpore sano.* That is why it is a shame that languages have suffered such a huge loss during the economic crisis in 2007-2009. Many language programs in elementary schools have been suppressed by local districts who are in charge of the curriculum choices and budgets. The first generation of students without any language exposure in early grades reached high school these past couple of years, and we are already seeing a decrease in the number of students learning French. Quotas are more and more insufficient to hire French teachers. Most language teachers must teach two languages to have enough classes. We are seeing more students without teachers officially applying for self-taught registrations, particularly for very demanding exams like IB. We are already helping them: PhilaFLAM has for example a partnership with a local public high school and one of our FLAM teachers offers the French International Baccalaureate lessons for their students. By teaching FLAM high school level students, we want them to not only continue to speak and study in French as long as possible, but also to "authorize" themselves to imagine studying abroad.

During one of the International College Fairs, I organized these past few years, one high schooler said that for the first time since she started touring universities, she felt like she could be among students like her: multilingual and international. She was among Third Culture Kids (or TCKs), a term coined by United States sociologist Ruth Hill Useem in the 1950s, for children who were raised in a culture other than their parents' or the culture of their country of nationality, living in a different environment during a significant part of their childhood development.

All Francophone universities, companies and governments in France, Québec, Canada, Switzerland, and Belgium, for instance, have a huge interest in attracting these students. FLAM students have the best of both worlds! And it is no surprise that universities, the ACUFCL, Campus France, for example, come to our events in greater numbers each time to present their post-secondary programs. During one of them, we invited our former students to talk directly to high schoolers about studying abroad. They were able to talk frankly and give very practical advice. They also confirmed that being bilingual gave them priority and sometimes unique opportunities that no other classmate had, in terms of internships and then their first jobs.

Universities and companies finally support the FLAM program

As president of the Federation FLAM USA, I am alarmed by the lack of financial support to help the increasing number of Francophone families who need a FLAM near their new home in the United States. The French government is helping as much as it can but with an average of about $15 per student per year, it is not nearly enough. They acknowledged before the pandemic that soon, if it were not the case already, there would be more French families in the FLAM organizations than anywhere else in the French education network in the United States. FLAM associations are teaching the future bilingual business managers and scientists in a world where French will be the most spoken language by 2050, and present on all continents. An investment that will benefit all of our local and international companies. The current economic development of new technologies indicates that companies are building plants in medium size cities, where private schools would be too expensive to create. FLAM would be the perfect solution to offer a French education anywhere in the world, easy and affordable for any company (and therefore family), anywhere their employees are going. The Federation FLAM USA is currently working with some companies to help by either creating local Saturday schools or, in the meantime, offering online classes.

It is a simple, inexpensive, and efficient solution. But it takes time, perseverance, and dedication, especially when there is still no recognition of the excellence of the education received, and of the impact of our work in some of French administrative organizations. But every day we continue, we persist, because we believe in this fantastic mission. I often say to families arriving in Philadelphia that participating in a FLAM association is one of the best adventures a French speaking parent can be a part of. Every Saturday, you receive hugs from one of the hundreds of students who still speak French because of you. Every year, you measure the impact of what you created when you see graduates studying abroad in a Francophone program or city and be proud of being bilingual. And every so often, you receive a very moving message from a parent who is so relieved and so happy that their child continues to progress in French and stay close to their family, their identity, and their cultural heritage. I am proud to be part of this incredible FLAM community and journey.

2. Francophone Immigration and Questions of Identity in New England: From Multiculturalism to Cultural Diversity
Emmanuel Kayembe

The first Francophone immigrants from Canada to New England worked hard to preserve their identity linked to their French roots. They treasured their cultural difference based on their Roman Catholic faith, French language and traditions. This claim to identity was in line with American multiculturalism in the early 20th century. Communities of different origins had the right to erect barriers protecting their native cultural institutions and to adapt their way of life to their own traditional norms, as long as they obeyed the law (Zunz 1987). However, multicultural policies failed as they did not favor a cross-cultural dialogue and did not build bridges among communities. They reinforced self-segregation tendencies within cultures instead. Current Francophone immigration from Africa is an occasion to rethink the concept of identity within an intercultural perspective, beyond the paradigm of cultural difference, which has led to interminable conflicts among nations: Blacks vs Whites, Americans vs Franco-Americans, Israelis vs Palestinians, etc. (Serres 1993).[1]

Ideology of difference as a paradigm of violence

When Francophone Canadians from Québec and Maritime Provinces started immigrating to the United States of America, two political ideologies confronted each other. The pluralist ideology incarnated by democrats, who supported identity claims of minorities, preventing forced cultural homogenization, and upholding the right to be different, and the political tendency of integration embodied by republicans, who were committed to a policy of assimilation (Zunz 1987: 430-432).

However, the dominant ideology remained that of assimilation. It slipped sometimes towards xenophobia and periodically exploded into violent episodes (Higham 1955). There was, indeed, a permanent and well-founded state of fear about a possible extension of French possessions in North America. The Franco-American immigration in Maine appeared, with the passing of time, as a Trojan horse capable of fostering the French influence and settlement. Strictly speaking, this perception was not a "conspiracy theory" from the American elite as David Vermette says(2019), but a real projection from the French-Canadian elite instead.It was based on political statements, strategies, and manifestos relating to the possibility of a territorial conquest of America as a mission-of-civilization. Works such as *L'Appel de la race* (1922), *La Vocation de la race française en Amérique du Nord* (1945), *Mission catholique et française en Nouvelle-Angleterre* (1962), as well as the acts and declarations from committees and congresses devoted to the future of French language in America, are evidence of the French- Canadian elite's political calculation, apart from the numerous annual reports on the Franco-American life. Some politicians rightly confounded the "*Franco-Américanie*" phenomenon to the apparition of a "*Québec d'en bas*" (Anctil 1979:39), an opportunity for French Canada to extend its boundaries over Canadian borders[2]:

> While the general phenomenon of emigration was still largely condemned as being a danger to French-Canadian society, Québec's elite began to view Franco-Americans more favorably. For some traditional nationalists, such as Jules-Paul Tardivel, emigration was to be part of a movement to extend the boundaries of French Canada and of Catholicism. Franco-Americans could maintain their faith and language and could even be the backbone of an apostolic reconquest of Protestant North America. In such a view, French Canadians in the United States became an important element in the developing "messianism" of French Canada (Bélanger 2000).

French and English presences in North America were both the consequence of a colonial expansion. They were based on the concepts of unchangeable identity roots and cultural barriers and, such as, they could not generate a culture of cohabitation and peace. French Canadians, who were Roman Catholic, considered the Protestant ideals of prosperity, ambition and acquisition of wealth as a sign of belonging to a corrupted world. In a famous discourse pronounced in Worcester in 1879, Ferdinand Gagnon, one of the fervent defenders of the ideology of "*survivance*," stigmatized what he called the "American materialism". He denounced with virulence Franco-Americans who were attracted by the American way of life, comparing them to fools, who wanted "to throw in the mud of the sewer of materialism a whole past of glory" and "to move towards a future of contempt and stigma" (Roche 1981: 51-52: my translation). For the French-Canadian elite used to depict the United States of America as a sort of Philistines' country, and the immigration as a descent into a modern Egypt: "They had left a country flowing with milk and honey to go and eat the Egyptian onions in abjection and tears" (Hamon 1891: xiii: my translation). Crossing the 45th parallel was for political leaders like entering a space of malediction, ruled by the devil. Lionel Groulx, the champion of French-Canadian ethnic purity and the author of *L'Appel de la race* (1922), spent all his life warning people of French descent not to be contaminated by "American materialism," whose long-term effects could undermine the Québec traditional society through Franco-Americans (Bélanger 2002: 92).

This very negative image of the United States of America finds its source in the rural-urban dichotomy derived from Catholicism, which teaches its followers to belittle wealth and to mistrust material comfort if they want to inherit the Kingdom of Heaven. In this sense, the lifestyle of people living in rural areas was considered as being full of peace, joy, honesty, compared to the lifestyle of people living in urban areas. The industrialization of the New World (*Novus Mundus*) was stereotyped as a sign of devil's activity, an extension of the corruption that removes human beings away from honesty, peace, happiness, etc.

One can say that Louis Hémon's *Maria Chapdelaine* (1924), for example, exemplifies in some way this myth of rural-urban conflict. This novel gives a broad outline of what was supposed to be the "French Spirit" (French Volksgeist), seen as a perfect incarnation of Catholic spirituality:

> The French character is just the opposite of the Anglo-Saxon American character. As much as one is cheerful, expansive, carefree, compassionate for the miseries of others, ready to make the most generous sacrifices, so the other is cold, focused, calculating, and selfish. It is therefore not to be feared that, for a very long time, Canadians will not be mixed up with Americans (Hamon 1891: 120: my translation).

The perception of Americans by the French-Canadian elite was a crucible of hatred, which drew an eternal line between two peoples without leaving room for a possible dialogue of cultures. This dualistic view, which puts what is good on the one hand and what is evil on the other one, on the account of the ideology of difference, was a key point of French-Canadian discourse about Americans, culminating many times in bloody clashes. Politicians and writers of Canadian descent repeatedly continued to label "Yankees" with all kinds of negative attributes. Louis Dantin, one of the most famous critics of Franco-American literature, called them "mercantilists", "thirsty for money", "crocodiles greedy for land", or used the Sermon of the Beatitudes to contrast the American "frantic quest for capital" and to condemn the cupidity of the chambers of commerce and banks (Roche 1981: 60-64). This cliché of Americans ended up limiting the possibility to know them better. It did not allow understanding the complexity of the cultural environment they were living in: "Giving a phenomenon a label does not explain it" (Caldwell).

On the contrary, cultural labels convey absolute images of nations and make impossible any cultural exchanges. They always spread hatred. Rosaire Dion-Lévesque, possibly the greatest Franco-American writer of all time, who gave a remarkable touch of interculturality to the Franco-American literature, refusing to be trapped in the net of essentialist stereotypes by crying out his love for America to the whole world:

I love you for your incredible cities
Which contain all the fairyland of the Thousand and One Nights [...]
Those who have seen in you only a vast pot
Where the raw essences of materialism stir [...]
Those do not know you (Santerre 1981: 141-143: my translation).

George Martin, one of the characters from Jack Kerouac's *The Town and the City*, points out as well this misrepresentation of American people as a nation stuck in materialism, revealing a hidden dimension of the American way life:

> All the fools in the world take us for millionaires living in mansions. They attack us because we are supposed to have so much money and to be so arrogant because of it. And what is it they are attacking? Some poor devil who works his heart out because his parents and his grandparents had to work so hard and taught him the life of work too. (Chassé 1977: 40)

The French-speaking Catholic Canadian was presented as a member of an elected race, invested with a divine mission, that of evangelizing the Protestant, who was accused of being a slave to selfishness and sensuality, a servant of pride and pleasure (Hamon 1891: 144). This discursive construction constitutes the very basis of colonial ideology. For Americans were assimilated into a degenerate race, caught up in evil practices that were not distinctly Christian:

> This people of the East, dechristianized in the long run, without fixed beliefs, slaves of selfishness which impose on them the disastrous practice of divorce and, what is even worse, the open revolt against the providential laws which guarantee the preservation and the propagation of the family, this people, I say, sees the Catholic Church at work; he is astonished and worried, even admires sometimes, but, entrenched in his pride, his disdain and his skepticism, the American, as a rule, does not convert (Ibid.: 144: my translation).

This representation built upon "theories of national superiority that justified colonialism as delivering the light of civilization to unenlightened peoples" (Dorsey & Collier 2018: 184). For Americans were depicted in a way that they appeared to belong to an inferior race. Religious hatred reached its peak: French-speaking Catholic Franco-Americans disliked English-speaking Irish Catholics and persecuted French-speaking Protestant Franco-Americans, who resided in the *Petits Canadas*. The Klan feared Catholicism would invade the entire region.

There were no victims on the one hand, neither executioners on the other, but only peoples relying on their own identity roots to tear each other apart in the shadow of a conspicuous religious fanaticism. Moreover, all these peoples were only together prolonging the war of religions, which opposed Catholics to Protestants and gave rise to the persecution of Reformed Christians in Europe.[3] As long as America was perceived as a religious refuge for Protestants who fled Europe to escape a bloody persecution, it is inconceivable to think that the Americans would accept without flinching the massive presence of Catholic immigrants from a country where Protestants were banned at some point in history! Religious persecutions targeted not only Catholics, but also Jews, Muslims, and atheists.

> Many of the British North American colonies that eventually formed the United States of America were settled in the seventeenth century by men and women, who, in the face of European persecution, refused to compromise passionately held religious convictions and fled Europe. The New England colonies, New Jersey, Pennsylvania, and Maryland were conceived and established "as plantations of religion." (The Library of Congress Exhibitions, undated)

From a paradigm of disjunction and reduction
to a paradigm of complexity

In today's globalized world, it is very important to reflect on how to think outside of the colonial mentality, founded on the binary dichotomy of "Us vs the Others" taken from a manichaeistic perspective. As Anne Marie Gaillard puts it, "Although ethnic identity is logically and historically the product of the differentiation of a group from another (I am what the other is not), this differentiation can only work if it is based on an appreciation of the other which is not negative: I am good, but the other is also good" (2019: 129: my translation).[4]

We learnt from Jacques Derrida that there is a solid link between "identity" and "hospitality". Our identities are linked to our capacity to welcome foreigners or strangers: "a home must have some kind of opening in order to be a home, meaning that the host must be hospitable to preserve his identity as a host. Thus, the stranger is the crucial character in the social order that will otherwise regard him as a parasite" (Rafn 2013). However, the Franco-American elite failed to leave any rooms for strangers (Irish, Italian, etc.) and fought for the purity of their race that was supposed not to be mixed up with the other peoples:

> Crossing two peoples is at the same time to change both their physical constitution and their mental constitution ... The characters thus remain at the beginning very vague and very weak. It always takes long hereditary accumulations to fix them. The first effect of crossbreeding between different races is to destroy the soul of these races, which is to say, that set of common ideas and feelings which make up the strength of peoples and without which there is no nation or country... It is therefore with good reason that all peoples who have reached a high degree of civilization have carefully avoided mingling with foreigners (Groulx 1922: 131: my translation).

The myth of ethnical purity was at the heart of Franco-American politicians' claims, which were founded on theories from the culturalist school of thought from the beginning of the 19ᵗʰ century. In this sense, every process of acculturation was understood as an attempt to undermine the authentic culture. In the Franco-American context, this involved not only the social and territorial organization, but also French language. Broadly speaking, the birth of *les Petits Canadas* was a consequence of a policy of segregation that provided a barrier to social intercourse. The role of "Little Canadas" was to slow down the acculturation of Franco-Americans and to protect them against the supposedly "corrupted" American civilization. Madeleine Giguère called these places "refuges from the cold, impersonal Yankee world" (1981: 10)! The strategy of spatial isolation for cultural purposes is part of colonial management of territories. Up to a point in time, colonial Great Powers used to systematically house peoples according to their race to avert the danger of *métissage*, namely through interracial marriages. On this matter, the position of French-Canadian politicians was not too far from the matrimonial conception of apartheid's artisans (Groulx 1922: 243; Comité Permanent de la Survivance 1945: 25).

Overall, the image of an unchanged and unchangeable Franco-American society was a utopia conveyed by the Franco-American elite, which stubbornly refused to recognize an elementary fact: all cultures are involved in a permanent process of acculturation that prevent them from narcissism. They are not impermeable to each other nor isolated by well-sealed borders. To the great displeasure of officials, the culture the Franco-American working class was living in was a composite culture, made out of elements from their French-Canadian heritage and cultural aspects from the host society. Their French was no longer as pure as the elite wanted it to be, with the passing of time.

Today, we need to build cultural bridges among communities, beyond the untenable and utopic policy of cultural purity. All cultures are impure, hybrid because of a global acculturation. The French language is today an impure idiom, a linguistic place of generosity and of hospitality. English has borrowed from French an impressive number of words called "Gallicisms". In turn, French is full of "Anglicisms". Francophone literature has revealed to the entire world the existence of not one French language, but a variety of French languages which express a cultural diversity throughout the world. It is time to think outside of prescribed and dichotomist identities, which steal our veritable identities, on the pretext of securing us. It is time to reach out to French-speaking immigrants from Africa and to welcome them as part of our cultural diversity in Maine. "We need to put an end to the idea of a border that defends and prevents. Borders must be permeable; they must not be weapons against migration or immigration processes" (Glissant 2008). We must put an end to the conception of identity as a single root and discover the relation that exists between our place and all the places of the world. We can gain an intercultural comprehension of identities by re-reading Rosaire Dion-Lévesque, who defined himself as a hybrid[5], a global citizen, sensitive to the misery and suffering of Others, namely Others from Africa:

> Like a polar night, / black was your skin /covered with dirty rags, /young African from Alabama, / once stranded in my town. //Our hands stretched out /In predestined gestures/And my solicitude/Flew to your misery//The alms that I gave you/By this already distant evening/Was only a few pennies/For your frugal meal//In exchange, /Black sun of my white night, /You gave me more than bread/Showing me/Your heart similar to mine. (Chassé 1977: 19: my translation).

A new Francophonie is emerging in Maine, as if paying tribute to the prophetic words of Rosaire Dion-Lévesque. Communities and humanitarian organizations are working together to host new Francophone immigrants from Burundi, Burkina Faso, Cameroun, Democratic Republic of the Congo, Djibouti, Gabon, Ivory Coast, Republic of Congo, and Rwanda.

Some people who are from Angola, but emigrated there from Democratic Republic of the Congo, are also able to speak French. Several projects and organizations are working with them as well as the other immigrants to help them succeed: the Greater Portland Immigrant Welcome Center, the New Mainers Resource Center at Portland Adult Education, the Immigrant Legal Advocacy Project, Hope Acts, the Catholic Charities Refugee and Immigration Services, the Maine Access Immigrant Network, the Maine Immigrant and Refugee Services, etc. The mission of all these institutions is for the most part geared towards strengthening the immigrant community through language acquisition, economic integration, and civic engagement. That is, to support Maine's economic development by facilitating the professional integration of immigrants and refugees. And by meeting employers' demands for a skilled and culturally diverse workforce.

Immigrant communities are organized in associations based on their nationalities. They are seen as an asset for the labor market. The state of Maine has unresolved issues with an aging workforce and lower birth rates, and some leaders are viewing immigrants as an answer to the state's struggles to attract younger people to live and work here. Immigration is seen as a kind of "magic wand that will bring young families to Maine to help communities build the next generation" (The New York Times). Immigrants have contributed hundreds of millions of dollars in taxes. Immigrant-led households in the state paid $ 437.7 million in federal taxes and 193.9 million in state and local taxes in 2018. However, it is wrong to see them only through economic lenses, as a solution for a declining workforce. For they brought with them new cultures, new ways to see the world, new skills. Franco-Americans have to see them as an unexpected boon for the resurgence of the French language in Maine, French as an international language of culture and not as an ideological and colonial medium. This Renaissance of the French language and culture should not be interpreted as cultural resistance, but rather a tool for "cultural dialogue", a way to build an inclusive world based on solidarity with diverse peoples, a third place outside of polarization. To reach this cultural objective, there is no need to resurrect the spectre of old monolinguist ideologies.

French must be seen as a plus, a precious key that can allow immigrants to open doors in job market. Although the newcomers have to quickly learn English to overcome language barriers and to enter the American workforce, they do not need to reject French nor stop speaking it at home with their children. For there is a growing need for translators and interpreters who can write and speak French: A general trend shown by a 2017 report by the think tank New American Economy[6] found that language skills are now essential in many professional sectors and a proficiency in French is a key advantage. For example, nearly 22,300 job offers published online in 2015 in the United States were looking for candidates proficient in French compared to 9,500 in 2010. French is the third most requested language on the American labor market, particularly in sectors such as insurance, healthcare, finance, and humanitarian aid. Supporting the teaching of French as a professional language therefore represents a challenge and opportunity in higher education for the future of French in the United States" (Cultural Service of the French Embassy in the United States, 2019).

There is an urgent need for solid programs of French for Professional Purposes in Maine. Consulates of France in the United States could support the development of French for professional purposes, notably through facilitating annual training workshops for high school and college teachers. A first step will consist in designing, for example, curricula of Healthcare Diploma of French and of French for legal purposes through the Franco-American Fulbright Commission.

3. I am an American and Very Much a Francophone...Malgré Tout
Etienne A. Kouakou

Growing up in Abidjan, the Ivorian capital, in the 1970s, it was natural for us children to interact with friends on the playground in French. After all, one of the most important legacies of the colonial era was the French language. Although we spoke a local version of the language, sprinkled with words from our local languages (some may say dialects, but this is a discussion for another paper), we were still able to communicate effectively. Later, we would learn what we considered standard French at school in order to prepare to assume, if necessary, important positions in the civic administration. But once at home, we were equally comfortable diving into our mother tongues, Baoulé in my case, or Bété, Sénoufo, Gouro, and others, for some of my friends. It all depended on their parents' ethnicities.

In middle school, I moved in with my older cousin and her husband, who was from the southern part of the country. His native language was Attie. At home, he spoke to us children in Attie while my cousin addressed us in Baoulé. Consequently, we were constantly immersed in two languages at home and French at school, where my cousin's husband was also our teacher. Personally, I had no trouble expressing myself in Baoulé and French. I also developed an acceptable passive proficiency in Attié, over the two years that I spent with my cousins, although speaking this language presented more challenges than simply making sense of it aurally. Our young brains were able to effortlessly absorb all these languages to which we were exposed.

In secondary school, I started learning English as a Foreign language, as is the practice in the Ivory Coast public schools. Unlike the local or indigenous languages and French, which we were able to learn by osmosis because we constantly heard them around us, learning English proved to be a challenge for most students. The main challenge, I suppose, was the lack of language immersion opportunities. By the end of secondary school, many students were able to speak some rudimentary English. The focus of the English curriculum was mainly on reading, grammar, and some occasional translation. There were two possible ways to develop real communication skills. You either joined your school's English club, where students met once a week to immerse themselves in activities essentially conducted in English, or you had to truly love the language and carve out your own path. I was of the latter.

Flash forward to years late in the United States, where I am, during one June morning in 1996, bound for a summer camp in Plymouth, Vermont. For the sake of brevity, and to avoid further digression, suffice it to say that I decided to stay in the United States at the end of my contract with the summer camp. Several years later, I got married and started a family. As a proud father and Francophone, I decided that the best I could do for my daughter would be to help her acquire the French language naturally, just as my friends and I had done decades ago when we were growing up. From the day she was born, Kaylin would hear only French from Daddy while Mommy and her siblings, and quite frankly everybody else in her immediate surroundings, would address her in English.

For more than nine months, things seemed to be going well. Kaylin would respond to simple commands or requests like "*Mets ça dans la poubelle*" or "*Tends-moi la main.*" Unsurprisingly, her first words were "*papa*" and "*maman.*" But my wife and I also noticed something unusual. Unlike her first two children who began to speak around Kaylin's age, we felt that Kaylin's speech was a bit delayed. She would say a few words, but she was not making complete sentences as one would expect from a child her age. My wife and I became concerned that she might have a language impairment. And unfortunately, this is when Mom undertook a new strategy. Kaylin would say "*maman*," and her mommy would redirect her, telling her to say "mommy" instead. Eventually, over the course of several months, I got exasperated and reluctantly gave up speaking to my daughter in French. Several years later, though, I would seek out events in French and bring Kaylin along with me, hoping that she might be able to strike up a friendship with a Francophone child or otherwise develop interest or curiosity in the language and culture. I remember one such function organized by the culture and education service of the French consulate in New York. I heard some of my African acquaintances address Kaylin in French just to fall back on

English when they realized she did not understand them. In hindsight, I realize that giving up my interactions with Kaylin in French was the worst mistake or decision I could have ever made. Had I persevered even as all the other members of the household interacted with Kaylin in English, she likely would have been able to understand some French even if she were unable to speak it.

As a Francophone who is used to various elements of the French culture, with language a prominent element, I must acknowledge the tacit bond that has endured whether I was conscious of it or not. One aspect of my Francophone background to which I have remained attached is the news and our customary news sources. When I first moved to the United States in the mid-1990's, the internet was not very popular; in fact, I do not think I had ever even heard the term used. This technology would become much more pervasive several years later as the world transitioned to the 21st Century in the year 2000. This is important to mention because the internet and the worldwide web would make is easier to access news sources from various parts of the world. In the mid-1990s, I had a difficult time tuning in to my Radio France International (RFI) for news from and about France, the Ivory Coast and the various African French-speaking countries. It was probably much easier to tune in to the BBC for world news. I do remember, though, that France 2, the French television channel, broadcast the news every evening from 7:00 PM to 7:30 PM. I always looked forward to the news in French not because I did not understand English (I had been an English teacher for five years before coming to the United States), but because I thought that France 2 was more likely to carry news about the Ivory Coast and the French-speaking world than any other local network.

Today, there is a plethora of news outlets, and the internet has turned the world into a global village. And today the possibilities are limitless. My preferences, however, are geared toward RFI, *France 24*, *Le Monde*, and any other French newspapers or networks available online. For news about the Ivory Coast, Africa in general, and French-speaking Africa in particular, my first stop is Abidjan.net, a website replete with links to various newspapers, as well as radio stations and television channels. Even after more than two decades in the United States, I am always very much concerned about what is happening in the Ivory Coast, but also about events in France. Indeed, as a Francophone, I feel a special bond to the country that lent my country its language, a country whose institutions usually serve as models for the institutions of my country.

On a personal level, my father fought alongside French soldiers in World War II and kept collecting his French army pension until he passed away in 2015. At the time he was recruited into the French army in the 1940's, the Ivory Coast was very much a *Territoire d'Outre-Mer*, an overseas territory administered by metropolitan France. I suppose that would have made Ivorians at least French "subjects" if not citizens. The fledgling administration at the time was run by French expatriates for the most part, with a limited number of locals serving in lower-level positions. Even the early educators such as elementary and secondary school teachers were mostly from France. Of course, the curriculum was very much French, and one would remember older Ivorians, those who grew up in the 1930s through the early 1960s, utter the phrase *nos ancêtres, les Gaulois*, a phrase that is very loaded from a historical standpoint. Beyond my personal bond, I know through my observations as an adult, that most of what affects France is likely to affect its former colonies or vice-versa. There are still military agreements between France and many French-speaking West African countries. Most infrastructure in the Ivory Coast was and continues to be built by French corporations. Even the CFA franc, the currency used in the Ivory Coast and many West African French-speaking countries was linked to the French franc and now to the Euro. Overall, it would not be an aberration to say that part of my heart beats for France. One just has to look at the way we root for France during the soccer world cup! For us, Ivorians of the Diaspora and at in the homeland, first is the Ivory Coast, then France, then Brazil or some other world-famous soccer nation. So, yes, the bond between France and the Ivory Coast, and I am certain with many other French-speaking countries, remains strong.

It is fair to suggest, at this point, that our connection to France has had an impact on who we truly are just as much as living in the United States as a Francophone raises an important identity question. After decades in this country would we define ourselves as exclusively American? And when discussing Francophone culture, should we not speak about cultures instead? In other words, is there such a thing as Francophone culture (singular) or cultures (plural)?

In essence, the *Organisation Internationale de la Francophonie* is an organization comprised primarily of French-speaking countries from various parts of the world. I do not want to delve into the history of the organization in this short essay. Suffice to say that it was spearheaded by Leopold Sedar Senghor, first president of Senegal; Habib Bourguiba, former president of Tunisia; Hamani Diori, former president of Niger; and Norodom Sihanouk, king, and former president of Cambodia. These gentlemen understood the necessity of bringing together citizens of countries that shared the use of the French language for linguistic, cultural, economic, and educational purposes.

Abdou Diouf, former president of Senegal and second Secretary General of the Organisation Internationale de la Francophonie once said, "*Une identité n'est pas figée, une identité n'est pas unique, elle est plurielle.*" Loosely translated, President Diouf was suggesting that a person's identity is neither static nor unique. Rather, it is plural or multifaceted. As such, one should speak of Francophone cultures rather than one Francophone culture. Let us not forget that the founding members were respectively from Senegal, Tunisia, Niger, and Cambodia. These individuals represented a variety of cultures and traditional beliefs. I would even suggest, as is suggested in the term "world Englishes," that even the French language stopped being "singular" the moment the indigenous people of the former colonies started using it. So, should we not talk of "World Frenches" as part of a conversation about Francophonie and Francophone cultures?

After the failure of my personal attempt with my daughter, I did not give up. On the contrary, I was even more determined to continue my own efforts to maintain the French language and make sure others, whether they were students or parents, could also find a way to continue practicing the language and cultures they had left behind. On a personal level, and this is relevant as a personal and professional endeavor, I made every effort to remain a true bilingual, but beyond this, I was willing to share my language skills with others that might be interested. Professionally, I had always wanted to become a translator or an interpreter. Unfortunately, there were no such opportunities in the Ivory Coast. Most students graduating from the English Department of the *Université Nationale de Cote d'Ivoire* usually ended up teaching English at a local secondary school, sometimes after completing their teacher education at the *École Normale Supérieure (*the teachers'college) in Abidjan.

Many would not even attend the teachers' college. Very often, students would take up a teaching position with no relevant teacher education background. By the time I came to the United States in 1996, my dream of being an interpreter and/or translator was very much alive. I started looking for opportunities to join a program that offers what interested me. I signed up for the French Translation program at New York University and completed five courses. I then sought internships in the field and was lucky to work with Christiane Milev, an accomplished translator of French at the time. The collaboration was short-lived, but it certainly opened my eyes to the possibilities. Specifically, it helped me navigate the application process for securing a position at the United Nations. I never was able to secure a firm position as a staff translator at the UN, but I was offered several interpretation contracts, which I gladly accepted, thinking, at the time, that they would eventually open better doors. This was in the late 1990s and early 2000s.

By the early 2000s, I had begun teaching, of all subjects, secondary school English at a local Catholic school. Imagine a Francophone teaching American children literature and writing in their own language! Initially, I was somewhat apprehensive and even doubted my ability, as a Francophone, to teach native speakers' literature and composition in their own language. After the first day of class, though, my confidence received a boost. I realized that speaking English as a native language--and I am convinced this applies to any other language--does not necessarily mean that one can read and write effectively in English. Urged on by this early success as a secondary school English teacher, I enrolled in the teacher education program at City College of New York shortly after completing my degree in liberal arts. By December of 2006, I had completed the coursework for the master's degree in secondary English education, had taught at the Catholic middle school for three years and gone on to teach at a Catholic high school.

The year 2009 may be considered an important one regarding my personal and professional efforts, conscious or not, to uphold the language in which I had been primarily educated. While teaching middle school English in Washington, DC, I decided to pursue dual certification in French and English as a Second Language. Already the holder of a permanent teacher certificate in secondary English from New York State, I only had to take the relevant certification examinations and submit the application to the relevant authority. I passed both examinations within several weeks and was soon awarded my French and ESL teaching certificates. The reason for pursuing teaching certification in French was simple. To me, it would not make much sense not to offer French, a language that I felt relatively comfortable teaching compared to English, although I had taught English as a Foreign Language in the Ivory Coast, ESL here in New York, and secondary English literature and writing in the local public schools. I owed something to myself and to my teachers, and maybe I felt that I had to uphold if not the French culture, at least the language that gave me my education in the first place. And how could I not delve into French culture while teaching the language? They go together! I was not able to use my French teaching certificate in Washington, DC, but it did come in handy once I moved back to New York after a one-year stint within the DC Public Schools (DCPS).

Back in New York in 2010, I secured a position in the French Heritage Program, which was then run by David Lasserre. At the time, I had never heard the term "heritage language," but after reading the job description, I pretty much had an idea of the student population within the program. Most students were from French- speaking West Africa, specifically from the Ivory Coast, Guinea, Senegal, and possibly Mali. I also had students from Haiti and students whom I would consider as Francophiles. These were native speakers of English who were interested in learning French. There were not many of them, but they certainly were a welcome addition. To the best of my recollection, most heritage students had a good grasp of French as a spoken language, especially the students who had been in the United States for a year or two. The longer the students had been in the United States and in the American school system, the more elusive French was to them. Maybe they had genuinely begun to forget the language of their countries of origin, or maybe they were just faking it just to fit in. The fact is that many students had a difficult time processing the simple reading tasks and assignments they had to complete. Luckily, most students were enthusiastic and active in class, which lent a joyous atmosphere to the class and created a positive learning environment for all. Needless to say, I always prepared my lessons enthusiastically and got on the subway to commute to the school with a smile every time I had class with my Francophone students.

I also remember writing a curriculum for the Monterrey French Immersion Program in the summer. My younger brother, who had received his doctorate from The University of Paris, La Sorbonne, had served as an instructor in the program previously, so I decided to join the program that particular summer. Eventually, I was unable to join as an instructor, but the program administrators decided to keep my curriculum, for which I was appropriately compensated. I believe that programs like these are a good way to provide some language immersion. The students come from various parts of the world (various languages are offered), but most important, from various parts of the United States. This is an indication that the French language and culture continue to entice everyday people, not just academics.

With this, I turn to the "Bilingual Revolution." I would suggest that a sound and thorough discussion of the future of French in the United States would be incomplete without due reference to the "Bilingual Revolution," a movement spearheaded by Fabrice Jaumont, the education attaché at the French consulate in New York, and his partners. It is important to mention that Dr. Jaumont also wrote a book by the same title. In this book, he provides ample advice to parents who want their children to attend schools that offer their general education curriculum and help immerse themselves in the French language and culture. The book provides detailed information on advocating for, setting up, and taking the steps for a bilingual program to thrive. In sum, this is a didactic book that is replete with useful information and practical steps for any parent or group of parents willing to make a difference in their child's education, specifically one that acknowledges and facilitates the acquisition or retention of their home language and culture. Thanks to the Bilingual Revolution, there has been a proliferation of French bilingual schools in the New York Department of Education (NYDOE) and beyond, so it might be relevant to give the movement some attention here.

Jaumont's opening chapter, "The Willpower of Parents: Yes, You Can" reaffirms my personal conviction that the French language, and any other language, cannot survive in a foreign land unless parents take an active part in ensuring its preservation through future generations. At the outset, Jaumont states that the past two decades have seen a proliferation of dual-language programs or schools in the United States and around the world. Most of these programs, he continues, were spearheaded by willing and determined parents who advocated for and usually played preponderant roles in their implementation. Several reasons moved these committed parents to action. According to Jaumont, the first reason is the parents' espousal of the cultures and languages specific to their community. The second reason is the willingness to create a bond between parents and their children's school. The last reason, he contends, is the necessity to establish a social, economic, and cultural environment that promotes a better understanding among the communities that are stakeholders within the school communities and the community at large (Jaumont, 1).

The above suggests that most of the parents who advocate for and take the steps to see dual-language programs sprout up and flourish in their child's school have clear reasons for doing so. They come from a culture and speak a home language that they want validated by the administration and other educators of their child's school. Moreover, what seems to be paramount is not a mere quest for acceptance and validation. The future of their language beyond the parents themselves is at stake. If their children's schools failed to implement the necessary bilingual programs, the result could be a linguistic and cultural loss for the child. And how might such a child communicate with their grandparents or other relatives who cannot express themselves in English, especially when they visit their parents' homeland? It is imperative, for the sake of communication within the family, to help the child not only speak their heritage language at home but continue the formal study of the language at school whenever and wherever that is possible. Dual-language programs can certainly offer such an opportunity.

Beyond the desire to preserve a language for cultural and other reasons pertaining to identity, we should bear in mind the important cognitive benefits attributed to bilingualism and biculturalism. Decades ago, the state of California decided to provide a brief period of English as a second language to their new non-native English students. At the conclusion of a period of one year, the students exited the bilingual program and joined the so-called mainstream classes. The move was known as Proposition 227 and received mixed reviews with supporters and detractors contradicting one another on the benefits of the proposition for students. Because of such programs, some parents might feel compelled or coerced to avoid using their native language at home, hoping to help their children make swift progress in English.

Today, thanks to the works of language acquisition experts, we know that multilingual students are in general better predisposed academically than their monolingual peers, and that they benefit greatly from instruction in their home language even as they learn English to join their native speaker peers in the general education classroom (I hesitate to call it mainstream; given the increasing number of multilingual learners poised to supersede that of native speakers. Mainstream might apply to a new category of learners.) Rather than promoting and implementing Proposition 227-like programs, the New York City Department of Education (NYCDOE) decided to support the innumerable English learners (ELLs) whose parents are native to more than a hundred countries. A quick look at the website of the NYCDOE is a great indication that they understand the importance of students to continue learning in their native languages even as they work on polishing up their English. The NYCDOE offers various programs for ELLs depending on the student population. Programs range from stand-alone ESL classes (pull-out) to in-class support (push-in) to fully bilingual immersion programs where students' schedule is equally divided between the languages of instruction. Additionally, the portion of their website dedicated to English learners is replete with resources for teachers, parents, and students.

Any educational program that acknowledges the students' home languages and works with willing parents to provide additional support in the home language and culture, in addition to the regular curriculum, is more likely to help our Francophone children preserve our linguistic and cultural heritage. Better yet, these programs, and more importantly bilingual immersion programs, will prepare the children of Francophone parents to excel academically and remain connected to and immersed, to a certain degree, in their home cultures. We already have the materials, facilities, and manpower (womanpower if you will), including faculty and other stakeholders, to provide the adequate education that our children need in addition to their general education courses.

Beyond the bilingual revolution currently in full swing in many of the nation's public schools, what boosts my confidence that the French language and Francophone cultures have a bright future in this country are the equally proliferating and sometimes well-established programs in French and Francophone studies at the tertiary level. Last weekend, I was at the University of Central Florida in Orlando, where my granddaughter was graduating. After the ceremony, I conducted a quick search about the offerings at this university. I was gladly surprised that they had a program in French and Francophone studies at both the undergraduate and graduate levels. In New York, many universities and colleges offer similar programs. Nationwide, there is no dearth of such programs that provide a platform for interested students to learn the French language and about Francophone cultures through literature, history, and study-abroad programs. A quick search yielded the following, and this list is nowhere near exhaustive: the City University of New York Graduate Center, Columbia University, and New York University (New York); Georgetown University, the Catholic University of America, and Virginia Tech (District of Columbia, Maryland, Virginia area); Brown University in Rhode Island; and the University of California, Davis. These are only a fraction of the numerous colleges and universities where French and Francophone studies figure prominently in the offerings.

With the Bilingual Revolution at the preschool, elementary, and secondary school levels (heritage programs need to be factored in as well) and the French and Francophone studies programs spread out in various colleges and universities around the United States, I am convinced that Francophonie and Francophilia are very much alive and will continue to flourish and thrive well into the foreseeable future. For more than three centuries, French was not only a language of education and prestige but also the lingua franca around the world. The luster may have dimmed somewhat, but the French language and culture continue to interest droves of intellectuals and others around the world. The same can be safely said for the United States as well. *Après tout, la Francophonie n'a pas que des États membres. Il y bien sept pays associés, ainsi que vingt-sept pays observateurs, ce qui fait sa force.*

Pour ma part, I am an American but still very much a Francophone *fier de voir davantage de programmes bilingues bourgeonner et se repandre* throughout the United States and the world. *Je demeure Africain et*

Francophone… et Américain et fier d'être tout cet ensemble. Sachons léguer notre heritage à nos enfants so that they, too, can embrace and keep it alive! Our children do not have the same opportunity to acquire languages by osmosis that I and many other Francophones had growing up in our respective countries. But if we convert into action our belief that our children need to retain their cultural and linguistic heritage, then we all need to foster the creation and development of even more French bilingual programs whether we are educators or interested parents.

4. Preserving French as a Heritage Language in the United States: The opportunity for another French Revolution in New York City.
Agnès Ndiaye Tounkara

In the introduction to their article on French Heritage Language Vitality in the United States in the Heritage Language Journal, published in 2013, Jane Ross and Fabrice Jaumont remind us that "the case of French is particularly interesting, because French heritage language speakers represent several distinct geographic populations and different historical circumstances, from recent immigrants to settlements dating back several centuries. Franco-Americans and Acadians in Maine and Cajuns in Louisiana serve as examples of revitalization efforts to protect and encourage the vitality of French as an indigenous language. In New York, communities of French expatriates and recent Francophone immigrants have collaborated to ensure French maintenance not only as part of their cultural identity but also as a path to academic and economic success and security."[6] In this chapter, my focus will be on New York's communities of recent Francophone immigrants as I have a personal connection to them as a Francophone immigrant myself and through my role as Program officer of the French Heritage Language program.

When people ask me when I am from, I usually say that I spent a third of my life in Senegal, a third in France and a third in the United States. That makes me Senegalese, French and American, a proud citizen of the world. I am also the mother of three children I am fighting every day to keep bilingual. Born and raised in Senegal, I went to college and lived in France for twelve years before moving to the United States. Strongly anchored in my Senegalese roots, I also embrace my French and American identities and value the power that comes with the ability to speak different languages and thus to see the world through different lenses. After working in the energy sector in France, a move to the United States allowed me to redirect my career towards my passions: education and the French language.

In this vein, I led the Education Department at the Alliance française of Boston for six years. I then moved to New York and joined a private bilingual school where I oversaw the extracurricular activities, promoting the French language outside of the classroom. I am now the program officer of the French Heritage Language Program, an organization which has been helping Francophone immigrants and young Americans with Francophone background to maintain their linguistic and cultural heritage.

When I took on this role in 2019, I was thrilled to have found another job that allows me to stay connected to the French language and to this unique and incredibly diverse community of French speakers around the world. From the Lebanese and Vietnamese friends I grew up with in Senegal, to a friend who was the only other African student in the first school I went to in France, to the very good friends from the Seychelles, Belgium or Iran that I made in Boston, to all those fervent American Francophiles who love French more than we do, I cannot think of another language which could have given me a more vital exposure to so many different cultures.

Growing up in Senegal, French was just the language we spoke at home, or should I say one of the languages we spoke, next to the Serer my father spoke with his family and the Portuguese Creole my mother spoke with her brothers, aunts, and cousins. Because they did not speak their respective maternal languages, they spoke French to each other and to me. I learned some Serer while visiting my grandfather in his little village, but I was never fully fluent; not as much as I was in Ouolof, the national language everybody speaks in the streets of Dakar, the language I used at the market and at the airport because I did not want to be treated like a foreigner.

French was also the language I used at school: I discovered *les Fables de Lafontaine, Molière*, and *Descartes* but I also read *Une si longue lettre* de Mariama Ba and *L'Enfant noir* de Camara Laye. All those wonderful novels shaped my identity. France was a natural destination for college, for me and many of my peers, at least the ones fortunate enough to have parents who could afford it. At the time, I did not fully realize how speaking French would dramatically ease the transition from Dakar to Nancy, a little town in the east of France. I went from the hot and humid days of Senegal to the cold and dry winters in Lorraine without blinking, or should I say, shivering. Going from my large extended Senegalese family to my smaller but no less warm French family, and from my mother's delicious thieboudienne to my host family's *quiche Lorraine* and *tarte à la rhubarbe*, I made them all mine.

School was very different and very familiar at the same time. It was in French, with teaching methods and materials that were not foreign to me. Of course, there were some ignorant questions and reactions along the way, I noticed the cultural differences, family dynamics I was not used to, the different ways people interacted. There was this moment when I looked around the first day of school and realized that I was a different color, I felt the weight of France's colonial past in some loaded conversations at work, but mainly, I saw intellectual curiosity and opportunities to tell people about myself and where I was from, as well as to learn about them. In all those conversations and encounters, some exciting and thrilling, some of them challenging, I was able to discuss, convince, debate, understand whom I was talking to and tell them who I was, all because we were speaking the same language.

In France, I never felt the frustration I still feel here in the United States, 20 years later, even as an adult fairly fluent in English. This feeling of having my exuberant mind trapped in the narrow prison of my English vocabulary, this feeling of not being able to be fully me. Throughout my travel and immigrant experiences, the French language has been the bridge which brought me back to my own roots and identity, connecting me to all the Francophones I meet and also leading me to meaningful professional opportunities. And this is why the work I do with the French Heritage Language Program is so personal, so close to my heart. Especially in New York, where we serve Francophone students from Africa and Haiti who do not have access to French classes nor to a bilingual education.

These students face greater challenges than I did arriving in France and in the United States: some of them were good students in their schools back home and found themselves in high school, a few years away before graduation, in classrooms where no one speaks their languages. Where very little of their academic capital is valued. They literally start from scratch and are sometimes held back because of the language barriers. They are also navigating new cultural norms and a new identity, in a socio-economic context which racialize them as Black. Like me, when they left their native country, there were sons and daughters, from a family and a specific village, from an ethnic group with a common language, traditions and values that they carry proudly with them, and all of that defined who they are. On their way to the "American dream," these students find themselves in monolingual classrooms where, all of a sudden, their complex and rich identities are too often reduced to being "Black "and "English Learners." Unfortunately, none of the boxes they check on the many forms (United States entry, schools, and colleges, etc..) they must fill out, give them the proper space to express what they really are: multilingual, from a culture, from countries, with rich histories and rich traditions. None of these categories really say whom they are while the many languages they speak do. Among them, French, a language they all share, is familiar in a variety of ways, and it makes them heritage speakers. Heritage language refers to a language with which individuals have a personal connection (Fishman, Heritage Languages in America). It is the historical and personal connection to the language that is salient and not the actual proficiency of individual speakers.[7] Some may be able to speak, read, and write; others may only speak or understand when spoken to. Some may not even understand the language but are part of a family or community where the language is spoken. Thus, it is part of their identity; and the vision of our program is that, in their American schools, the French Language can be the bridge to their Francophone peers, the bridge to their cultural heritage but also the bridge to their academic and professional future.

Through the French language, our students form, within their schools, a community, in ways that would not be possible if they were all speaking in their maternal languages. It is often, in French, that our students, from Mali, Senegal, Togo or Ivory Coast find each other and connect. These students are among the 2,000 students identified as French speaking students in New York's public schools. We know that this number is an underestimation as it is blind to the students' multilingualism; it only captures those who declare French as the language spoken at home, ignoring the majority of those who choose to list English or Wolof, Fulani, Haitian Creole, or Ewe (one of their native languages) on a questionnaire that only allows for one answer.

Like Ross and Jaumont explained: (...), several waves of immigrants from Africa have brought more French heritage language speakers into the country, many of whom also have another home language. It is precisely this diversity that renders determining the exact numbers of French speakers in the United States a complex task, because so many are also speakers of additional languages including Haitian Creole, Wolof, Bambara, and Arabic, as well as English, and also because many have been reluctant to report their home languages. And like them, I suspect that there are more French speakers in these areas than officially recorded, if the large number of undocumented residents were included.[8]

They have recently arrived in New York from Francophone Africa or Haiti and attend high schools where they are very rarely offered language instruction, the focus being on English language acquisition. Our program, born through a partnership between the Cultural Services of the French Embassy and the FACE (French American Cultural Exchange) Foundation, aims to fill that void.

> In November 2004, representatives from the French Embassy, various foundations, and New York University met in order to plan a project to serve recent Francophone immigrants within public high schools in New York. The French Heritage Language Program was the result of this plan aimed at offering linguistic and cultural enrichment while also facilitating English language acquisition by students of Francophone origin studying in New York public schools. The program's main objective is to promote bilingualism by helping students maintain or develop linguistic proficiency in French and keep a connection to their respective cultures and identities, while increasing their opportunities for success in their new environment.[9]

Our program has served more than 4,500 young boys and girls over the past fifteen years, in New York but also in Miami, Boston and Maine. The students meet, after school, under the guidance of a teacher, to maintain or improve their French by working on cultural projects to keep them connected to their cultural heritage. But our mission goes beyond maintaining the French language: as Maya Smith perfectly put it an article published in the Critical Multilingualism Studies Journal in 2017[10], "The FHLP not only provides free French language training, it also creates a space where these students can construct their identities as multilingual speakers and learn the value of their various cultural background."

Our curriculum leverages each student's linguistic assets and explores African and Haitian arts and literature through projects. Because our classrooms are very heterogeneous, our collaborative project-based approach is particularly relevant. We give them access to the growing and diverse artistic and literary body of work through book readings, movie projections, fieldtrips and workshops with artists and authors from French speaking peoples around the world. The French language does not belong to France anymore but to the 300 million people who speak it around the world, (the majority of them soon to be in Africa)[11], it is the language of La Francophonie, this multilingual space where many cultures cohabitate, with the French language in common. It is the language connecting these students to their heritage; it is also the language that can propel them in a globalized future where more than 470 million people will speak it too.[12]

A survey[13] conducted among 75 of our students in 2016 showed that 70% of their parents said it was important for them to maintain their French; 40% of them cited the program as a space where they feel the most comfortable speaking French; 23% thought it was helping them learn English; another 23% said it will help them get a job. Indeed, French can play a major role into building their academic success and easing their access to college through the AP French and the Seal of Biliteracy, by giving them the opportunities to leverage their bilingualism and obtain language credentials. The AP French (Advanced Placement French Language and Culture,) is a class that lets United States high school students earn credit for a college-level French class. It culminates in the AP French Exam, which is generally considered equivalent to a college-level French 301 final exam. Not only does it require to read and write at a certain level, but it also implies an ability to follow a college level course and to perform high level thinking around themes spanning from Identity and Families and Communities to Global challenges. Each year, we prepare students by offering courses and two intensive workshops during the school holidays. A typical American high school student usually gets at least four to five hours of instruction per week to prepare for this exam. Our students only meet once a week for two hours at most. On average, 75% of our students pass the exam (have a score between three and five, the maximum) which can result in college credits.

The Seal of Biliteracy and the Global Seal of Biliteracy (for language learners who do not have access to the Seal of Biliteracy programs offered by the states) are language accreditations which provide students with recognition of their language skills and the opportunity to demonstrate them to universities and employers. To qualify, students have to meet graduation requirements in English and show credentials in French. For the FHLP students, it means scoring at least at the Intermediate High level of the AAPPL (The ACTFL Assessment of Performance toward Proficiency in Languages) in French, equivalent to the B1 level within the Common European Framework (CECR). The test measures their proficiency in four different modalities: Interpersonal listening and speaking, presentational writing, interpretive listening, and interpretive reading. Our students 'performances on this test are on par with the national average for students enrolled in AP classes and in heritage classes, with only an average of two hours of French classes per week, compared to five or six hours per week for students in those classes.

Through the French language, students also break racial and socio-economic barriers; for example, when students from a high school in Brittany (France) visit our students in the Bronx every year and discover their common humanity by sharing and comparing their lives. Or, during a two-day visit to Lafayette College in February 2019, when our students got a real taste of life on campus. There, they were paired and roomed with students from the Lafayette College French Department and created long lasting connections with their roommates; they received   a comprehensive overview of the complex college admission process in the United States from an admissions officer from the university, and even sat in a French class, getting access to a world their circumstances had thus far put out of reach. Once again, through the partnership created with Lafayette College, the French language was the bridge that provided access to a world that seemed out of reach for most of these black students from the Bronx and Brooklyn. The visit helped them understand that their multiculturalism was valued, their bilingualism was an asset and that they have something unique to bring to a college classroom. In a perfect world, a program like ours would not exist and all these students would be in bilingual programs where their linguistic assets will be leveraged and where they will be an asset for the entire community. The benefits of a bilingual education and the maintaining of heritage languages have been proven by researchers and scientists around the world, by data: cognitive benefits, better academic results, fewer school dropouts, increased creativity and critical thinking, open-mindedness, and cultural awareness, all result from fluency in and connection to more than one language.

In New York, the Bilingual Revolution[14] began years ago and is still under way: a grassroots movement led by parents and community leaders have already brought high quality bilingual education to more than 2000 students in eleven schools in Manhattan and Brooklyn. Yet, there is still a lot of work to be done: 70% of the dual language programs are for elementary or middle school students. According to the *2020 NYC Department of Education English Language Learners demographic report*, 43% of the students in the public schools speak a language other than English.[15] Only 6.21% of the students who speak another language at home have access to bilingual programs. The department, however, recognizes that strengthening students' literacy skills in their native languages has a positive impact on their English learning and on their social emotional well-being. This occurs though developing linguistic self-esteem and deep connections to the language.

Moreover, none of the eleven French dual language programs are in the Bronx, despite the more than 22,000[16] French speakers (age five and over) identified by the 2018 United States Census Bureau American Community Survey. Among the declared languages spoken at home, French is in eighth place in the city as a whole (Haitian Creole is in 6th place) but French moves up to fourth place in Manhattan and the Bronx, even to the second and third in certain districts, thanks to the French-speaking Haitian and African communities. And this number will only grow: slightly more than two million immigrants from sub-Saharan Africa lived in the United States in 2018. While this population remains small, representing just four and a half percent of the country's immigrants, it is rapidly growing. Between 2010 and 2018, the sub-Saharan African population increased by 52 percent, significantly outpacing the twelve percent growth rate for the overall foreign-born population during that same period. The greater New York and Washington, DC metropolitan areas were the United States cities with the largest number of sub-Saharan immigrants in the 2013-17 period, with the Bronx being the second county in the country, by concentration, of sub-Saharan Africans.[17]

In a positive shift towards a more inclusive model, New York city has made Culturally Responsive Sustaining Education (CRSE)[18] the gold standard with the belief that all the students' cultures are equally important assets, which should be leveraged in the classroom. The Culturally Responsive Education framework is a deep and positive shift from a world where there are dominant cultures and marginalized ones, to a world where all cultures are valued equally, a world in which schools acknowledge, value, and leverage the wealth of knowledge that every student brings into the classroom, including their linguistic assets.

Our programs are designed to build their literacy skills, with inclusion of their cultural heritage in mind. As suggested in the "CRSE framework", they use a curriculum with many narratives and voices from the students' backgrounds and cultures. They create more opportunities for them to present the Seal of Biliteracy in English and French, more opportunities to take the French AP exam, especially since they belong to the highly under-represented group of black and Hispanic students who have very little access to it. Making the shift to a Culturally Responsive Sustaining Education (CRSE) in New York's public schools requires offering more French heritage programs, not only in the International High Schools[19] where we traditionally offer our programs but in all communities with a high concentration of French speaking communities. This should ensure the commitment of the schools' leadership and the Department of Education.

The French Heritage Language Program is a program that has been proven to meet the needs of heritage speakers and is the fruit of a solid public-private partnership through the FACE foundation and the cultural Services of the French Embassy. If we are able to mobilize parents' support by communicating to these often-first-generation immigrant parents that their children are not at a disadvantage in bilingual programs, then all the ingredients identified by Ross and Jaumont[20] to create successful linguistic opportunities that will further strengthen these communities in New York City are here: it is time for another French Revolution.

5. Sisyphus on the Bayou: Pushing back against the rolling good times and the absurdity of writing about being French in English.
David Cheramie

Most people know about the myth of Sisyphus today due to the book of the same name published in 1942 by French existentialist author Albert Camus. Its subtitle, Essay on Absurdity, gives away much of the plot. Since it is not a novel, we can forgive him. We are familiar with the story of Sisyphus being condemned, for all eternity, to rolling a boulder up a hill, only to have it tumble back down just before reaching the summit. An absurd endeavor indeed. What most people are less familiar with is how Sisyphus got himself into that predicament or even who exactly he was.

According to legend, Sisyphus was the first king of Ephyra, the original name of the ancient Greek city-state of Corinth. His kingdom was prosperous, but he was also a conniving, evil tyrant who thought nothing of killing people who came to see him just because he could. It was not so much his murderous ways that first angered the gods (who are themselves known for wiping out large swaths of humanity on occasion) but his lack of hospitality. But that was not enough to earn him his eternal punishment. One day, Zeus transformed himself into an animal. This time, he turned into an eagle and kidnapped Aegina the nymph, daughter of Asopus, the god of rivers. Learning of her abduction, her father followed them to Ephyra where Sisyphus, ever the shrewd dealmaker, gave information to the aggrieved parent about what direction he saw a large bird carrying a woman in his talons in exchange for a water well to be placed inside the city. When Zeus found out he had been ratted on, he ordered Thanatos, the god of Death, to chain Sisyphus up and bring him to the underworld. When presented with the chains, Sisyphus asked Thanatos to show him how they worked. Death tutored him so well in the art of locksmithing that Sisyphus chained him up instead and fled the underworld, preventing Death from doing what he does best, making dead people. With no one dying any more, chaos soon ensued. Aries, the god of war, would have none of this since no one was dying in battle, his main source of amusement, as one might imagine. It got to the point where he went down to the underworld himself to free Thanatos so he could go back to his killing ways.

Since people were dying again, Sisyphus knew he was only delaying the inevitable divine punishment awaiting him. Before he perished, he asked his wife, Merope, to throw his cadaver into the streets which in those days were probably little more that open ditches. For all of this reputation as a good leader, he probably still had a lot to learn about urban planning, especially if he had to strike a bargain with a god to get fresh water in town. Be that as it may, he knew his body would eventually wash onto the banks of the River Styx. Once among the dead, he went to see Persephone, the queen of the underworld, to complain to her that his wife had not given him a proper burial. Moved by his plea, she gave him permission to return once again to the land of the living, provided he came back once he was humanely inhumed. Being the consummate politician, he naturally broke his promise and once again cheated death. Zeus sent his messenger, Hermes, to bring him back to Hades to receive his eternal punishment. This time, though, Sisyphus resigned himself to his fate and began his longtime love-hate relationship with a steep mountain and a large rock. What does all this have to do, as you may rightfully ask, with French in Louisiana? Let me illustrate with another story involving real people and real events.

The other day I came across a digitized edition of my hometown newspaper, the Lafourche Gazette. The date on it was May 12, 1976. Blazoned across the right side of the front page is the title "French President to Visit South Louisiana," announcing Valéry Giscard d'Estaing's imminent arrival to the Bayou State. Upon an official invitation to mark the bicentennial of the American Revolution by then President Gerald Ford in acknowledgement of France's longstanding alliance with the United States, Giscard d'Estaing would come to America accompanied by the French First Lady Anne-Aymone Giscard d'Estaing to celebrate their country's crucial role in the American victory over the British. Among the stops they would make outside the nation's capital were New Orleans and Lafayette. The article goes on to talk about our French-speaking governor, without naming Edwin W. Edwards, the French-speaking University of Southwestern Louisiana president, Dr. Ray

Authement, the mayor of Lafayette, the Honorable Kenneth Bowen and, *cela va de soi*, the Council for the Development of French in Louisiana (CODOFIL), chaired by the former Congressman, James Domengeaux. There was obviously much planning invested in bringing the President of the French Republic to an area of the United States where French was still spoken on a daily basis by a million or so inhabitants.

While VGE, as the French press had dubbed him, never made it to my hometown of Golden Meadow, I do recall the visit of some French journalists a few years before. They were probably among the 150 journalists invited to the first *Hommage à la musique acadienne*, later to be known as *Festivals Acadiens et Créoles*, that was held in Blackham Coliseum in Lafayette on a dark and stormy night in the spring of 1974. I was coming to the end of my freshman year at Golden Meadow Junior High (Go Lions!) where I had taken my first ever French class, French I with M. Lefort. Admittedly, I was unable to converse with the journalists and do not remember much about their visit except for the Marquisat Red Burgundy served at the reception. Even though I had a rather large vocabulary (i.e., I knew many words, but could barely construct a complete sentence) and was the top student in the class (it ain't bragging if it's true), I was just beginning to stare at that boulder I would later be pushing up that hill for all of my adult life. Even though I could not speak French fluently yet, I had always known what it was supposed to sound like, so pronunciation was never a problem. For example, the vowel sounds like "u" and "eu" that bedevil most Anglophone students of French were already familiar to me, especially in the curse words which, of course, we learned first. I would later go on and receive a Ph.D. in Francophone Studies from the hands of Dr. Authement, speak French with ex-Governor Edwards and become the director of the organization Mr. Domengeaux founded. I did not know it at the time, but I had just been condemned to this eternal struggle for trying to cheat the death of French in Louisiana.

I, of course, was not raised speaking French, even though it was my parents' first language and the only language one of my grandmothers ever spoke. The reasons for this break in the oral transmission of the language have been well-documented; there is no need to go into any detail here because those causes held true for me and most other members of my "lost generation." Nonetheless, as I began pushing that boulder, I came to understand, over the course of forty-plus years of living and breathing the French language, the immense gravitational forces pushing back. In keeping with the traditional figure in Louisiana folklore of Lapin, the underdog (or should I say under-rabbit) who far outwits his bigger and stronger rivals, we have had to invent strategies that would allow us to protect and preserve our French language and customs from the far larger and powerful forces of American assimilation. Here is a short list of some of the accommodations we have had to make in order to prove our American bona fides, and not have us suspected of fomenting rebellion, insurrection and succession, something we have been known to do over the years.

Reciting the Pledge of Allegiance and singing the National Anthem in French are de rigueur guarantees against any suspicion of separationist inclinations *à la québécoise*. Trotting out the French Immersion students in performative displays of patriotism were proof that we were no threat. While no longer banished from the public space, we often find French nonetheless in certain safe spaces like French Tables and bilingual signage. No worries about encroaching into conquered territory. As long as it is not around the kitchen table, French is in a tolerable space. "I am going to say this in English, so everyone understands" is often heard in arguments for the use of the French language. Even though we have come full circle from when speaking French in public was frowned upon to having people tell me they wish their parents had taught them to speak the language, much more is being said about French than in French. From my point of view, the underlying message is that we can delude ourselves into believing we can actually promote French in English.

While there is certainly a rich homegrown plethora of cultural expressions, especially in song lyrics, the translation of mainstream American culture into French seems to be a strong current. One needs to look no further than the translations of such hit novelty songs like Ray Steven's *The Streak*; *The Cajun Streak* by Belton Richard was a big hit. Recordings and performances of contemporary songs as diverse in style and genre as *All Along the Watchtower* (*La Tour de Garde*), *Three Little Birds* (*Trois Petits Tchocs*) or *When the Levee Breaks* (*Quand la Levée Casse*) into French by Gen X and Millennials add to desire to situate our culture and our language squarely in our American experience. Personally, nearly all of my cultural touchstones are the usual Anglo-American ones of my generation: U2, The Ramones, B-52's, etc. Although I enjoy traditional Cajun and Zydeco music, I cannot say it is often my first choice when searching for things to listen to on YouTube or Amazon Music. It is not even my first choice in Francophone music with my taste going more towards Brel, Piaf, Gainsbourg and Françoise Hardy for continental French, and classic Acadian acts like 1755, Edith Butler and Suroît. More modern singers like Lisa LeBlanc and Radio Radio are also among my favorites. In my defense, I do listen to less traditional Louisiana Francophone musicians like Zachary Richard, Feu Follet and Île Dernière. Perhaps it is because they allow making the connection between these two worlds I am constantly oscillating through. This duality is perhaps best exemplified in how the Louisiana Purchase is translated as *La Vente de la Louisiane*. It is as if I am constantly being bought and sold, culturally speaking.

At this point, we can take this effort to integrate French into the public only so far. French will never be allowed to go beyond second-tier status, not even coming close to challenging English's primacy, even on the part of many who would consider themselves to be activists. There will never be a separate French-language public education system, Francophone healthcare nor any governmental services of any consequence offered in French. While the continued use of the language seems to be predicated on its economic viability in society, on a veritable ecosystem created by and for Louisiana Francophones, there is little to no indication it will progress to the point where, for example, we will have a full-fledged Francophone university any time soon to train the professionals necessary to form this kind of society.

Performative French then, especially the Pledge of Allegiance in French and other displays of patriotism, will only contribute, in my opinion, to the continued ostracization of the language. We try to reverse engineer French from English as we can see when, for example, on the Cajun French Virtual *Table Française* Facebook page, people ask for literal translations of English expressions such as "Holy Crap." This process of imposing an Anglo-American template on a Creole reality has missed the mark. A language is the expression of the culture it comes out of. "Raining cats and dogs," according to some etymologists, may come from the old English word "catadupe," meaning a cataract or a waterfall. Seeing that French would not share that original word, it is understandable that *Il pleut des chats et des chiens* is not the correct translation. However, *Il pleut comme une vache qui pisse*, gives greater insight into the overall sensibilities of Gallic cultures as opposed to Anglo-American ones.

We are not the same people from one language to the other. For me, learning French was like opening the floodgates that released a repressed part of my inner self. Like many of my generation who learned French as a second language, it was not so much that we acquired French, but that something that had been wadded up in a tight ball inside of us had finally been unfurled. Without access to the French language, we have no access to that part of our personality. However, we like to pretend we do. Even still, we have to cope with what was aptly called "linguistic schizophrenia". Without a complete valorization of the French language, both our particular way of speaking the language and its "standard" form, we will not only be put in an inferior position vis-à-vis English, but also forced to waste time and energy with internecine battles needlessly dividing ourselves from ourselves and from other French speakers around the world. That psychological healing can only come from being as wholly and as authentically ourselves in both languages.

Given the long hiatus of education in French in Louisiana, key phrases like *lagniappe, couillon*, (with extra points for creative spelling like coo-yon), the suffix -eaux being substituted for the letter "o" everywhere (e.g., Geaux Saints, Sneaux Balls, etc.) and my personal nemesis *Laissez les bons temps rouler* all play into this illusion of "Frenchness." What would French look like if we had been educated in French? What if in Louisiana a deal had been struck with the French-speaking Catholic population like with the Québec Act of 1774 which granted His Majesty's subjects the right to practice their religion in their language? Considered to be one of the most intolerable of the Intolerable Acts, it was enacted in reprisal to the Boston Tea Party and other acts of insurrection against the Crown. The importance of the Catholic Church supporting the preservation of French in the Maritime Provinces was also paramount. While an interesting thought experiment, pondering this question for too long is vain at best and counterproductive at worst. Our time going forward would much better be spent by developing new strategies, like the ones to combat coastal erosion, which prioritize the consolidation of what is salvageable.

There are no indigenous rocks or mountains in Louisiana, so my punishment is different. The fact of the matter is that most Cajuns and Creoles have made the choice of English generations ago, or should I say, that choice was beaten into them. As alluded to earlier, we have heard the story *ad nauseum*. Our parents (grandparents, great-grandparents) were punished and shamed for speaking French. They spoke to us in English but continued to speak French among themselves to keep secrets from us. Normalizing this behavior towards a language and its culture is a power play meant to drag an otherwise well-functioning society kicking and screaming into another. Reading this chapter in our history through post-colonial glasses is not beyond reason. Having to write this essay in English is proof of that we still have a long way to go before we can attain any measure of peace with that fractured past. The fact of the matter is that I have never felt at home in English. I always knew that I was French, even if I could not speak it. Writing about my experience as a recovered Louisiana Francophone in English is, and I do not think I am exaggerating, at best betrayal, at worst treason. Speaking the language that was imposed by force upon us, even speaking and writing it well, gives me no satisfaction, no sense of accomplishment. Seeing anything I write in English along other Anglophone writers gives me no sense of being a part of that same family, no sense of accomplishment. Indeed, I am always the outsider. Do not get me wrong, there are naturally dozens of English-language writers I admire and look to for inspiration. But, as a good friend of mine told me long ago, "I am an American, *mais je suis pas américain.*" Nonetheless, it is only when I am among other Francophone speakers, writers, and poets, even if I know I am as far away from the talent of most of them as one can get and that we may have greatly divergent tastes and opinions, I know that I am among my people who speak the same language, both literally and figuratively.

The way thought bends around the noun-adjective agreement to make sure there is an accord; the way the *passé composé* cradles adverbs between the helping verb and the past participle; the way subject-object-verb syntax establishes first a relationship between the subject and the object before defining the nature of that relation: they all create a musicality, an ambiance, and a texture that place me in my environment. For example, let us take a simple sentence like I love you. The subject I declares its action, in this case to love, first. I must first establish that I am doing something, and that is loving. We do not know yet what I love until I announce the object of my love, in this case, you. On the other hand, in French, *je t'aime*, we first establish that there exists a subjective I, *je*, and an objective you, *te*, bringing you into proximity to me, into a direct relationship with me. Even further cementing our relationship as uniquely between you and me before we know what action it will take, is the elision of the e before the vowel commencing the verb to love, aimer. *Je t'aime* nearly combines into one word, especially when spoken sincerely. *J't'aime* resonates as one syllable, one movement, one expression of two becoming one. I love you are certainly beautiful words in and of themselves that are not said enough, even between people who truly love each other. But as the Avett Brothers sing, they are three words that have become hard to say and even harder to see as anything other than three separate words.

Joseph Campbell wrote that mythology is the penultimate truth because ultimate truth cannot be put into words. The question Camus posed in the opening lines of his book was whether life was worth living. Knowing that we will never attain the ultimate truth nor reach the pinnacle, the question we need to ask ourselves, *Franco-louisianais*, is whether or not life is worth living in Louisiana without French. Like King Sisyphus, we have cheated death time and time again, as illustrated by the bon mot Zachary Richard and Barry Jean Ancelet (and I on occasion) often recount whenever someone asks about the viability of the French language: "*Chaque fois qu'on veut fermer son cercueil, le cadavre se dresse et demande une autre bière.*" (Everytime someone wants to close its coffin; the body sits up and orders another beer.) But for how long? Will French live or die, or will it exist in a zombie-like comatose state somewhere in between?

If we really want to relieve French of its existentialist crisis and revitalize it to the point of truly having *droit à la cité*, perhaps Sisyphus is not the right metaphor; perhaps we need to think of it in terms of Groundhog's Day. Every day we wake up to the same scenario, going through more or less the same motions. Yet, at the end, Bill Murray's character has his *prise de conscience* and learns something new every day, slowly making progress towards some far away but attainable goal. Then, perhaps, I can imagine myself happy.

6. French: Louisiana's Most Renewable but Undeveloped Natural Resource: Cultural Tourism as a Revitalization Tool for Louisiana Heritage Languages
Joseph Dunn

Louisiana, New Orleans, Baton Rouge, Lafayette: These place names loom large in the collective imagination of Americans and people around the world. While we now usually only relate to them in English, there are definite clues about their origin when we read: *La Louisiane, La Nouvelle-Orléans, Bâton-Rouge, Lafayette*. How often, though, do we see or hear these original orthographies or pronunciations outside of historic documents and texts in archives? Taking it a bit further: The Bayou State, Cajun, Zydeco, Laissez les bons temps rouler, Creole, Fleur de lys, Acadians, Gumbo, Zachary Richard, Jambalaya, Tony Chachere's Creole Seasoning, Boudin. These, among other words, catch phrases and names have been ubiquitous in Louisiana tourism promotion campaigns since at least the mid-20th century, playing on the state's French history, heritage, and culture to entice visitors to travel and spend money in restaurants, attractions, and accommodations. This messaging has and continues to create the perception in French-speaking countries and regions that Louisiana is indeed a Francophone space, where they can consume tourism products in French. The reality is often quite different.

Les chiffres - The Numbers

Tourism and culture are in the top five economic engines of the State of Louisiana, accounting for 242,000 jobs in the tourism sector and 171,486 in the cultural sector, and nearly $20 billion in direct spending in 2019. In March 2020, the Governor of Louisiana closed the state due to the COVID-19 virus. This mandated shut-down was implemented just at the beginning of the spring tourism and festival season, which usually draws significant numbers of international visitors, including many French-speakers.

The closure also coincided with the announcement by the Lieutenant Governor, the elected state official charged with overseeing the Department of Culture, Recreation and Tourism, that numbers in 2019 had exceeded previous records with 53.2 million visitors and direct spending of nearly nineteen billion dollars.[21] According to statistics provided by and compiled from various sources by the Louisiana Office of Tourism, approximately 352,200 tourists from Francophone countries or regions visited the state from 2015 through the spring of 2020, spending approximately $40,638,820.[22]

L'université - University

Despite these Francophone visitation and economic impact numbers, a quick glance at the coursework necessary to obtain a bachelor's degree in hospitality management at one of several Louisiana universities that offers such a program reveals that none of them requires the study of a world language. This sometimes contrasts with the messaging used to recruit students, as illustrated by this text from the Hospitality Management Major page on the website of the University of Louisiana at Lafayette (ULL):

> Tourism Right Here in Lafayette. Lafayette's location in the heart of Cajun Country attracts thousands of visitors who spend hundreds of millions of dollars every year. Our culture is known for its delicious food, unique landscapes, and welcoming people. You will learn how to share that culture with people who are just visiting or who call Lafayette home.[23]

Even the University of Louisiana at Lafayette which styles itself the "*Université des Acadiens*" and which is located in "the heart of Cajun Country" does not require French for its tourism and hospitality students.

Les écoles – Schools

Much has been written, broadcast and publicized about Louisiana's French immersion schools. These model educational environments in which more than 5,000 Louisiana schoolchildren spend up to seventy percent of their day learning academic subject matter *en français* are prized as the incubators of Louisiana's future generations of French-speakers.

For parents, the bilingual child equates to higher potential for secondary education scholarships and higher earning potential in adulthood. For administrators, bilingual students mean higher standardized test scores. In addition to those enrolled in immersion, more than 30,000 students study French as a second language in junior high and high school classrooms.[24]

That being said, the number of students who study Spanish is double and perhaps even triple that of those who study French. Surprisingly, French is no longer offered as a language option in many Louisiana schools, even in areas that are historically Francophone. In an online discussion group, one person remarked about this very topic, "Central Lafourche High School in Mathews does not have a French teacher." Lafourche Parish is one of the most French-speaking regions of the state.

The elimination of French as a second language programs in Louisiana schools might be attributed to the ever-increasing Hispanic populations and the economic impact of Spanish-speakers. Anecdotally, students, parents and administrators consider Spanish to be more "useful" than French because in Louisiana, as elsewhere in the United States, Spanish is a language of mass consumerism. French is not. This tug of war between French and Spanish classrooms leads to questions about the end goal of opening and maintaining French immersion environments when there is no pathway to higher education or professional development in French, even in tourism, one of Louisiana's top five industries.

Les lois - Laws

In the legislative restructuring of the Council for the Development of French in Louisiana (CODOFIL) in 2010, among the agency's mandates is the creation of a "Francophone Friendly" label for festivals and businesses.[25] Article 6 of LA R.S. 25:651 (2010) calls for CODOFIL "To develop a certification system whereby vendors, festivals, and restaurants may be designated "Francophone Friendly" and design and issue a marquee that may be displayed by each certified entity."

Subsequent community outreach to identify tourism services and other entities that offer oral or written service in French led to the launch of the initiative OUI! in 2019.

Per CODOFIL's website, "With the *OUI!* Initiative - formerly called *FrancoResponsable* French-Friendly - CODOFIL seeks to identify and catalog Louisiana businesses that can offer services in French. To be part of this network, a business must be able to interact with clients in French (at least one French-speaking staff member) and/or supply written materials in French (menu, brochures, website, etc)."

Additionally, the "Louisiana French Language Services Act: Act 106" enacted in 2011 (LA R.S 25:671-674), calls for the identification of French-speakers in state government offices "[t]o the extent practicable, to provide state government services to French speaking citizens and visitors in the French language" and "To assist Louisiana citizens who speak French in dealing with and receiving services from state government so as to support the long-term sustainability of Louisiana's historic French cultural heritage."

Specific to tourism, the text also reads, "To assist French-speaking visitors to the state and thus to promote an increase in tourism and greater investment in the state from Francophone countries" and "[t]he department shall urge the convention and visitors' bureaus throughout the state to implement a similar program." As a non-funded mandate, the Louisiana French Language Services Act has not been implemented since its adoption into law in 2011.

Le marché du travail - The Job Market

Even with the *OUI!* initiative and the adoption of the Louisiana French Language Services Act, there remain no mandated positions, hiring practices or tax incentives for employing Francophone workers in Louisiana.

The adoption of these laws has not led employers to actively recruit and hire French-speaking staff, which would professionally and economically validate them in their Francophonie. To date

(2021), anyone who might be inclined to request and consume services in French in the public or private sector has no way to visibly identify French-speaking personnel.

Le français au travail - Where French Works

CODOFIL's *OUI!* initiative has been successful in compiling an inventory of 88 Louisiana tourism-related businesses that can provide verbal or written service in French.

> Lodging (hotels, bed & breakfasts): 16
> Restaurants: 24
> Attractions/Welcome Centers: 48

Of the attractions and welcome centers, thirty-seven employ French-speaking staff or rely on Francophone volunteers, while twenty-four provide written materials in French (brochures, exhibition panels, websites, etc.) However, this service cannot always be guaranteed.[26] Among the most successful historic sites proposing tours in French are Laura: Louisiana's Creole Heritage Site ("Laura Plantation") in Vacherie, LA and Vermilionville in Lafayette, LA. Since opening to the public in 1994, Laura has actively marketed its ability to provide daily tours in French by creating a fully bilingual website and welcoming French-speaking tour operators, travel agents, print and broadcast media to discover the diverse Creole history of the former sugar plantation. Prior to the outbreak of the COVID-19 pandemic of 2020, Laura offered tours in French three times per day, seven days per week. Between 2015 and 2019, Francophone visitors from France, Canada, and elsewhere accounted for more than 12% of annual visitation, supporting two full-time bilingual administrative staff members, as well as five part-time French-speaking historic interpreters.[27]

Two hours to the west of Laura sits Vermilionville, a living history museum and folklife park. According to its website, "Since its opening in 1990, the historic village has become one of Lafayette's premiere tourist attractions welcoming more than 50,000 visitors each year from around the world."

Vermilionville employs five French-speaking staff, including its executive director. Though exact numbers were not available, Francophone visitors account for roughly 60% of the site's international visitation annually.[28]

Prochains pas - Next Steps

One of the biggest challenges to the full development of a French-speaking cultural tourism economy in Louisiana is that the educational, political, and social labeling of French as a "foreign language" over the past century has resulted in a disconnect between the state's diverse populations and their relationship to their own French and Creole-speaking history and culture. The tourism leaders and decision-makers at the state and local levels who mass market Louisiana worldwide are, by and large, monolingual anglophones who do not recognize the economic potential of French. From the classroom at the elementary, secondary, and university levels and into the workplace, methods and strategies must be developed to reintroduce French and Creole as homegrown, renewable assets in the same way that music, cuisine, and other aspects of Louisiana culture are presented as consumable products.

As we continue to collect data on enrollment in immersion and French as a second language classrooms, as well as the numbers of Francophone tourists and spending, we can begin to envision the creation of cultural tourism networks in which multilingual Louisianians can take leadership roles and provide services *en français*, thereby economically validating the teaching and reacquisition of Louisiana's French and Creole heritage languages and their reintroduction to the marketplace.

7. The "cadaver" is thirsty: Perspectives on language activism in Louisiana
Marguerite P. Justus

A week before the COVID-19 lockdowns began, I was sitting at a French Table in a small South Louisiana town. *Les Tables Françaises*, as these grassroots meetups are called, form an essential pillar of language maintenance and revival in the state. This particular group was new, and at this inaugural meeting we went around the table introducing ourselves in French. The organizer, a local priest, explained what had inspired him to start a new group in this particular area. I introduced myself as an employee of the Council for the Development of French in Louisiana (CODOFIL) and expressed my delight at being able to add another group to the calendar of French Tables I maintain on our website. To the left of me, an older couple introduced themselves and explained a bit about their childhood and the way they had seen the language shift happen in their lifetime; they were native Louisiana French speakers. Next was a young woman in her twenties, sitting beside her grandfather. She said bonjour, and then switched to English, quietly stating: "My name is Yvette Cormier,[29] and I do not speak French."

She went on to explain that she would like to learn and had come to the meetup with her French-speaking grandfather for this purpose, but the way she had phrased her first statement stuck with me. It reminded me of media depictions I had seen of Alcoholics Anonymous meetings. She communicated her situation with a kind of somber simplicity, tinged with self-consciousness. The feeling is not unfamiliar to me. At some point in early childhood, I came to understand that my maternal grandparents had grown up speaking a different language than I had, and from that point on, there was always a question in my brain: Why did I not speak French?

My mother's family had lived in South Louisiana for hundreds of years. They had spoken French for hundreds of years. I still lived in South Louisiana. Why did I not speak French? I am fortunate to be able to ask this question in the past tense - I spent my teen years and early twenties learning the language - but for many of my friends, this disconnect with French is still an issue. I have heard the French language described by Louisianians as a "phantom limb" or a "missing piece." People wonder to themselves: I hunt like my PawPaw. I fish, dance, cook like my PawPaw. Why do I not speak French like my PawPaw?

The most common answer to that question involves French-speaking children being punished in the Louisiana public school system during the first half of the 20th century; this was the answer I was given when I asked the question as a child. As I got older and studied 20th-century Louisiana, however, the answer became more complex. The rise of the oil industry run by Anglo-Americans, the effects of the Second World War, the expansion of highway systems, the advent of television - all these things and more played a role in language shift in Louisiana.

When seen this way, the problem of language shift feels much less straightforward. Consequently, the possible solutions seem more intangible. It can be demoralizing to consider all the forces we are fighting against when we continue to speak French in Louisiana. Some pessimism is to be expected when working with a minority language, particularly one that finds itself "competing" with a hegemonic lingua franca like American English. We can feel a sense of loss over the decline in speakers. We can lament the differences between the way our elders speak and the language as it is taught in a more formal school setting. We can complain about those who have seemingly "given up" and fully "Americanized." It would be unrealistic to say we should not feel pessimistic at all.

Ironically, an antidote to this pessimism lies within the problem itself: Nothing is more motivating to me than thinking of the countless Louisianians I have met who hate the fact that they do not speak French. I still hear the sentiment echoed by people, from teenagers to retirees: they know their families spoke French, they know they do not, and they are genuinely bothered by that. As long as it bothers us, we stand a chance of correcting it.

One Obstacle at a Time

In some people, the desire to speak their family's heritage language is intense, almost primordial. As a high schooler, I took French classes but also immersed myself in Francophone movies, music, books, and radio programs because something in me would not sit still until I could communicate in this language. I have many friends, bilingual Louisianians in their twenties, thirties, and forties, who had a similar feeling when learning. Still, this is not everyone's experience. The desire for French does not always translate to successfully learning it.

I am certain that if learning French were commodifiable - if you could master the language simply by paying $800, for example - language decline would immediately reverse in Louisiana. The cost could double or triple, and I fully believe people would still scrimp and save to buy back this part of their heritage. Unfortunately, language learning does not work this way. You can pay for a class or for a linguistic stay in a Francophone country, but you cannot purchase a skill; you can only build one through your own efforts. There are so many obstacles that it can seem as if the only people who make it through, who learn French on purpose despite the Anglo-centric world around them, are those who have that unrelenting determination to do so. Yet, to pin it all on motivation would be both misguided and unproductive. If the only paths to fluency are to be raised in the language or to possess an inexplicable zealousness for learning it, language "choice" might as well be predestined.

On the other hand, if we accept that language learning and language use are choices, then a key part of helping people to choose French is to remove obstacles. The obstacles are myriad. Finding the time is a major one for most adult learners. Finding the money for classes, instructional resources, or immersive travel can be difficult, and the United States is so accustomed to the primacy of English that there is not a cultural norm of learning other languages; if it is not through a class, some sort of language learning software, or study abroad, many Americans do not know how to navigate the language learning process. Some learners who have begun the process find they have an aptitude for languages, while others find the opposite. The latter may abandon the project quickly, deciding that they are "no good" at languages in the same way that some people struggle with math or writing. Varying aptitudes may play a part, but the accompanying mentality ("I am no good, so why bother?") presents a far bigger obstacle. Even if someone works around all these obstacles and manages to reach a level of competency in French, it can be a challenge to try to put that French to use. English is everywhere, and people who do not habitually go against the grain to use their French can begin to lose their language skills.

One effective way to remove several of these obstacles at once is to start with young Louisianians. A student learning French at school has time set aside for learning and no additional financial burden. This is true of French as a Second Language classes but even more so for French Immersion programs where students' French learning is integrated into their other subjects. Louisiana boasts a healthy French Immersion presence in the public school system, with over 5,000 students currently studying in French immersion across thirteen parishes.

Various nonprofits and language schools fund scholarships allowing Louisianians to study French abroad, though the demand for these scholarship programs often outstrips the supply. CODOFIL also encourages the use of French in public spaces through programs like the Oui! Initiative, an online database of Louisiana businesses that can offer services in French. If you discover through the Oui! website that the barista at your local coffee shop speaks French, you may decide to order in French on your next visit.

One major obstacle that CODOFIL is working to remove right now is the lack of guidance for independent learners of French. CODOFIL is launching a new website in 2021 called "Learn French, Louisiana!" The site is a curated catalog of learning resources for both International and Louisiana varieties of French[30] and puts a particular emphasis on free or low-cost resources that are easily accessible. The resources it highlights include everything from YouTube channels to children's books to podcasts to smartphone apps. There is also a blog section on the site that reflects on the lived experience of language learning, normalizing the struggles learners face and building a sense of community around the process. Learning French as a Louisianian is not just a pastime; Louisiana learners of French are part of a movement.

A New Wave

In recent years, the energy behind the movement for French in Louisiana has intensified. CODOFIL celebrated its 50th anniversary in 2018. French Tables have expanded, with new ones cropping up in small towns like Erath and bigger cities like Baton Rouge. A few years ago, as this new wave was starting to build, I asked a long-time activist for French in Louisiana what sort of shifts she had noticed in the community over the years. She replied that she was both impressed and excited by the way young Louisianians are engaging in very tangible ways with the language. She talked about periods where French Louisiana language and culture were enthusiastically celebrated, but with more of a focus on cultural pride. The moment we are currently living goes beyond pride; activism has to be active.

In December 2018, two Louisianians in their early twenties founded *Le Bourdon de la Louisiane*, a curated webzine entirely in French and Kouri-Vini (Louisiana Creole) that has a particular focus on Louisiana topics. Its name is a nod to the last regularly published French-language newspaper in Louisiana, *L'Abeille de la Nouvelle-Orléans*.[31] *L'Abeille* published its last article in 1923, but nearly a century later, Le Bourdon's contributors are writing online articles that spark fascinating debates. Authors ask why the state's vital records office does not allow for accent marks on birth certificates (effectively relegating every Aimée to be Aimee) and debate the pros and cons of choosing particular dates for an inclusive national holiday that would unite the Louisiana Francophone community.

Earlier that same year, two other Louisiana twenty-somethings met for the first time at a French Table and realized during their conversation that they knew of no French-language podcast made by Louisianians. Not content to simply critique, they signed up for a membership at the local open-access media station and started the podcast *Charrer-Veiller*. The co-hosts discuss amongst themselves and invite guests. Depending on the episode, they may talk about *loups-garous* (werewolves), people's experiences learning French in Louisiana, or *Ti-Wayne* (a calqued nickname for the rapper Lil Wayne).

Media startup *Télé-Louisiane* also began in 2018 and a separate media company, New Niveau, was launched in 2020. Télé-Louisiane began its programming with a series of sixteen French-language interviews filmed during *Festivals Acadiens et Créoles 2018* and continues today with programs like *Les Aventures de Boudini et Ses Amis*, an animated cartoon that is being integrated into elementary French Immersion classes. Meanwhile, *New Niveau*'s programs include *Les Nouvelles-Orléans*, a bi-weekly sampling of local news headlines, and *Le Tac-Tac*, an editorial-style series that touches on themes like Louisiana exceptionalism and the role of codeswitching in a bilingual society.

Télé-Louisiane and *New Niveau* also provide platforms for independent creators to showcase their work. *LACréole Show*, the brainchild of a French-speaking Louisiana high school student, is featured on both websites. In addition, the activists behind *Télé-Louisiane* and *New Niveau* are not limiting themselves to a single avenue for engaging with French. The founder of *Télé-Louisiane* is involved in community organizing efforts to expand French Immersion in schools. The creators behind *New Niveau* write and perform original indie pop in Louisiana French with their band *Sweet Crude*.

Indie pop in French may be new to Louisiana, but the French language has a longstanding relationship with traditional Louisiana music. That relationship has continued to flourish. Young people continue to pick up accordions, fiddles, and rubboards. They continue to learn the traditional canon, and many continue to add to it. Musicians like Louis Michot, Kristi Guillory, Cedric Watson, and Blake Miller have been mixing their original creations with traditional standards for years. Artists like Jourdan Thibodeaux and Sweet Crude are writing songs not just in Louisiana French, but about it. "*Tu vis ta culture ou tu tues ta culture - y a pas de milieu,*"[32] asserts Thibodeaux in his original song *La Prière*. Sam Craft of Sweet Crude ends the song *Finger Guns* with a refrain that feels like a cry for urgent action: "*On est la dernière génération! On est la dernière génération!*"[33] Louisianians are writing music, and at times, they are writing anthems.

The popularity of music as an oral form of literature is complimented by a resurgence of writing in French. In 2019, after a decade of hibernation, the University of Louisiana at Lafayette's Francophone literary review was revived by a group of motivated graduate students. *Feux Follets* - as the review is called - publishes poetry, short prose, and visual art pieces in a yearly edition that is released both as a physical paperback and online. *Ô Malheureuse! French Writings by Louisiana Women* is another noteworthy recent publication. What began as an open call for contributions from female Louisiana writers on the blog *La Prairie des Femmes* evolved into a paperback collection of writings published by UL Press with over forty contributors of various ages and backgrounds. *Les Éditions Tintamarre*, the French language publishing house based out of Shreveport, is releasing fresh printings of 19th-century Louisiana authors alongside newer works like Nathan Rabalais' *Le Hantage*. The poems in it may be interspersed with black-and-white images of cemeteries, but *Le Hantage* is brimming with the word play of a very much living language.

These are only a few examples of the creative momentum currently surrounding French; new initiatives have been emerging in various domains, whether it be the arts, education, or public planning. In 2017, the French Culture Film Grant began funding the creation of short narrative films and long-form documentaries that focus on language and culture in Francophone Louisiana. The Alliance Française de Lafayette has recently added Louisiana/Cajun French and Kouri-Vini language classes to its continuing education efforts. The city of Lafayette is installing bilingual wayfinding signage in 2021. The modern-looking signage features French more prominently than English. The old refrain that generations of Louisianians heard so often - that the future was in English, and only in English - is starting to feel inaccurate.

None of this progress would be possible, however, were it not for the work of previous waves of activism. The project for bilingual signage in Lafayette relied heavily on the 2010 Dictionary of Louisiana French as a reference; the dictionary took a team of volunteers over a decade to compile and has become a powerful tool for legitimizing French in Louisiana. Young musicians may be experimenting and writing their own lyrics, but the path for this was laid out for them by artists like Zachary Richard and Michael Doucet. The activist mentioned at the beginning of this section, the one who praised young Louisianians for their initiative, was herself a French teacher and inspired young people's activism for several decades.

The Real Stakes

If I am expounding on the numerous success stories in the Louisiana French movement, it is not to give the impression that everything is going well. The challenges Francophone Louisiana faces are very real. Every ten years, census numbers give a sobering account; we cannot seem to create new speakers of French at the rate at which we are losing the older generation of native speakers. Yet, every time I hear a Francophone foreigner reference the "*Cajun mort-vivant*"[34] or a neighbor sighing that the language is "dead," I cannot help but think of these perspectives as myopic. My mind immediately goes to Zachary Richard or Barry Ancelet quipping: "*Dès qu'on est prêt à fermer le cercueil sur le cadavre de la Francophonie louisianaise, ben, le cadavre se lève, pis demande une bière.*"[35]

War feels like an imperfect metaphor for the linguistic situation in Louisiana. Tensions between Francophones and Anglophones are not a major issue. There is no nascent separatist movement for French Louisiana. Nevertheless, 'war' feels like the appropriate metaphor to describe the experience of working against language shift. Any battle lost can feel like the end, but it is only a battle.

In reality, so many of the battles are psychological. One of most important tiny battles I regularly fight is to remind people - myself included - of the real stakes involved in speaking French. At times, the question of which language to speak can cause anxiety. Does everyone in this group understand French? Would it be weird if I spoke French now? Is my French even good enough? It provokes something akin to the fight-or-flight response. In those moments, I have to remind myself that this response feels like danger, but it is not actually dangerous.

If I speak French to someone and they do not understand me, nobody dies. If I try to shift a conversation from English to French and it ends up feeling awkward, nobody dies. If I conjugate a verb incorrectly, nobody dies. Conversely, every time I choose French, I am making that language alive in Louisiana. I have won that day's tiny battle. At French Tables, on social media, and in our creative endeavors, battles like this are fought and won every day.

8. Speaking from the margins of the margin: An African American Perspective on learning French in Louisiana
Jerry L. Parker

Conversations on race in America are hard. Regardless of background, environment, and beliefs toward race, racism, prejudice based on race, implicit bias, systemic racism, and social injustice these conversations carry what I find to be a burden of defining. This burden includes the duty of defining one's position on race, defining one's boundaries on what is acceptable to say about race, and defining what constitutes a racist from an individual who has unique experiences. In this chapter, I seek to expand the conversation into foreign languages. Specifically, I take a unique approach by focusing on my experience in relation to learning French as an African American male second language learner living in Louisiana.

To approach this chapter, I use an autoethnography approach (Belbase, Luitel, & Taylor, 2008). I will first establish the general educational context for African American children in foreign languages, specifically in higher education. I will then give my personal experience with learning French and the trials and tribulations of being an African American man in a very white dominated field. I will then end with recommendations on how to diversify the field with more African American students.

Previous Research on African American Students in Foreign Languages

The research on African American students' attitudes toward foreign language education is at most a few decades old. In fact, Moore (2005) found that in the two leading academic journals in foreign languages, Modern Language Journal (started in 1925) and Foreign Language Annals (started in the 1960's), there only existed five articles related to minority students. Of that, three dealt specifically with Black[36] students and two were coauthored by Moore (Davis & Markham, 1991; Moore & English, 1997, 1998). With the rise in recent efforts toward diversity, equity, and inclusion, more work needs to be produced; hence, the purpose of this chapter. However, before more can be done, the sum of the existing literature must be considered.

One of the earlier studies was conducted by Lassiter (1989). In her dissertation she wanted to understand if race was a factor in learning a second language among university students. She discovered that Black students were more focused on learning languages as a tool for communication while white students were more focused on cultural awareness and the study of languages because of previous exposure via schooling, travel, and social exposure to bilinguals. Black kids on average suggested that bilingualism would make them more marketable and would be more beneficial for going to graduate school or professional school. She concluded that both black and white students had positive attitudes toward learning a language but that it was white kids' cross-cultural awareness which most likely contributed to their larger enrollment in courses.

In more recent years, Moore (2005) conducted an exploratory survey where she collected data over a two-year period. There was a total of 128 Black respondents (37 male and 91 female). The majority of these students stated that they were only studying a language because it was required for them to graduate. Additionally, they were most interested in learning Spanish, French, Japanese, and German. They further suggested that their experience with learning a language was neither good nor bad. There was also no correlation between them choosing to take a certain language and their parents' previous experience with languages; however, they were commonly discouraged by other students who believed languages were too hard. The respondents in contrast felt that study abroad should be mandatory for all students and that to increase enrollment there was a need for more offerings, more emphasis on culture in the classroom, less concern with grammar accuracy, and more awareness of the benefits of learning a language.

More than half a decade later Watterson (2011) also sought to gauge Black students' attitudes toward studying foreign languages. It was discovered that Black students do not normally feel a connection to foreign language study because they do not see a direct connection between their Afro-diasporic heritage and the course content. Glynn (2012) echoed this same sentiment while investigating the experience of various ethnic groups during foreign language study. In surveying and interviewing urban and suburban African American students, it was determined that students felt that teachers harbored negative feelings toward them and that issues of systemic exclusion were a contributory factor to the low number of African Americans enrolled in foreign language courses.

Glynn called for the development of a system for recruiting in elementary and junior high and the providing of equity and differentiated instruction in teaching. Glynn also stated that there was a need for foreign languages to be required for graduation along with support for families and schools to maintain them. Lastly, it was recommended that less dependency on the textbooks, a shift away from Eurocentric curriculum and toward culturally relevant pedagogy, a shift in attitude toward language study in the whole school, and a focus on critical pedagogy and social justice were needed for all students to succeed in foreign language courses.

Pratt (2012), in looking specifically at Spanish, also concluded similar findings. In surveying students in a district of 7,069, only 1,034 (15%) identified as African American, while 3,122 (44%) identified as Hispanic or Latino, and 2,737 (39%) identified as white. Of this population, 422 (14%) African American students were enrolled in Spanish courses in comparison to 1,484 (49%) white students and 1,073 (35%) Hispanic/Latino students. Her survey results concluded that the African American students were mainly studying Spanish because of economic/career benefits, family background, a like of the language, requirements for entry into college, it seemed fun or interesting, and various other extrinsic factors.

As it related to African Americans continuing the study of Spanish beyond what was required, Pratts' findings concluded that their main focus was on their grades, teacher remarks and support, satisfying college entrance, knowledge of the language, variety in the activities, career benefits, group activities and projects, and their enjoyment of the language among other things. Moreover, as it concerned their college motivations, the African American respondents cited mainly the possibility of good grades, enjoying the classroom activities, encouragement of the high school teacher, wanting to continue what they started, possible career benefits, being comfortable, the difficulty of Spanish, relevance to other academic subjects, the reputation of colleges and universities, and clear signs of progress in Spanish as factors that determined if they would either continue or stop their study of Spanish.

The Black experience was also a topic of interest for Calhoun (2012). However, this study centered on Black foreign language majors' lived experience. In interviewing three students, this study found that identity among Black foreign language majors was a more complex conversation than just race. There were multiple aspects of daily life that drew them toward majoring in foreign languages. Pollock (2018) also sought to look at the Black experience and found that multiple factors contributed to students' willingness to study a language including: educational experiences in K-12, family support, peer support and the instructor. Specifically, having a Black/African American instructor would have positively affected their attitude toward foreign language learning.

Although brief, the review of previous literature shows the progression of research on Black students across the past few decades. Each study more or less concluded the same ideas that are still being echoed in the literature. Black/African American students face no specific intellectual problems in learning a foreign language (Hubbard, 2014). They are just as likely to gain fluency in a language as any other race of children. Black/African American students are less likely to study a foreign language and to continue it through year three or beyond at the high school level due to a plethora of reasons (Glynn & Wassell, 2018). Black/African American students constantly receive counseling against taking foreign language courses because others believe it would be too hard for them or is a waste of time and has no benefit for them (Hubbard, 2014).

To assure equity and meaningful participation for all racialized minorities in foreign languages we must address issues of inequality and inequity directly (Anya & Randolph, 2019). Although the argument by educators against such conversations is that it is too political and has no place in schools, students will still go through socialization via a particular lens (i.e., race, gender, sexuality, socioeconomic) whether we talk about it or not. Specifically, racism and race are engrained in all aspects of American society. Hence, Juneteenth, Martin Luther King Day, Hispanic Heritage Month,

Asian and Pacific Islander Heritage Month, and Black History Month being federally recognized celebrations. Colorblindness is a deliberate choice to ignore student differences and how they operate individually, systematically, and institutionally (Anya & Randolph, 2019). To further contextualized the research on African American/Black student interest in foreign languages in the following section I present recent data from the both the National Center for Educational Statistics (NCES) and the Louisiana Board of Regents (LBoR).

Contemporary Enrollment Trends in Foreign Language Education

During and post-COVID-19, America was in a transformative period. Americans took more interest in issues of diversity, equity, and inclusion in all aspects of society including the education system. As it relates to the current study, research on African American[37] students and foreign language education is centered around the notion that "schools are institutions that respond to and reflect the larger society" (Nieto, 1992 pp 21). Thus, when considering the data on African American students in foreign languages, there are some interesting realities of American society that must be faced.

In looking at recent data published by the National Center for Educational Statistics, as shown in Table 1, the number of Black students who have graduated with a bachelor's degree in a foreign language within recent years is almost non-existent. To further disaggregate the data, Table 2 presents the number of female graduates in foreign languages from 2017 through 2019.

The data on Black female foreign language graduates is a little more promising. Of the 23,143 individuals who identified as female, those who identified as Black females made up five percent of the total female graduates. This in comparison to white females who made up more than half of the total female population and Hispanics/Latinas who made up a little less than one-fourth of the total number of female graduates. Black females are still trailing behind Asian and Pacific Islanders and Alaskan Indian/Native American but had slightly more degree earnings than biracial and non-resident female students.

Table 1. Foreign Language Undergraduate Graduation rates of between 2017-2019

Total	White	Black	Hispanic	Asian/Pacific Islander	Alaskan Indian/ Native America	Biracial	Non-resident
2017-2019 33,549	19,198 (57.2%)	1,172 (3.49%)	7,733 (23.04%)	2,128 (6.34%)	86 (.26%)	1,499 (4.47%)	1,333 (3.97%)

Table 2. Female Graduates in Foreign Languages by Race between during 2017-2018 & 2018-2019

Total	White	Black	Hispanic	Asian/Pacific Islander	Alaskan Indian/ Native America	Biracial	Non-resident
2017-2019 23,143	12,897 (55.72%)	1,157 (5.00%)	5,640 (24.37%)	1,462 (6.32%)	56 (.24%)	1,007 (4.35%)	927 (4.00%)

Jerry L. Parker

Table 3. Male Foreign Language Graduates by Race between during 2017-2018 & 2018-2019

Year	Total	White	Black	Hispanic/ Latino	Asian/Pacific Islander	Alaskan Indian/ Native America	Biracial	Non-resident
2017-2019	10,406	6, 301 (60.55%)	415 (4.00%)	2,093 (20.11%)	666 (6.40%)	33 (.32%)	492 (4.73%)	406 (3.90%)

Table 4. Foreign Language Graduates in Louisiana by Race between during 2009-2019

Year	2009	2010	2011	2012	2013	2014	2015	2016	2017	2018	2019	Total
Black	9 (9.77%)	15 (13.39%)	9 (7.69%)	12 (14.46%)	12 (12.90%)	8 (10.81%)	8 (10.26%)	5 (6.50%)	4 (7.55%)	4 (7.41%)	4 (5.71%)	90 (9.88%)
Non-Black	84 (90.32%)	97 (86.61%)	108 (92.31%)	73 (87.95%)	82 (88.17%)	66 (89.19%)	70 (89.74)	72 (93/51%)	53 (91.38%)	50 (92.59)	66 (94.29%)	821 (90.12%)
Total	93	112	117	83	93	74	78	77	58	54	70	911

Retrieved from nces.ed.gov

It is well known that females overall are the largest population of students in higher education and Black females are the largest growing number of degree earners. In comparison to the total population of graduates, Black females earned only 3.45% of all bachelor's degrees in foreign languages during the two-years between 2017 and 2019. However, they earned 98.72% percent of the foreign language bachelor's degrees earned overall by black students over the two-year period. This is in opposition to black males as presented inTable 3.

Those who identified as white made up the largest population among those who identified as male and who graduated with a bachelor's degree in foreign languages during the 2017-2018 and 2018-2019 school years. The second largest group of graduates was Hispanic/Latino men followed by Asians and Pacific Islanders. Black males earned the second lowest number of bachelor's degrees in foreign languages, ranking above students who identified as biracial and as non-residents. The Department of Education data speak to an issue that has been of concern to scholars nationally for decades. Of further interest would be looking at these trends state-wise. For the current conversation, I divulge into Louisiana's numbers.

Undergraduate Foreign Language
Graduation Rates in Louisiana

Language and language education is a very unique thing in Louisiana. We know from studying 20th century sources that many indigenous languages such as Choctaw, Chitimacha, Atakapa, Tunica, Biloxi, and Natchez were some of the earliest languages spoken in the region (Dajko & Walton, 2019). More prominently, Louisiana is well known for having strong cultural and linguistic communities related back to their French and Spanish heritage. Louisiana Cajun French and Louisiana Creole French, which scholars typically refer to in combination with lexicon from the Native Americans as Louisiana Regional French, and Isleño Spanish of St. Bernard Parish still have a strong presence in contemporary times and is spoken as either a first or second language by many Louisiana natives.

Considering the state has such as strong linguistic influence one would think bilingualism would be a large aspect of the majority of citizens daily life. However, this is not the case. In looking at data related to the completion rate for foreign language majors over a 10-year span we see the same trend as with the national data among Black students. As suggested in Table 4, Black students on average are not earning bachelor's degrees in world languages at rate near as profound as other races of students in Louisiana.

In Louisiana, almost one-tenth of foreign language graduates over the past ten years identified as Black. This is in comparison to White, Hispanic, Asian, and other races of students who made up 90% of all total majors. In looking across the years, the average number of Black foreign language graduates was 8.18. The median number of Black graduates was 8. The mode or the most common number in a graduation cohort was 4 students. The range was 17.

As a point of comparison, over the past ten years, the average number of foreign language graduates who identified as white or another race was 74.64. The median number of white and other graduates was 72 with a mode of 66. The range was 58. Although the numbers can appear to be inflated when considering Black students were compared against the total of all other racial groups (i.e., white, Asian, Pacific Islanders, Biracial) when comparing the number of Black graduates in other fields such as Political Science, Communication, and even English these numbers are still significantly low. Just as the field of education has a teacher shortage, the data presented here tells us that foreign languages have a Black student shortage. The problem with not addressing shortages is that eventually they turn to non-existence.

As Anya and Randolph (2019) advocated, the core of the matter lies at addressing access, opportunity, and success. We must understand more of why minoritized groups choose to and not to participate in foreign language education because awareness helps to create a positively impactful experience. Dually, ACTFL (2021) declared "no individual should experience marginalization of their contributions or talents because of their unique attributes".

Clearly African American students and specifically African American males have little interest in pursuing a major in foreign languages. The question for foreign language advocates, social justice leaders, and educators alike is why? What is so unique to these programs that is turning African Americans off from the possibility of being bilingual? When considering the data that have been presented, it is clear that the more understudied topic is the lived experience of African American foreign language majors. I commit the rest of this chapter to giving my experience in learning French as a Louisiana native as a response to the aforementioned question.

The Margin

The French language arrived in North America in 1604 when French citizens came to Canada. (Ancelet, 1988; 2007; Brasseaux, 2005; Klingler, 2003). Living in this territory was rough because they were not prepared for the harsh winters. They also did not know how to grow and hunt their own food; thus, they eventually returned to France.

A second wave of French settlers arrived in 1632 in Acadia in an attempt to build a settlement. Unfortunately for them the British had taken control of the territory by 1755 after the Twelve Years War. Anyone who identified as Acadian and would not convert to Protestantism was arrested and later deported. Some of these individuals returned to France while others resettled in the New England area or went to Louisiana in search of religious freedom under Spanish rule. This group, later known as the Cajuns, settled in southern Louisiana and built communities while adjusting to growing food, trapping, and hunting as they did in Canada. Francophone culture in Louisiana flourished throughout the 19th century. Because of its proximity to the Caribbean, Louisiana also began to assimilate linguistic and cultural aspects of the Antilles resulting from immigration caused by the Haitian Revolution (Ancelet, 2007; Brasseaux, 2005).

Across the years southern Louisiana developed a unique culture consisting of a mix of Colonial, Creole, and Cajun French dialects that are still spoken today. There was also a lot of social and racial mixing and interracial relationships during the period, so it was rare for there to be any pure form of the three. Still today it is very common for there to be white creoles and Black Cajuns living in various parts of the state. The title "Louisiana Regional French" has therefore been developed by academics to describe the dialect of French that developed in southern Louisiana (Lindner, 2008; 2013), although others argue that Cajun French and Louisiana Creole (also called Kouri Vini) are two separate languages. With Americanization and the growth of industrialization, English became commonly spoken in Louisiana except among Black Creole societies and the poorer Cajun communities in the southern part of the state (Ancelet, 2007; 1988; Brasseaux, 2005; Klingler, 2003). Post-Civil War Louisiana saw a greater increase of native Louisiana French-speakers assimilating into the English-speaking mainstream society. Jim Crow laws and segregation caused the Black French speakers or *gens de couleurs libres* to be re-identified in the American context as African Americans and Cajuns as white. The Indigenous were classified among these groups based on their skin tone and/or their willingness to assimilate or remain on the reservation.

In 1916, English became the mandatory language of education which further pushed the assimilation of French and Creole-speaking children (both Black and white) into mainstream English-speaking culture or excluded them as participants in only Francophone Louisiana society. Hence, the first margin was created. Post-World War II Louisiana experienced a linguistic and cultural revitalization with the young soldiers returning from France (Ancelet, 1988; 2007). The "Cajun Renaissance" was also started. During this time individuals identifying as Cajuns and Creoles started to take pride in their language. In 1968, the Council on the Development of French in Louisiana (CODOFIL) was created with the mission of cultivating French in Louisiana to be widely spoken again and to preserve Louisiana's French heritage (Ancelet, 2007; Lindner, 2008). The main efforts of CODOFIL can be seen through its teacher program.

Speaking from the Margin of the Margin

It should be clearly understood that "to be in the margins is to be part of the whole but outside the main body (hooks,1989 pp. 20)." As a Black bilingual I have lived my entire life as a participant, but also as an observer. Being born and raised in Louisiana has shaped me in so many ways including why I chose to become bilingual. I am among a small number of African American second language learners from and currently living in the Deep South. My journey to the margin of the margin starts in childhood.

I was always interested in foreign things in my younger years. I vividly remember as a child that I was fond of Hong Kong cinema, Chinese food, pagodas in Japan, and the pyramids of Egypt. My parents did not encourage or punish my behavior, rather they just let me be. As I matured into my teenage years, my mother was also in school earning her bachelor's and master's degrees. In her undergraduate career, she was required to take a French course. After she finished the course, she kept her textbooks which I would read with amazement. I was always interested in what these foreign words were, how to pronounce them, and how to correctly use them. This is what sparked my interest in languages.

The Early Years

Growing up in Louisiana during the 1990s, I always knew French was here, but it was just a normal aspect of life. Mardi Gras, Lafayette, and boudin were normal words used in our daily jargon. Names such as Herbert (hay-ber), Boudreaux (boo-dro), and Decuir (duh-kweer) were commonly heard and pronounced in French style. No one in my family nor any of my classmates ever thought anything special of these words. It was partly because we did not realize they were unique to us.

As I progressed through my early years, I was constantly told by family to become a doctor or lawyer, as many kids in the Deep South are, not just African Americans. It was not until later in life that I realized that I was a prime example of the words of Carter G. Woodson (1933):

> When a Negro child finishes his education in our schools, he has been equipped to begin the life of an Americanized or Europeanized white man, but before he steps from the threshold of his alma mater, he is told by his teachers that he must go back to his own people from whom he has been estranged by a vision of ideals which in his disillusionment he will realize that he cannot attain.[22]

I was in essence being groomed by my friends, family, and teachers, to grow up, become successful and then give back to both my local community and my family. Because of our past, in Louisiana race and community lines merge when it relates to finances. Poverty has no race, nor does it discriminate. A high school education, going to college, and creating a successful life is a luxury only afforded to a few.

What many outsiders may not know is that in the state of Louisiana, for many years, in elementary school students were required to take thirty minutes of French every day. In actuality, my classmates and I would spend these thirty minutes goofing off, laughing at the funny sounds, and trying to figure out what was for lunch. None of us took it seriously and the teacher was only trying to live the American dream and give his best attempt at teaching.

Coming of Age

Throughout my middle school experience, I did not take any courses in foreign language. Our school offered them, but I was not encouraged by my counselors to do so. I formally started my academic study of foreign languages as a high school sophomore. I took Spanish I and to be blunt, I hated it. I had no idea what was going on and why I was forced to take this course. I showed up everyday, made jokes with friends, and suffered through. I was an honors kids, so I had bigger concerns than some random Spanish class.

My Spanish teacher was also my English teacher, so I had to see her twice a day. She was one of the most interesting women I had ever met in my life. She was very eccentric, but she had a heart of gold and treated everyone like her kids. She would fuss at us and then minutes later call us her pumpkins and reminded us how much she loved us and was proud of us. Regardless of race, gender, sexuality, or whatever else, older women from Louisiana are nurturers. Everyone is their child, and they love and support you through life. I have been re-taught this many times along my journey.

By seeing her two times a daily five days a week I got to know her very well. Interestingly, she was also a French teacher at the school, and she was my first time being exposed to the notion that people could speak two or more languages fluently. She served as my first role model for bilingualism and trilingualism. I remember having a conversation with her as I prepared to fill out my schedule for Junior year and asking what elective I should take. She suggested that I take French. I still today never regret following her advice.

My Junior year I was enrolled in French I and Spanish II. At this point in life, I wanted to be an American history teacher and was excited to be enrolled in Advanced Placement United States History. While APUSH, as we called it, was stimulating, I absolutely loved my French class. The sounds, the words, the phrases, everything about French made me happy. My French teacher was also so sweet and kind and truly did make my experience even better. She was also friends with my Spanish I teacher and Spanish II teacher. She spoke a little Spanish as well. It really did make a difference in my learning because I had a community of commonalities with her.

During my Senior year, my high school required that all graduating seniors take an internship course called "Windows to the World." In this course we had to job shadow someone working in a field that we wanted to pursue after graduation. At the time my mother was working at a local Historically Black [College or] University (HBCU) and was able to connect me with the department head of foreign languages.

The department head was a tall, beautiful African American woman from Mississippi. She had curly natural hair and dressed in eloquent pants suits. She had learned to fluently speak both French and Spanish and was a professor of both at the university. Throughout this year she mentored me in language teaching and taught me so many lessons about being a college professor, Black and bilingual, and an educational leader. She embraced me as her own grandchild and instilled in me the courage, grit, and tenacity to continue the legacy of Black second language learners in the south. Little did I know this would eventually become my reality.

My classmates thought it was cool that I was in both French and Spanish and job shadowing a college professor. It was rather normal to them because as an honors kid I was perceived as an overachiever. I now understand that no one really saw that as a future for me and neither did I. It was not until I gained my first and only true exposure to Louisiana Regional French in an academic space at ALCFES (*Association louisianaise des clubs de français des écoles secondaires*—the Association of Louisiana High School French Clubs) that my perspective changed.

During this event I was introduced to terms such as *piastres* (money) and *asteur* (now). I was taught about the various places in Louisiana where French was used, what certain street and city names meant in French, and aspects of Cajun and Creole culture. From there, I carried the title of "Francophone" proudly. Upon graduating, I had my plan. I would go on to a regional in-state school and would double major in French Education and Spanish Education and I would minor in Italian. I would go on to teach French and Spanish and eventually make my way back to my high school and start an Advanced Placement program in each.

My Undergraduate Experience

I entered my undergraduate program with my plan, but little did I know three years later I would be leaving with a Bachelor of Arts in French with a minor in Spanish, Francophone & Creole Ethnic Studies, and International Studies. At the time Louisiana higher education was going through budget cuts and many degree programs including French were casualties. However, because of this I was able to become co- president of the French club, president of the Spanish club, and join many other organizations. I met my dearest friends and many associates. I lead the fight to save our French program, and most importantly, I made a lasting impression on my department head who eventually became my boss. I taught languages at the local lab school and worked to develop a program that still exists over a decade later. My undergraduate years were very bright but there were some dark spots

During my undergraduate program, I was educated by scholars holding advanced degrees from Yale, Penn State, LSU, and the University ofMaryland. Throughout my formation, I was nurtured in Parisian French and culture. There were various days that certain professors would mention words, phrases, and cultural tidbits directly related toLouisiana Region French. But it was not until my last semester that I took actual coursework.

The course was entitled *Eloge de la créolité* (In Praise of Creoleness), named after the seminal text written about the Caribbean. This course focused on Creole culture in Louisiana. While it was educational, it did not develop my knowledge of how to speak and interact with others in Louisiana Regional French. Moreover, in my undergraduate career I was always searching for myself in French. My elementary school teacher was an African-French speaker, but I never knew anything about his culture. I was longing to see myself in the curriculum. I was looking for a connection between my heritage and culture and the great works of France since that was all I had known. I never found them in my undergraduate years, but I was determined to do so; thus, I enrolled in graduate school at another regional, institution in the heart of Francophone Louisiana.

Graduate School & Doctorate Studies

My graduate institution is still one of the leading programs in French and Francophone Studies. During my time there, I was surrounded by avid Louisiana French scholars, activists, bilingual politicians, and even bilingual grocery store clerks and other service workers around the city. I took numerous courses on or related to Louisiana French and sat in on many lectures and scholarly presentations related to the topic. Additionally, I studied under the tutelage of multiple prominent Louisiana French scholars who taught me the value of my state's culture, heritage, and our French dialect.

During my first semester I took a course on Louisiana Creole. This is when the many years of searching for myself in French finally culminated. This course was taught by an older, Black Louisiana creole. She looked like and reminded me of my grandmother. She was soft-spoken but was filled with so much wisdom and knowledge of her people. She taught me who I was and where I fit in the French-speaking world. During that same semester I also took a literature course on the French Caribbean. I was able to see so many aspects of Louisiana in the literature and culture of these works. This course was taught by an older white man originally from California, but I felt as if I was working with a Caribbean islander. He was so well read on the topic and worked to expand my understanding and personal interest in the Caribbean.

My graduate school experience gave me more courage to carry the torch forward. Post-graduation, I went on to start teaching at my undergraduate university and constantly working to improve French in Louisiana through activism work and infusing it into my teaching. I also completed my Ed.D. in Educational Leadership at this university while also teaching. I wrote my dissertation on the inclusion, exclusion, bias, and distortion of Caribbean and Louisiana content in French and Spanish textbooks. I have published articles on the teaching of French and have worked to develop the student experience to be more enjoyable.

Transgressing the Margins of the Margins

In looking back on my experience with French in Louisiana and being on the margins I have always carried my language skills as a badge of honor. When I introduce myself to people and they find out that I am a university faculty member they are normally shocked. In all honesty, I noticed they are truly shocked when I start speaking and they hear that I am very articulate. I am 5'11, dark-skinned, and athletically built so I do not fit the model that has been perpetuated by society for individuals who look like me.

The conversation usually progresses into "What do you teach?" to which my response is foreign languages. From there, "Oh, what language do you teach?" To which I respond, "French and Spanish." I have been running this obstacle course for decades at this point. For many years I thought I was alone. I felt as if I were the only African American person who majored in Foreign Languages and/or who is a language teacher. But, through the power of social media I have learned that we as a community exist.

A few years ago, I ran into my elementary school French teacher at a conference. He did not recognize me, but I vividly remembered him. It was an honor to stand among him as a colleague and to show him that his hard work was not in vain. I graduated college, majored in French, and am now teaching French at a university. Seeing him was a reminder to me that representation matters. Seeing someone who looked like me doing a job mattered. Diversity in foreign languages matters.

My path in the school system changed my life. I would not be where I am today if it were not for the love, support, and mentorship of those select individuals along my path. However, "despite the contemporary focus on multiculturalism in our society, particularly in education, there is not nearly enough practical discussion of ways classroom settings can be transformed so that the learning experience is inclusive" (Hooks, 1994 pp. 35). In looking at my story, I testify to the fact that success can be found for black students, specifically Black males, in foreign languages. There is a space of cultural and social belonging for us.

My story also speaks back to the previous literature about how and why community support and representation matter. Black students' strongest reason for choosing to or to not study a foreign language comes from their environment. From my experience, I was surrounded by individuals who were bilingual and saw potential in me to follow my dreams. I was discouraged along the way and told that there was no money in education nor foreign languages. Conversely, I was also encouraged to be unique and stand out from the crowd.

To increase the number of Black foreign language majors our field must progress in its thinking. First, we must work to nourish all students regardless of race. In our schools and community there is a need to work together to build, strengthen, and reinforce language programs. Students need to see the practical, social, emotional, and cultural benefits of bilingualism and biculturalism. Through community building efforts students will see the interconnected nature of language and their immediate society.

Language advocates must also work to have everyone change the language used to talk about foreign language courses. Languages are not "hard" to learn. It is not "impossible" to learn them in a classroom. It is very likely that you will go somewhere or meet someone who speaks the target language. There is also a need for increased awareness of the career possibilities of being bilingual. In looking at my story, I would have never known that learning multiple languages was possible had it not been made aware to me by multiple individuals across multiple years.

Exposure and innovation are also key areas of foci. The boom in technology has allowed individuals to see and experience all parts of the world from the comfort of their own home. During COVID-19, we saw an increase in videoconferencing and social media exposure. These tools should be welcomed and utilized for demonstrating to all students that true fluency is an obtainable goal for everyone.

Along with technology, it can also help to create better access in our teaching practices. Black students often cite high-quality instructional practices as a reason for studying a foreign language. I can attest to this as well. My experience was filled with unique approaches to teaching, but with today's technology, I am able to do so much more.

Increasing students' exposure to the language and language community via Youtube, Wordpress, and Google Earth provide concrete examples of the abstract grammar rules and aspects of culture traditionally taught in textbooks.

Most importantly, building a stronger network to cultivate our students will transgress the margins. In my experience, all my educators worked with one another across levels to ensure I was brought to the next level and set up for success. At each level I was offered advice on where to go next and how to best achieve. As a university faculty member, I still receive such mentorship as it relates to my own activism and scholarly agenda. All students, and more specifically Black boys, at all levels need the same support I was given to walk a similar path. French is a learnable language for everyone regardless of race, gender, sexual orientation, or any other aspects of identity.

Conclusion

Targeting higher education is the most essential to promoting and retaining diverse groups of learners, particularly Black students. Specifically, it is the alignment of the mission, goals, and objectives of each university's curricula and making connections to Louisiana French that give promise to preservation for generations to come. Although between 2010 and 2011, Louisiana's higher education system experienced the closure of a large number of bachelor's degree programs in French and French education (Louisiana, 2010), post-COVID-19, the possibilities of what universities can and cannot do are endless. Likewise, with the increase in efforts toward diversity seen nationally there is now institutional support to have our programs reflect our immediate communities.

I write this chapter in response to the idea that "often when the radical voice speaks about domination, we are speaking to those who dominate. Their presence changes the nature and direction of our words" (Hooks, 1989 pp 16). Hence, in considering my experience and the data presented, I expect many of my readers to be anything but other African American males.

I also expect my readers to take my experience along with the data presented and my advice for advocacy, and consistently work to increase representation of all minorities in foreign languages. Regardless of any data, all students can learn French. In 2020, in an interview with *TeleLouisiane* I coined the term *Louisianaphonie*, giving a name to the phenomena that Louisiana has so many languages spoken here. To grow and strengthen our *Louisianaphonie* we must first increase the reach and impact of our speakers. That starts through a focus on diversifying our supports.

Lâche pas la patate pour la diversité dans la communauté Francophone en Louisiane.

9.   We Are Pointe Au Chien
Georgie V. Ferguson

I am a proud member of the Pointe-au-Chien Indian Tribe. Indian-French language is part of my identity, even though I am not a fluent speaker. The fact that I am not a fluent speaker is in fact inextricably linked to our history, and the ongoing threats we face as Indigenous living in the Gulf of Mexico. As an Indigenous woman, I have always walked in two worlds. Wherever I am, I carry Pointe-au-Chien with me. I bring my own personal experiences, as well as perspective on the experiences of my grandparents, my parents, and my children.   My observations spanning these four generations offer a comparative lens through which I can share insight and context for the rapid shift that has occurred in language, environment, and lifestyle during this relatively short period of time. It is my honor to offer you this glimpse into my world. The world I come from. When walking in two worlds, this is the one I call home.

The Pointe-au-Chien is a tribe of Indigenous people that have lived in concert with the land and waterways of the Terrebonne Basin in South Louisiana since before the arrival of the Europeans. We speak a unique Franco-Indien dialect of French that is distinct to our Indian community living on Bayou Pointe-au-Chien. While we primarily descend from the Chitimacha and Biloxi peoples, other petit nations in the Mississippi River Valley intermarried with our ancestors. Our ancestors spoke their own tribal languages as well as the Mobilian language used for trade. The French language was also a dominant language used for trade during both the French and Spanish colonial periods. Some of our ancestors married Francophones who lived amongst our people. Our dialect of French evolved to include an amalgamation of traditional Indian words incorporated from the Indigenous languages traditionally spoken by our ancestors. There ar several communities in South Louisiana, including other Tribes along nearby bayous, who speak variations of French influenced by a variety of historical factors.

Linguists have suggested that the tribes in Terrebonne and Lafourche Parishes may be home to the most linguistically continuous and well-preserved groups of Francophones in Louisiana. This comes as no surprise to me, given the level of fluency and number of monolingual Indian-French speakers from our community, as well as the overwhelming preference for French being spoken in the homes of tribal members in Pointe-au-Chien. This can be attributed to a variety of socio-historical factors. The tight-knit social structure of our tribal community and the fact that, until recent decades, tribal members remained physically and socially isolated from neighboring Anglophone communities, has contributed to our ability to retain our spoken language. Racism and the denial of education, which I will discuss more later, were also factors contributing to the continuation of physical and social isolation. Not only is our dialect of Indian-French distinct, but according to some reports, being a Francophone was once associated with being Indian along the bayous of the Terrebonne Basin.

During the 1960s and 1970s, folks were beginning to travel outside of the community and interact more often with non-Indians, and if you were heard speaking French in the distance, non-Indians would immediately assume you were Indian before seeing you. Our tribe was once a community that French. For example, my grandparents *only* spoke Indian-French. They did not speak or understand English. My mother's first language is Indian-French, and it was not until an Indian mission school was built in Pointe-au-Chien, and Indian children were allowed to attend that school, that the English language was first introduced to our people. At that time *none* of the Indian students (*or their parents*) spoke English, yet they were not allowed to speak French in school. In fact, they were disciplined, often harshly, for doing so. Furthermore, it was not until the end of policies that prohibited our people from attending high school in the late 1960s and early 1970s that the ability to understand English began to increase among tribal members.

Many from my generation speak Indian-French as their first language, most have learned both Indian-French and English and are fluent in both; and sadly, some of us, like myself, who didn't grow up in Pointe-au-Chien, have not quite developed the level of fluency of our peers. My children and others from their generation have had a similar experience to ours, in that language development is largely dependent upon proximity and frequency of exposure to spoken French.

I have fond memories of being surrounded by my family speaking rapidly in Indian-French as a child. Indian-French is still the preferred language spoken in the homes of the Pointe-au-Chien and at Tribal Council meetings. I always feel a great sense of pride and respect when I am in that environment. Our *tribu*, the Pointe-au-Chien, and most of our approximately 800 members, still live primarily in our vibrant community on (or in close proximity to) the beautiful, once lush and fertile, bayou of the same name. Bayou Pointe-au-Chien is located at the tip of "da boot". Louisiana is often referred to as "da boot" due to its shape, and opens up into a series of lakes and estuaries that feed into the Gulf of Mexico. It is also the dividing line between two parishes in South Louisiana, Terrebonne and Lafourche. Our Indigenous francophone community once occupied a much larger land mass that has eroded exponentially in the past several decades, and continues to do so daily. The community surrounding Bayou Pointe-au-Chien was once home to a vibrant and flourishing landscape.

However, our traditional homelands are located in the fastest eroding basin in the United States. Some of our tribal villages have already been lost due to coastal erosion and salt water intrusion. Our Tribal homelands and freshwater tributaries, which have been inhabited by our people for generations, are now completely submerged. The residents of the once thriving villages that existed on these lands have migrated to higher ground over the past several decades as the land their homes were built upon has become partially submerged. The threat continues in real time as our lands continue to be washed away. Despite the massive land loss, the majority of our tribal community continue to reside in what is called "Lower Pointe-au-Chien", because of its proximity to the Gulf of Mexico and separation in proximity to "upper Pointe-aux-Chenes" by several miles of marshland.

Over the past several decades some have had to build homes for their growing families further "up the bayou" due to land loss. If you were to look at the map, we are now surrounded by water. Our homes now line the bayou in the only habitable village that remains, where you will often find the elders of our tribe sitting outside in the shade conversing in our unique dialect of Indian-French on any given sunny afternoon.

Traditionally, our ancestors were farmers, fishermen, hunters, and trappers. During the 1850s, Tribal leader Alexander Billiot and his brother had a lucrative sugarcane farm. The sugarcane operations were so successful that the brothers were able to sell their sugar in New Orleans, where being a Francophone was an asset. Our people lived in palmetto houses until the early 1950s. In fact, my mother lived in a Palmetto house during her childhood. This traditional dwelling is made of saw palmetto, which is a fan palm. Whole branches typically cover a frame of willow, and the floor is made of mud. A coal oil lamp was used for light in the evening. Cooking was done outside over an open fire, and a bucket was used to retrieve fresh water from a well dug outside. Most tribal members over the age of sixty were born at home with the assistance of a midwife. Traiteurs (traditional healers) treated sickness through the use of Indigenous knowledge of medicinal plants and prayers.

Our lives have always revolved around the natural resources in our environment. Many villages, sacred sites, and areas where we once lived and worked, are no longer habitable. We are concerned about the impact of numerous canals built for oil and gas that have widened, bringing in salt water, and further deteriorating our lifeways. Most of our tribal area has been excluded from the Morganza to the Gulf levee system, and we are now the front line for tropical storms and hurricanes. In 2021, the second eyewall of Hurricane Ida made direct impact on our community and in the aftermath all but fourteen homes were destroyed. Despite the rapid changes and ongoing systemic and environmental threats to our natural habitat and way of life, we continue to adapt and fight for the ability to restore our wetlands and maintain our culture.

In addition to advocating for more protection, inclusion in restoration plans, and funding to make our community more resilient, *we along with other Tribes in Louisiana and one in Alaska, filed a complaint with the United Nations to address the human rights violations and social injustice caused by the government's failure to protect our communities.* (UUSC, 2022). Along with the obvious threats we face related to the environment, we also face longstanding systemic threats to our language and culture. Because of policies in place by the State of Louisiana and Terrebonne Parish, Indians from Pointe-au-Chien were prohibited from attending high school until the late 1960s and early 1970s.

Our people remained segregated and largely isolated from the non-Indian community until the time that public schools in Louisiana were finally integrated. When my mom started school, she attended a small Indian school across the bayou. Since there was no bridge connecting one side of Pointe-au-Chien to the other, people traveled by boat. My mom spoke (and understood) only French, but school was taught in only English, and the students were punished if they spoke French at school.

The state mandated that only English be spoken in Louisiana's schools, and Terrebonne Parish has not provided any bilingual language programs. These policies have had a direct impact on the spoken language. For example, my grandmother was monolingual, and my mother was also monolingual until forced immersion into the English language by the Indian school as a child. As a result, my mother is bi-lingual.

Students from French-speaking homes in our community today face additional barriers to developing and retaining our Tribe's unique Franco-Indien language if they are required to travel outside of the community to receive an education. Tribal members are working diligently to protect our tribal language. We are not sitting by idly but are taking active measures to protect our traditions. To address the swift environmental and social changes our tribe has faced in recent decades, the Pointe-au-Chien Indian Tribe holds a culture camp each summer for children ages 8-14 where we celebrate our unique heritage and language.

The children's families, community members, volunteers, and members of neighboring tribes join us to support and share in the celebration of our language, culture, and heritage through a variety of activities. Many of our activities are centered around the French language of our people.

Our youth are given lessons in Indian-French, which teach and highlight our unique Tribal language. One of my sisters wrote a song for the camp in Indian-French that celebrates our Tribe's heritage. It is rehearsed throughout the week and the children perform it on the last day of camp each year. Tribal children are also taught oral history. Through traditional storytelling activities, our Tribal Elders share their experiences as children in all facets of life. Each child is also assigned an ancestor to learn about throughout the week and at the culmination of camp they each share what they have learned with one another and the community. Traditional activities during camp are presented in English and French. Some of the traditional activities include: boat rides to view historical and sacred sites no longer accessible by land, building traditional palmetto huts, and learning about traditional plants and medicines. The campers are also treated to traditional meals prepared by Elders. Many of our activities serve to develop strong connections between our youth and our elders, so that the process of passing knowledge to the next generation is not impeded by externally introduced barriers to our way of life.

A proud and resilient people, we continue to exist as distinct in language and culture despite colonization efforts, massive land loss due to coastal erosion caused by man-made environmental impacts, and lack of status as a federally recognized tribe. In spite of the exploitation of our Tribal People, land, and waterways, and the denial of educational opportunities *especially in our native Indian-French language*, we actively maintain our resolve to persevere, adapt, and sustain our Indian-French language, cultural knowledge and traditions. Today, the township of Pointe-aux-Chenes (including both the Pointe au Chien Indian community and Indian and non-Indian residents living in upper Pointe aux Chenes) is a community of mostly Indian-French and Cajun-French speaking residents.

A majority of the children in our unique pocket of the world either speak fluently or come from homes where Indian-French or Cajun French is spoken. In fact, it has been a source of pride for the community that the Pointe-aux-Chenes Elementary School has consistently reported the largest percentage of native 'spoken-French' speakers than any other school in the state of Louisiana.

This observation by a tribal member highlights the importance to our people of our Indian-French language:

All the elders speak French where as you go into other communities, they may start in French but before the end of the conversion they switch to English. That is not the case here. I think we are the only community that are more comfortable speaking French. I think the only reason we don't have our tribal meetings in French is because not everyone understands. If they do, everyone speaks too fast for them to understand. Not many that come to the meeting don't understand but there are a few.

As I mentioned earlier, my mother's first language is Indian French, as is everyone's in our tribe from the generation before mine. They did not speak English until it was forced upon them at the Indian mission school, and her parents, my grandparents, spoke Indian-French exclusively, as did most everyone from their generation and before.

One of our Tribal members noted the following about her husband's experience:

They couldn't speak French at school. Although he and his cousins used to talk in French and got caught and would get punished and had to write "I will not speak French at school" 500 times. It was automatic with his friends from down the bayou to speak French. He feels more comfortable speaking French [than English] when he is with his friends and family. He feels it has to be French down here That's why we need a French immersion school. Children need to speak French.

It is difficult for me to imagine what it must have been like to experience forced language immersion, without the consent of your parents, and without the ability for your parents to communicate with those enacting that kind of atrocity. To be punished and physically "disciplined" for speaking your native language instead of a foreign language that you don't know how to speak, much less understand, is still difficult for me to think about for too long. It is important *to remember*, though.

These events, and the laws that supported them, are at the root of the rapid shift in language fluency that occurred within my generation, and threatens to impact future generations of our people. Mandates by the State of Louisiana prohibited the French language from being spoken in school. These mandates created disparities and barriers to education across all Francophone communities of South Louisiana. The mother of a good friend of mine, who is Clifton Choctaw, recently shared with me that they have experienced a trajectory of language loss that is similar to that of many French Acadian communities that live in close proximity to them. The older tribal members speak French, but the younger generation does not.

A tribal member active in the initiative to save our school shared this account of how these mandates impacted her family and compounded the existing barriers to education our Tribal members were already facing.

> *I learned English in school also. I think everyone our age and older learned English in school and got punished for speaking French. One of my older brothers ended up quitting school the last time he got caught speaking French. The principal was not there that day and the teacher in charge said she would report him to the principal, and he would get a paddle so he didn't go back to school.*

Although our Indian French language *is* distinct, we did not, and do not, exist in a vacuum. Although we remained isolated from the community of European, English-speaking settlers that occupied the area for many generations, the use of French among the petit nations was widespread. There are a number of tribal communities along the bayous of the Terrebonne basin, and many of the bayou tribes have kinship ties.

There are multiple accounts, especially among the Pointe-au-Chien, of the language spoken in Pointe-au-Chien being immediately identifiable among other French speakers familiar with the area. Our Tribal community has one of the most distinct and identifiable dialects of spoken French in Louisiana. For example, this account of both past and present experiences from a prominent tribal member:

My French language experience is the same as everyone else in our Community. I was raised speaking French and learned English in our Indian school. What I can add is French in our Community was different than other communities. For instance, in the early 1970s a group of us went to the Montegut gym to play basketball. While there, a lady working in the gym asked us what language we were talking. We told her French and started talking to her in French. We found out that our dialect was a little different and we were talking too fast for her to understand. Another instance is, I call a lady who had grown up in PAC but moved to Alabama years ago. While trying to tell her who I was I said a few words in French and her response was, you're from Pointe-au-Chien. She had recognized my PAC French dialect. Nowadays when we're having a meeting or around people who don't understand French, I'll turn to someone I have talked French to all my life and automatically speak French to them. It is just a habit I can't break.

One of the benefits of Louisiana's widespread use of French is that despite differing dialects there is a strong sense of community among the Francophonie of Louisiana. We are excited to be engaged with the Consulate General of France in Louisiana, Tele-Louisiane and our recent work with CODOFIL, whose support of the preservation of language fluency among French-speaking Louisiana Tribes aligns with our mission to retain our Language, and cultivate an active environment that facilitates retention despite ongoing risks to extinction. These organizations have spoken out in support of our efforts to establish a French Language program in our school, and Tele-Louisiane is partnering with our tribe to offer weekend French classes for local children.

When you realize that your language, and your people, face extinction there is a real sense of urgency, responsibility, and in the case of non-Indian-French speakers like myself, sometimes misplaced guilt, about the impact of our lack of fluency. One thing that is important to keep in mind is that the loss of language that has occurred was through no fault of our own, nor was it something that we desired to happen. The importance of acknowledging this cannot be overstated.

The motivation and sense of empowerment that results from recognizing this fact is crucial to the fight for Language resilience across the Indigenous French-speaking communities of South Louisiana and beyond.

Our experience has equipped us to recognize this and fight to protect our language and culture, and ensure that our children are provided the opportunity to not only speak, but access education that celebrates the Indian French language of our people.

10. Crossroads of the Francophonie
Scott Tilton

Growing up in Louisiana, one recognizes quickly that this state is as much a lifestyle as it is a place. Before COVID-19, the annual calendar was marked less by the months than by festivals and celebrations: Mardi Gras falls around February, Jazz Fast in April, and a list of must-see events rounds out the rest of the year. What gives us a passion for living in a place where the culture is always on display also periodically raises the question of what underpins that culture.

On the face of it, one may say Louisiana is Southern. It certainly does not get more geographically south than here. And Louisiana shares a lot in common with the American South – football, different foodways, and a certain propensity to say "bless your heart" when we get upset. However, the second one drives across our state border and reads on the bright blue welcome sign, "*Bienvenue en Louisiane*," it becomes abundantly clear that what stands out about the state is at times how much it can differ from the American South. One night dining in the boisterous atmosphere of a Creole grand dame restaurant such as Galatoire's or Antoine's in New Orleans, which evoke the Old-World charm of a Parisian brasserie, can make that abundantly apparent. You could also walk through the French Quarter or the Faubourgs Marigny and Trémé to understand that the urban landscape evokes more Havana and Cap-Haïtien than Charleston.

What becomes clear when one looks at the local culture is how much of it is influenced by being Francophone. While being Francophone in America may seem like an anomaly, a constellation of communities scattered across the country have spoken French for centuries. But in an era in which many people have not had the opportunity to learn French, and thus the identity surrounding language becomes less strong, the question can be asked: is being Francophone in the United States a relevant moniker today? When one looks at the richness of the United States' Francophone communities and the opportunities being connected to the global Francophonie brings, the answer becomes a resounding *oui*.

Louisiana serves as a great case study. In the past many Louisianans spoke French. An estimated one million spoke French as recently as 1970. Being Francophone in Louisiana has never reflected a singular identity or reality. As early as our founding, what became clear was that the linguistic diversity of the Gulf South would never be easy to label. Beginning in the 1720s, people brought to Louisiana under the evils of chattel slavery would begin to develop a beautiful language that would become Louisiana Creole, which is still spoken today. The Acadians, who would leave the shores of Canada and find their way to the coastal tapestry of Louisiana starting in the 1750s, would bring a French that reflected the blend of French from western France. The African, French, Spanish, German, and indigenous peoples who used the term Creole to define their diverse culture would speak different varieties of French that flourished across the Gulf South.

This unique Francophone world never disappeared – not even after Louisiana became part of the United States in 1803. The language was taught in schools, used in politics, and shaped the culture of the region throughout the 19th Century. In the aftermath of the Civil War, French-speaking Afro-Creole activists, many of whom who had lived in France in 1848 when that country finally abolished chattel slavery, drew on transatlantic philosophy to fight against slavery in American and get involved in post-war politics. These activists used *La Marseillaise* as their anthem and wrote newspapers in French such as *La Tribune* to express their aspirations for *égalité*. It was the creeping in of Jim Crowe and other reactionary politics targeting the diversity of Francophone Louisiana that undermined these Francophone cultures. By 1921, a bitter date whose centennial we marked this year, Louisiana's reactionary assembly passed a new constitution that banned French in schools. From there, increasingly restrictive policies took force. By the time we reached the 1950s, the rapid decline of French & Louisiana Creole created a modern myth of the inevitability that French would be on its way out in Louisiana. True Americans only speak English, right?

Well, in recent decades, a resilient revitalization reemerged in Louisiana that has successfully advocated for Louisiana French & Creole. The people who have advocated for French & Louisiana

Creole are no less American than their monolingual counterparts. They defend an open view of the United States where linguistic diversity can exist. Today, nearly forty schools have French immersion programs, and a new generation is learning the language. There is a growing hipster movement because young people have been able to take ownership of being Francophone and build visibility for the language. With a new generation that wants to be involved in building Louisiana's Francophone future, there is a need to create a space that is inclusive and has a clear vision of better future that the French language can offer a young Louisianan in her teens today.

Becoming Part of the Francophonie

This vision led my husband, Rudy Bazenet, and me to launch and direct an initiative that successfully saw Louisiana become the first United States state to join the International Organization of the Francophonie. La Francophonie is the second largest international organization after the United Nations. Based in Paris, the organization brings together 88 countries and regions, representing one billion people, and 16% of the global economy. La Francophonie promotes multilingualism and cooperation among the parts of the world where French is spoken. When Rudy and I launched the initiative, I was living in Paris doing my studies. I am originally from New Orleans, where I grew up learning French, and so I had the great fortune of studying at *Sciences Po* for my master's degree. It was in attending a conference on the economy of the Francophonie in Paris that first instilled the idea of having Louisiana join the organization. Rudy and I were fortunate to serve as coordinators of the initiative. We notably helped figure out the procedure by which Louisiana could apply, and then coordinated action between the State of Louisiana, the Senate, and the State Department to get the authorization for Louisiana to join. Receiving authorization to apply was a long but necessary process, as Louisiana needed approval from the federal government first to be able to formally apply to become a member of the Francophonie. As the initiative advanced, enthusiasm grew as it became clear that the grassroots movement for French in Louisiana was able to work towards a common goal – one that had never been achieved before. It was in working with the Council for

Development of French in Louisiana (CODOFIL) that we successfully submitted Louisiana's candidate in April 2018 and were accepted into the Francophonie in October 2018.

Louisiana's joining the Francophonie is a milestone for four main reasons:

- First, it is a recognition that Louisiana has a vibrant Francophone heritage that is shaped by the migration of people and ideas from different parts of the French-speaking world – West Africa, the Caribbean, Europe, and Canada.
- Secondly, it also means that the United States is present in the Francophonie. The United States has always been a Francophone country, even if that heritage is not valued in a monolingual space. As such, developing our voice as a Francophone country through Louisiana's presence in the organization helps build recognition for the eleven million Americans who speak French today.
- Thirdly, for our ongoing efforts in Louisiana to revitalize French, it is momentous in that we can further promote employment, education, and culture by developing exchange and dialogue with French-speaking countries. It is one thing to work with Québec through bilateral U.S.-Canada ties, but it is much easier to leverage our shared language connections when both Louisiana and Québec are in the Francophonie.
- Lastly, the initiative showcases how civil society has a critical role in language revitalization. Since we joined the Francophonie, there has been a flourishing of new organizations led by young entrepreneurs across the state. How to create a space for these new organizations and provide them the resources to grow will be critical for ensuring the long-term sustainability of the revitalization movement.

Towards Creative Placemaking for French

I must add a disclaimer here. For a long time, I resisted the idea of coming back to Louisiana, preferring to stay among the Haussmannian boulevards of Paris. I will also say that it took filling out so much paperwork and standing in interminable lines to get the correct visa that I wanted to stay a little while to honor the process. But Louisiana always had a way of drawing me and Rudy back.

After the Francophonie initiative, Rudy and I kept thinking about what infrastructure would need to be in place to ensure the continued momentum for French and Creole in Louisiana. What we reflected on was that a whole generation of young people who want to see the language continue must at some point make a sacrifice professionally if they want to launch a project. In a state where an estimated 150,000 to 200,000 people still speak French, it is not the largest market, and we are also not in a state the size of California or New York, where you can find a nearly inexhaustible pool of people who may be interested in your business or nonprofit. Adding to that, since English is spoken universally in Louisiana, it is not always clear who speaks French and where you can find them. French thus can be hidden in plain sight meaning the person next to you may speak French, but it would be awkward to insert the fact that you speak French into the conversation.

To tackle these issues, Rudy and I produced the idea that creating a tangible space where placemaking for Louisiana's heritage languages takes place –you can walk in and know you can find people speaking the language and that cultural activities are happening. We also thought that building a fund to incubate projects and ideas that will support the language would be invaluable for mitigating the risk that young professionals must take to be able to dedicate their careers to language revitalization. As such, we founded the Nous Foundation in June 2020. We worked on the project for over two years before launching, which involved speaking with people on the ground in Louisiana and many evenings figuring out how best to serve the needs of the community that we want to help.

We break our mission into three aspects. First, we promote Louisiana's French & Creole-speaking cultures. Second, we connect Louisiana and the United States to the Francophone world by developing partnerships and demonstrating dynamism of the Francophonie. Finally, we are raising funds to build a physical cultural center in New Orleans that will bring together a café, concept store, and event spaces to have workshops, language tables, and exhibitions.

Since launching, we have built a community of 10,000 individuals. We also helped found an international network of Francophone cultural institutions called the *Réseau international des maisons des Francophonies* (RIMF), which brings together 35 cultural institutions around the world, of which only two are in the United States. We have been organizing dozens of seminars and workshops that have brought together activists and the broader public to help spur important conversations that need to happen to move forward: overcoming debates about identity, pessimism that French and Creole are inevitably going to disappear, among many other challenges to tackle. Broadly speaking, the Nous Foundation has been successful, which indicates that the numerous other visionary projects out there to support our heritage languages are viable careers. We have been able to raise funds during a pandemic and hope to open our cultural institute next year. French and Creole are languages of opportunities.

A More Inclusive Future for American Francophones

I am personally very optimistic about the future of language revitalization in the United States. There is growing recognition that minority languages, whether French, Navajo, Gullah English, and many others, need to be supported to ensure the cultural diversity of the United States. And with most people connected online, there is an unparalleled access to exchange ideas and successful revitalization programs that can be used to support French & Creole in Louisiana. And based on what we have seen in Louisiana, the appeal of being Francophone is widespread. The interest in French in Louisiana is carried as much by people of Acadian or Creole descent as those who moved from other parts of the United States and other countries. Redefining French in the American context as a radical openness to those who want to learn the language and or are interested in the diversity of Francophone cultures can be a unique way to build visibility.

There are challenges ahead that can be overcome by building an inclusive Francophone identity that bridges socio-economic fault lines in today's America. One of the pitfalls to avoid is placing French in opposition to English. We should not define French in the United States by what is not. All too often the actors who promote the Francophonie globally do so by bashing English. This is off-putting to the large numbers of potential French speakers in the United States who will not want to invest in learning a language that is seen as an exclusive club. French has a unique North American identity and has been spoken across the country since before its founding, but that legacy alone will not continue the transmission of the language if people think that they must choose between speaking English and learning French. Adieu to English bashing.

Another pitfall to avoid is making speaking French too associated with exclusive communities. There are a million reasons to learn French, each as valid as the other. Perhaps someone's grandmother was Acadian and now the grandchild wants to learn, or someone could have just moved to New York from Senegal. It can also just be a lifelong dream to travel to Paris. The reason I raise this is because in Louisiana a discourse has arisen that sometimes looks down at people's motivations for learning French as if someone who is not zealous about keeping local heritage alive today cannot be an advocate for French down the road. This train of thought has led people to define French speakers as being *Louisianiste*, the goal of this terminology is to demarcate clearly that people who speak French somehow are more invested in supporting Louisiana than non- French speakers. This is a fallacy that builds barriers and turns people away at the door.

There is also a need to bridge the geographic gap between the French constellation in the United States. French seems to have spread along the waterways of North America. Whether talking about immigrant communities in East Coast cities, people who studied French out of passion, the descendants of *Québecois* who moved to New England, or Francophone communities in the former Louisiana Territory, we truly scattered all over. We are not clustered in one area like today's Latinx communities, whose communities are present in the American Southwest, which facilitates language transmission. To continue the transmission of French, we need to be adept at using social media to promote a shared Francophonie and be in touch with each other. Our organization, *Nous*, wants to practice what it preaches. We work with groups such as *Le Caribou à Lunettes* in Detroit, and the French-Canadian Legacy Podcast up in New England. We are brought together by our shared love of French, even if I say that I walk on a banquette and not a trottoir. Being Francophone in the United States today by definition means that you are part of a diverse, inclusive, and ever-changing community. Embracing that image and helping Americans realize that speaking French is uniquely American and connects us to a vast Francophonie will offer an open image for our future.

En conclusion

In Louisiana, we so often hear among younger generations how they are sad that their grandparents spoke French or Louisiana Creole, but they did not pass it along because of shame. While historical remembrance of that shame has not gone away – Louisiana is awash with disparaging jokes of French-speakers that implies that they are not intelligent – a new generation is ready to throw off the shame and get to work learning French. This is true around the United States. The value of learning another language is becoming recognized. Making an inclusive argument that being Francophone and American is not a contradiction, but a long-standing tradition, is a way to attract new speakers.

Now that Louisiana is in the Francophonie, we can expand the conversations that we are having in the United States to contribute our voice. We are not a forgotten linguistic community, nor are we disappearing. We are resilient as communities scattered across this country. We may not always think about it this way, but with eleven million French-speakers, we are one of the most Francophone countries in the Western Hemisphere. The United States, like Louisiana, is at the crossroads of the Francophonie: we welcome Francophones from around the world while reasserting our own unique Francophone heritage. Embracing our position within the broader Francophonie will give added meaning to being Francophone in the United States today.

11. *Fais-toi plaisir, lis en français !* – Living and passing on the French language and cultures through youth literature. *Mélissa Baril*

"Mom, if the French had won the war against the British, we would all be speaking French now in the US!" Smiling, my 11-year-old son, came up with that big eye-opener this year. Of course, that is a naive comment. This sentence is hard to understand… Here, we are talking about events from 300 years ago, and we cannot change the past. What can we do with the future then? Today and tomorrow, how can we live, connect, share the French language and its myriad cultures in our day to day? How can we envision our future, as a community, living in the United States?

As a native French speaker, I do not struggle with locating my roots. On the other hand, my children, and their children, and then their children again, may. That is scary to me. So, the challenge is not just to count on the foundation we are building. It is to fill up their backpacks with knowledge, tools and pride in the Francophone world. It also means that it must be attractive, useful, dynamic, young, moving and colorful. Here are the actions I believe can promote the learning and use of French as a lively, modern, and pluralistic culture.

Impact of French in my Life

I am from Québec. My husband is from France. The kids were born in France. French is our essence; it is a given. French is understood as a language with diverse accents and expressions within our family. We now live in Michigan. Work, school, activities are all in English. We, as parents, are pursuing a goal: cultivating an attachment to our roots, even while developing a sense of belonging to our new country. And finding the right balance between these different cultures. It may become a real battle to keep it up. When we landed in Detroit a few years ago, I was surprised. There are so many French-speaking families here! For one, the automotive industry is attracting foreign companies calling for expatriates who come and go. But you do not have to dig very deep to also find seeds that were planted long ago in Détroit, which I like to write with an accent, as is it the French word for strait. Beaubien, Lafayette, Riopelle, Rivard, Vincennes Streets. Belle Isle. Grosse Pointe. Go up North and you will also come across Marquette and Sault-Sainte-Marie. The impact of French is all around us. Then why am I struggling to find resources to connect my kids to the Francophone cultures the are familiar with?

The Caribou in Action

As a parent – and as a French teacher to my kids, one thing struck me. There is no dedicated French bookstore nor library. How am I going to get new books, here in Michigan? When you struggle to find resources to link your kids to your culture, you feel isolated, disconnected, maybe discouraged. In September 2017, I was contacted by Nadine Robert, an author and publisher from Québec, who was coming to Detroit for a specific event sponsored by the Québec Government in Chicago. "Would you have time for a coffee?" she asked. Wait. What? A children's author speaking French coming to Detroit? We are not going to just have a coffee, dear, we will have you meet with as many families as possible! And that is how in a few days, arrangements were made with the media center of a public school to host a reading workshop with this artist on a Friday night. Even parents participated, and the English-speaking media specialist got to know books in their original version, which she bought in English for the school.

– Mélissa, when will the next event be?

Yes, that was the outcome of that evening.

The message was clear: What is next? We need more!

That is how the Caribou à lunettes started. I opened the boxes of books I already had and shared with other families. Surprisingly, through word of mouth, more and more families came. I started offering creative workshops around literature as well, for children and teenagers. Some kids from bicultural families, for whom French is not the main language, came to realize that the language is shared by many other children, that it is lively and useful, and that it can be learned in a fun environment.

Organizing events to meet with authors and illustrators has been another constant objective. It has a spectacular effect on people. A book is then not just about a stack of sheets of paper glued together. It is about another human who created something to talk to readers, to talk to you. It is about connecting people. And therefore, a kid is much more inclined to grab that book and read it. And parents too.

March 2019. Lucile de Peslouan is visiting and ready to start the creation and publication of fanzines[38] with teenagers about feminism and social roles. But parents are not leaving the room. They want to meet her too, to listen, participate. We ended up creating two groups, one so that parents could also share about the topic and create their own fanzine. So much energy and willingness to be together, in French! With the pandemic, virtual life took the forefront. I launched an online bookstore to support parents and teachers in their search for books in French, offering quality, diverse, and inclusive stories. French books are so much more than stories about the Eiffel tower or Jacques Cartier! Workshops and conferences with creators were offered online in March for the *"Mois de la francophonie."* The Caribou allows me to encourage authors, illustrators, and publishers from different horizons, and help the community discover them, broadening the idea of a global Francophonie. The Caribou is about actions to promote youth literature in French. But beyond that, it is to create a space of connections with French-speaking cultures, with people.

Thoughts for the Future

Now, what is next? That is again the question. Once upon a time, there were eleven million Francophones in the United States. They all got married, had kids, and lived happily ever after. Fairy tale? If there really are eleven million people speaking and learning French here, as the *Centre de la francophonie des Amériques*[39] is suggesting, that is more than in Canada! What can stop us then to bloom? Are We Afraid to Speak French? If you want a language to live and flourish, speak it. What I see locally is that some are ashamed of their French. There is an underlying judgement: my French is not good enough, my French is not as nice as the one we speak in Paris, my accent is incorrect. Stop! That is what we call linguistic insecurity.

I know what it feels like. So many times, while living in France, I was told how 'cute' my accent was, that I was not using the correct word, that this expression was wrong or local, that we could not say this or that. Even though French is my mother tongue, even though I have a bachelor's degree in French writing and proofreading, even though I had worked fifteen years as a communication and publishing specialist, I doubted myself! I doubted myself so much that I signed up for a grammar and proofreading class in a Parisian school of journalism. You know what? I learned one thing: "my" grammar was the same. I already knew everything that was taught. (And I was more inclined to feminize the vocabulary and use gender-inclusive writing.) My French was absolutely "right." Because there are multiple "right" French languages.

All languages evolve. French is moving. French is pluralistic. Let us be proud, let us assume our personal, unique, diverse French, here, without seeking comparison or approval from somewhere else.

> *Le français a, en lui, un potentiel merveilleux. Cet attrait a déjà été là. L'histoire nous l'a enlevé. Les têtes couronnées qui ont associé le français à leur propre prestige ont obligé les Francophones à lui mettre une perruque et, depuis, on semble avoir oublié qu'il est beau sans cette perruque. Qu'il est un superbe troubadour. Qu'il est inventif, et qu'il peut même être un tant soit peu sournois et voler les mots des autres langues, sans les leur rendre. Et, surtout, qu'il peut être bon même quand il est mauvais. Que l'idée du mauvais n'est qu'une idée. Que si on veut que ce mauvais soit du bon, on n'a qu'à décider que c'en est, et c'en sera.*[40] (Anne-Marie Beaudoin-Bégin, *La langue affranchie*, p. 112).

[French has a wonderful potential. This attraction has already been there. History has taken it away from us. The crowned heads who associated French with their own prestige forced Francophones to put on a wig, and since then we seem to have forgotten that it is beautiful without this wig. That it is a superb troubadour. That it is inventive, and that it can even be a little sly and steal the words of other languages, without giving them back. And, most importantly, that it can be good even when it is bad. That the idea of the bad is just an idea. That if we want this bad to be good, we must decide it is, and it will be.]

Buy Local!

Every community has its specific features, historically, geographically, socially. Within the United States, some regions have stronger French roots than others. Immigration is also playing a big part in bringing a new energy. Where do we start or inspire the movement?

Setting up actions locally, adapted to the needs of the regional community will quickly make a great impact, bringing people together. Do you like food? Why not stop by Baobab Fare in midtown Detroit for East African meals and meet with Nadia and Mamba who speak French? Do you like basketball? Then, why not meet with Sekou Doumbouya from the Lakers after a game? (That was the plan if the pandemic had not postponed the event... Now, I guess, we will also have the chance to meet with Killian Hayes in Detroit!)

My focus is youth. They are the future. How can you draw their attention? How can French be attractive to them? How can they value their multiple cultures?

The learning of French is an important matter and a worry to me. Teachers ought to know there are more tools than just the program workbook with the Eiffel tower on the cover. There are so many other sources of support to help students acquire the subject. I am looking forward to creating a hub to present more and more of them. And to show the kids that French is a dynamic language used around the world. Again, learning is always more powerful in action. Arts and culture are my favorite gateways as they imply pleasure. Artists bring inspiration, they are role models. Activities around music, theater, dance, crafts, food, books (of course!) are tools to foster knowledge and a sense of belonging. Moreover, if all this is linked to the local environment, it will be more tangible. In Detroit, it is easy to organize meetings around history or with businesses with French origin products or French-speaking owners. And the Canadian border is a bridge or tunnel away, where on the other side, there is a Franco-Ontarian community, also standing for their rights, for their schools, and organizing activities in French. No need to travel far away! Let us take ownership of our local Francophonie, to show a reality that is close to people. It will give it more weight and meaning.

Vous parlez français aussi?

The millions of French speakers in the United States are diverse and scattered. Do we know each other? I have been told by a Michigander that she was not aware there was a French community in Maine. When you know there are other people like you, in your own country, you feel relieved, understood, reassured, empowered, content, happy. Not alone.

Let us look closer again. Multiple communities, within our local community do speak French. Yes, there are historical French regions with native families passing on their heritage. There are expatriates from different French-speaking countries, coming and going. Immigration and long-term residents also enhance and multiply the cultures, opening up our vision of the French world. And there are so many students learning French, and their teachers! We have our own French world within the US. But what we are missing is a bridge between all of us. A link (or multiple links) to connect and share, within our local communities and between the different areas in the country. If we can get together, we will be stronger and feel more encouraged. Foreign organizations already exist to support their citizens and promote their part of the world. Partnering is certainly a must in building up awareness, consolidating and strengthening the foundations.

What's Next?

French is not about the past, the war, the time of our great-great-grand-parents. It is happening now, and not just in schoolbooks, but in all areas of life. This is one key to foster interest. French is so much more than one specific country. And it is alive within the U.S. That is another key: empowering local actions and endorsing local culture and needs. Working together, joining forces instead of competing, no matter where your French comes from, will accelerate the movement. We need to be in action. We need to create a new wave of enthusiasm. In my case, youth literature is my driver, my accomplice. It is a means to value the diversity of the language and its cultures, to foster awareness and openness to the world. The Caribou will continue to promote fun reading and learning in French, in the Detroit area and on a larger scale, to build strong bridges between people. I could never recommend enough the documentary Baggage[41] from Melissa Lefebvre and Paul Tom, produced by Picbois Production, and viewable on Vimeo. It is based on a school play and gives voice to teenage immigrants in a high school in Montreal.

As shown in the film, you do not have to split yourself into the many pieces of multiple cultures you are built on. You can be 100% American *and* 100% French or 100% Canadian, 100% Cajun, 100% Lebanese, 100% Tunisian, etc. Multiple cultures add up to make the person you are. What richness! Let us take ownership and be empowered.

12. French Heritage in Minnesota
Mark Labine

In the beginning, they spoke French. For some two hundred years before it officially became a member of the United States, French was the most commonly spoken European language in the land we now call Minnesota. This reality was effectively documented by William H. Keating in 1817 when he made the following observation while part of a military excursion up the Mississippi River with Major Stephen Harriman Long:

> Not being previously aware of the diversity in the character of the inhabitants, the sudden change from an American to a French population, has a surprising, and to say the least, an unpleasant effect; for the first twenty-four hours, the traveler fancies himself in a real Babel.[42]

The official state motto of Minnesota is a French expression, *L'etoile du Nord* which means the North Star. This honors the historic French origins of the state. Historical records show that the preferred language of business in Minnesota during its territorial and early statehood period was often French. As Judge Charles Flandrau commented about the early days of St. Paul in 1855:

> Nearly all the people were French, and that language was quite as usually spoken as English. The town of Mendota was almost exclusively French and half-breed Sioux, the latter speaking French if they deviated from their native tongue.[43]

This French accent in Minnesota should not come as a surprise to anyone studying the early European migration and exploration of North America. French-speaking explorers are known to have reached Minnesota as early at 1659, when Pierre-Esprit Radisson (1636–1710) and Médard Chouart des Groseilliers (1618–1696) explored the eastern shores of Minnesota along Lake Superior.

In their 1659 voyage, Radisson and Groseilliers came to explore and trade for furs and would eventually be key players in the organization of the Hudson's Bay Company. Other French explorers would follow, and in 1680, Father Louis Hennepin, a French-speaking Catholic priest, traveled up the Mississippi River and discovered a waterfall located near present-day Minneapolis he named "Les Chutes de Saint-Antoine." The anglicized version of this name still exists today.

In 1683,[44] an explorer named Pierre-Charles Le Sueur with four French companions, came to the place "where the waters meet," which the Dakota called *Mdote aka Bdote*. The town of Mendota, Minnesota is named after this Dakota expression. These early French explorers observed a huge river flowing into the Mississippi at this junction which the Dakota called *Wakpa Mni Sota*, or "land where the waters are so clear they reflect the clouds." Pierre Le Sueur named this River the Rivière St-Pierre and for years this river was called the Rivière St-Pierre or St. Peters River. We know this both from his recorded recollections, and from early maps created by French map makers, such as the French cartographer Guillaume Delisle, (1675–1726).[45]

After Le Sueur, a fur-trade business developed between the French and local Native American tribes. Names of the first Frenchmen entering Minnesota territory as explorers and fur traders are familiar names, such as Radisson, Duluth, La Salle, Joliet, La Vérendrye, Perrot, and Le Sueur. Others less known came also, some as licensed traders, but many more as *coureurs des bois* (unlicensed fur traders), who operated without the consent and authority of the French authorities in Québec. One estimate is that, by 1700, there were perhaps 400 contracted or licensed voyageurs and likely more than 3,000 unlicensed *coureurs des bois* operating in French claimed lands. Undoubtedly, some of these traders operated in present-day Minnesota.

The French began to build trading posts that would eventually be spread out all over present-day Minnesota. Pierre La Vérendrye built Fort St. Pierre in 1732 at the outlet of Rainy Lake, and Fort St. Charles on Lake of the Woods the same year. Another La Vérendrye fort was built on the Roseau River. René Bourassa, who had traveled west with La Vérendrye, built a fort in 1736 at the mouth of the Vermillion River near Crane Lake. In 1727, Fort Beauharnois, sometimes referred to as the "Sioux Post," was built on Lake Pepin near present-day Frontenac, Minnesota. The first commander was René Boucher de La Perrière. Later, Jacques Legardeur de Saint-Pierre was commander of this fort. This post was designed to only trade with the Dakota, who were one of the dominant tribes in Minnesota.

The Treaty of Paris ending the French and Indian War in 1763 gave England claim to the vast interior of North America.[46] The British thereafter began taking over French posts throughout the region. This caused problems as the Natives had established good relationships with their French trading partners, and many of the French had intermarried with women from the local tribes.[47] British traders soon found they could not trade with the Native American tribes without help from the French Canadians, who continued to be the majority of traders heading west.

After the American Revolution, the United States claimed the region west of the Mississippi. When the Jay's Treaty was signed in 1794, British and French-Canadian traders were allowed to continue trading in the Midwest.[48] The War of 1812 disrupted the fur trade and many French-Canadian fur traders in the Minnesota region fought on the British side. After the treaty was signed ending the war, the United States retained the western region and Congress passed an act excluding foreigners from the fur trade in American territory. John Jacob Astor's American Fur Company purchased posts of the North West Company south of the border, but by this time the English had moved the center of their fur trade north of the Canadian border to places such as Fort William.[49]

After the War of 1812, a frontier skirmish, called the Pemmican War, broke out between the fur traders of the North West Company and Hudson's Bay Company. This war would last several years. In the Battle of Seven Oaks on June 19, 1816, twenty-one Red River settlers and Hudson's Bay employees were killed. The conflict ended in 1821 when the North West Company and the Hudson's Bay Company merged.[50]

One of the effects of the Pemmican War was that many French-Canadian fur traders, who worked in the Red River land and were part of the Selkirk Colony, migrated down to Fort Snelling, and many of them ended up working for the American Fur Company located in St. Peter, (present-day Mendota). This colony, established by Thomas Douglas, 5th Earl of Selkirk in 1811, was made up of Scottish, French-speaking Swiss, and French Canadians. Between 1821 and 1835, it is estimated that 489 refugees from Selkirk's Colony arrived at Fort Snelling, and they continued to come in following years.[51] These early Selkirk colonists became the nucleus of the first

European settlement of Minnesota. They built chapels in St. Peter and St. Paul[52], and their Catholic faith brought French-speaking clergy who ministered to their early congregations and organized educational institutions that exist to this day in Minnesota.

The year 1837 was a turning point for Minnesota when treaties gave ownership rights of land to the United States. When the Dakota and Ojibwa signed a treaty with the U. S. government for all the land east of the Mississippi, people started moving into this area to establish permanent settlements. Most of these people were not French-speaking, so the era of French being the dominant language in the area would transmute into history. Its heritage and mark on the Minnesota culture and landscape would remain, however.

One obvious remanent of Minnesota's French Heritage is the numerous French place names throughout the state. Many retained their French spelling, although many others were anglicized.[53] An example of some French names anglicized are Rainy Lake (formerly Lac la Pluie), Lake of the Woods (formerly Lac du Bois), Maple Lake (formerly Lac aux Erables), and Thief River (formerly Riviére Voleuse). Here are examples of place names in Minnesota with French origins:

Accault Bay, Argonne, Audubon, Bain, Battle Creek, Baudette, Beauford Township, Beaulieu, Beaudry, Bejou, Belgium Township, Bellaire, Belle Fontaine, Belle Plaine, Belle Prairie Township, Belle River, Belle Rose Island, Bellevue Township, Benoit, Bernadotte Township, Big LaSalle Lake, Birch Coulee, Blanchard, Boisberg, Bois Blanc Lake, Bois de Sioux River, Bois Forte, Bois Franc Creek, Brule River, Brule Mountain, Burdette, Burau, Cannon River, Caribou Lakes, Chaudiere Falls and Portage, Chapeau Lake, Cloquet, Cloquet River, Cloutier's Island, Coteau des Prairie, Dalles of the Saint Croix, De Forest, Delorme, Demarest, Des Moines River Township, Demontreville Lake, Detroit Lakes, Desnoyer Park, Du Forte Lake, Duluth, Dumont, Duquette, Emard Township, Embarrass Township, Faribault, Flacon Portage, Flandreau, Folles Avoines, Fond du Lac, Fortier Township, Fremont, French, French Creek, French Lake, French Lick, French River, Frenchmans Bar, Frenchy Corner, Frontenac, Gentilly, Gervais Lake and Township, Girard Township,

Goodin Island, Gooseberry River, Grand Cote, Grand
Marais, Grand Portage, Gratiot Lake, Groseilliers and
Radisson Lakes, Hennepin, Henriette, Huot, Isle, Isle
Royale, Jessenland Township, LaBathe Island, LaBelle
Lake, Lac qui Parle, Lac Plé Lake, Lac Vieux Desert Lake,
La Crescent, La Croix Lake, La Crosse Township, Lafayette,
LaFleche Prairie, Lafond Ave, Lafontaine, Lagarde,
Lambert Township, Lamoille, La Grande Prairie, Lake
Antoinette, Lake Fremont, Lake Gervais, Lake LaBelle,
Lake Marquette, Lake Pepin, La Porte, La Prairie, Lake
Superior, Lake Traverse, Lake Vadnais, Lake Vermillion,
Larpenteur, La Salle, La Salle Lake, Le Center, LeClaire,
L'Etoile du Nord, Le Homme Dieu Lake, Lemond
Township, Le Sauk Township, LeRoy, LeSueur, Little
Canada, Little Marais, Louisville Township, Maine
Township, Marcoux Corner, Marillac Lane, Marine on
St. Croix, Marquette, Mille Lacs Lake, Montcalm Place,
Neville, Nicollet County, Nord Lake, Orleans, Otter Tail
Point, Pape de Terre, Parent Lake, Pelland, Perrault, Peltier
Lake, Pettit, Picard Lakes, Pig's Eye Lake, Plantagenet Lake,
Platte River, Pomerleau Lake, Pomme de Terre Fort, River,
and Lake, Portage de Rideau, Portage River, Portage Lake
and Township, Poupore, Prairie, Prairie Island, Rabideau
Lake, Racine Township, Ravoux Street, Renville, Revere,
Robert Creek, Rochert, Rondo (Rondeau) Neighborhood in
St. Paul, Rolette, Roseau, Saint Anthony, Saint Clair, Saint
Cloud, Saint Croix, Saint Francis, Saint Hilaire, Saint
Lawrence Township, St. Louis County, River and Township,
Saint Paul, Saint Peter, Saint Vincent, Saulteurs, Terrebonne
Township, Tetagouche Lake, Tettegouche State Park,
Traverse County, Traverse des Sioux, Vadnais Heights,
Vermillion, Voyageurs National Park, Wyandotte
Township, Zumbro.

The French legacy in Minnesota was also present in the early
formation of European communities established in the State in the
19th century. The French Canadians were participants in three
phases of early European settlement in Minnesota.

The first phase of French-Canadian settlement occurred in
the 1820s and 1830s. Although what was to become Minnesota

remained officially closed to settlement, isolated agricultural outposts were being formed in the State at fur trading posts, at the Fort Snelling military reservation, and in what United States treaty makers labeled the Half-Breed Tract around Lake Pepin.[54] French-speaking fur traders and their families who had established ties in the territory by working at fur trade posts and who had children with native American women began to plant crops, raise livestock, and build homes. Many of the French-speaking colonists in this first phase were members of the Selkirk Red River Colony. These early settlers traveled south by Ox Cart to establish temporary housing in the Fort Snelling military reservation between the years 1821-1837.

The second phase of French-Canadian settlement in Minnesota occurred between the years 1837-1862 after separate United States treaties with the Ojibwe and Dakota opened up land between the St. Croix and Mississippi Rivers. There were two treaties in 1837, one with the Ojibwe and one with the Dakota. This second phase of French-Canadian immigrants began to migrate to the United States and Minnesota in the 1840s. The French-Canadian population in New England almost doubled during that decade.[55] Members of the Selkirk Colony, many who were French-Canadian and who had been squatting in the Fort Snelling Military Reservation, made up part of this second phase as they settled in the Mendota and St. Paul area. French Canadians also arrived in substantial numbers to Midwestern states such as Michigan, which by 1850, boasted a French population of about twenty thousand.[56]

The third phase of French-Canadian settlement in Minnesota came after the United States government passed the Homestead Act in 1862 and continued making treaties with the Native American tribes for their lands. This opened up additional land opportunities for settlement. The land opportunities, a robust United States economy, and a difficult economic depression in Canada from 1873 to 1896, all resulted in a large-scale immigration to the United States, including many French Canadians.[57] It is estimated that over one million French Canadians emigrated to the United States between the 1840s and 1930s. This group were not related to the fur trade and were generally farmers by occupation. Many of them came to Minnesota, some immigrating first to New England, and then re-settling in the Midwest. They ventured to Minnesota primarily because of the perceived economic opportunity provided by the large amount of land available at cheap prices.

In 1891, the Twin Cities area of Minnesota contained approximately 18,000 French Canadians. Outside of the Minneapolis-Saint Paul metropolitan area, a number of small French-Canadian settlements were established, with the largest settlements being in Polk County in the Red River Valley.[58] In the 1900 census, Minnesota shows the second highest concentration of Francophones in the United States. Below is a list of seventy-nine settlements in Minnesota where French-speaking Catholic churches were established. This means that the French-speaking population was large enough to support a church. French Canadians also settled in other places, in smaller numbers, where they did not have the numbers needed to establish a French-speaking church. These populations are harder to trace. As a result, some of these smaller settlements may not be listed here. The seventy-nine settlements include the following:

Afton, Albertville, Anoka, Argyle, Badger, Belle Prairie Breckenridge, Brooks, Brown's Valley, Buffalo, Centerville, Chaska, Cloquet, Corcoran, Crookston, Dayton, Delano, Delavan, Dorothy, Duluth, East Grand Forks, Elk River, Faribault, French Lake-Annandale, Fort Ripley, Gentilly, Ghent, Grand Marais, Grand Portage, Green Valley, Greenbush Township, Hamel, Henderson, Hugo, Huot, International Falls, Iron Range, Lake Benton, Lambert, Little Canada, Little Falls, Louisville, Marshall, Medicine Lake, Medina, Mendota, Minneapolis, Minnesota River Valley, Oklee, Oakwood, North Dakota, Osseo, Red Lake Falls, Red Lake Indian Reservation, Red River Valley, Saint Anthony (Saint Antoine), Saint Boniface, Saint Paul, Saint Vincent/Pembina, Somerset, Wisconsin, Stillwater, Terrebonne, Tower, Two Harbors, Wabasha, Warroad, Waverly, White Bear Lake, and the White Earth Reservation.

In addition to the seventy-nine settlements with sizable French-Canadian populations, the French were very involved and instrumental in setting up schools and providing education opportunities to Minnesota residents in the nineteenth century. The French-speaking Sisters of St. Joseph of Carondolet started the first school in St. Paul on November 7, 1851. They went on to provide instruction and administration to 78 schools in Minnesota. In addition, they founded the College of St. Catherine in 1905, an institute of higher learner that still exists today as St. Catherine University.

The Franciscan Sisters operated the Convent and Academy of St. Anthony in Belle Prairie, Minnesota and taught all classes in French for a number of years.[59] Other French religious orders involved in providing education to Minnesota include: The Institute of the Brothers of the Holy Family (founded in the diocese of Belley in France); the Crosier Order, (founded in 1210 in France), which formed the Crosier Community of Onamia, Minnesota. the Brothers of the Christian Schools, also known "De La Salle Brothers;" the Congregation of Holy Cross or "Congregation a Sancta Cruce" founded in Le Mans, France; the Grey Nuns from Montreal, Québec; and the Sisters of St. Joseph of Médaille who taught in sixteen schools in Minnesota.[60]

In addition to the important French influence on education in Minnesota, numerous organizations were formed in Minnesota by French or French Canadians. French Canadians founded more than three dozen French language newspapers in the Midwest in the nineteenth century, mostly in Michigan, Illinois,[61] and Minnesota. Most were short lived, but Le Canadian in St. Paul survived more than two decades.[62] Below is a list of some of the organizations in Minnesota that were related to the Franco-phone language or culture:

> Afoutayi Dance, Music and Arts Company; Alliance Française; Association of French-Canadian Pioneers (formed in Duluth in July, 1911);[63] Club des Bons-Vivants, (a French speaking club said to be open to persons of good nature with smiling faces and happy characters);[64] Club Democratic Franco Americaine, (a club of French-Canadian democrats formed in March 1884);[65] Commanderie de Bordeaux aux États-Unis d'Amérique (organized in 1957); Echo de l'Quest; Franco American Literary Club of Sister Cities; French-American Heritage Foundation, (formed in February 2013); French American Chamber of Commerce; French-Canadian Dramatic Club; French Club in Duluth, (formed in the early 1900's); French Sister Cities, including Foumies, France to Fridley and Tours, France to Minneapolis); Initiatives in French Midwest; International Organization de la Francophonie, (created in 1970); La Société Candienne Française (1979-2001); Lafayette-

Papineau Republican League of Minneapolis[66] (formed in 1898); La Voix du Lac Newspaper published in Duluth (1892);[67] L'Etoile du Nord Newspaper (1874-1876);[68] Le Canadien Newspaper (1877); Le Citoyen Americain Newspaper (1884);[69] Les Amis de la France; Le Courier de Duluth Newspaper (1890); Le Franco Canadien (1877);[70] Le National Newspaper (1877);[71] Les Amis du Theatre (early 1970s); Les Veillees Canadiennes Newspaper (1852); L'Association des Français du Nord; L'Oeil Newspaper (1893); Les Survivants, a group formed in Minnesota and dedicated to French-Canadian culture and language; Minnesota Chapter of the American Association of Teachers in French (AATF); National Huguenot Society; Poulenc Academy; Saint Vincent de Paul Society; Saint Jean the Baptiste Society (1834); the Société de Bienfaisance Franco-Canadienne de Saint Paul;[72] Société des Voyageurs (1976;, Théâtre de la Jeune Lune; Théâtre du Monde; Union Francaise (1867);[73] Union St. Jean Baptiste (1870-1900);[74] and Union Catholique de l'Abstenence Totale (1871).[75]

The French legacy is still alive in Minnesota and according to the 1980 United States Census, approximately 8.2% of the population in the state had French origins, mostly from French Canada. Residents with French origins also include French Huguenots who were part of the early settlement in the United States, immigrants from West Africa where many countries speak French, and Haiti, among others. There are a number of options to learn, or practice, French in Minnesota, including French immersion schools, French language courses in universities and community colleges, local community education classes, informal conversation groups, private tutors, self-study, and online resources. French Mass can still be heard on Christmas Eve at the Church of St. Louis, King of France, in St. Paul, and on Sundays, at St. Boniface Church, in Northeast Minneapolis. Our Lady of Lourdes Church in Minneapolis still carries a strong French heritage legacy.

Each year, *L'Association des Français du Nord* (AFRAN) sponsors a Chautauqua Festival featuring French heritage in Huot, Minnesota. The French-American Heritage Foundation and Alliance Française sponsor several French heritage and French cultural events throughout the year, including Fête St. Jean-Baptiste at the Sibley

Historic Site, in Mendota, and Bastille Day. There are a number of fur trade festivals or rendezvous that take place each year in Minnesota that celebrate of legacy of French Voyageurs.

The French-American Heritage Foundation has listed seventy-one French heritage sites in Minnesota. These sites are listed in Chapter eighteen of *They Spoke French*, a book published by the Foundation. The French Heritage in Minnesota is rich and an important part of our state's history. It has many different faces and influences and the immigration of French-speaking emigrants to Minnesota continues to this day. This heritage should not be forgotten. It should be understood, valued, and enjoyed.

13. Rethinking the approach to Franco-American Culture in New England
Timothy Beaulieu

Around a million French-Canadians came to the United States between the 1840s and 1930. The French-Canadians, now known as Franco-Americans, discussed in this chapter worked in the 19th- and 20th-century mills of New England. Their story goes something like this: They lived in small enclaves near the mills called *Little Canadas*. Their lives were primarily conducted in French and centered around work, family, and religion. They resisted assimilation into the larger American culture longer than most immigrant populations and their story, strictly speaking, ends in the 1960s. They are now Americans like any other, only with hard-to-say names pronounced with a French accent that not many in the States can master. The End.

That is the general story I have encountered over my years becoming more familiar with my heritage and somewhat lost culture. A quick look at my background, so you get to know the person who is presenting you with these ideas about the Franco-Americans. I am basically your mild-mannered, everyday 3rd-generation Franco- American. I have a great wife and kids; I work in an office. I'm basically living the *Rêve Américain*. Growing up I knew my name was French, but from where? It was not until my twenties that I learned our ancestral story when my grandfather decided to talk about it a few years before he passed away. It is hard for some to believe, but there are millions of people in New England whose personal history unfolds in similar manner. How do we start this process sooner, or help support those who do find out about their French-Canadian roots in this imperfect way? I have been observing the culture closely since about 2010 and became a member of the Franco-American Centre of New Hampshire (FACNH) in 2014. Despite this, I am relatively new to the Franco-American world, as I said. So, I served on the FACNH's board of trustees from 2015 until 2021. In 2015, I came up with the idea for NH PoutineFest and launched it with the FACNH in 2016. It is a several thousand-person festival that mirrors similar events in Québec and in the Midwest of the United States. NH PoutineFest is currently the largest poutine festival in the United States. It is a big celebration of a Québécois food and the Franco-American culture of New Hampshire.

Current State of Affairs

We are currently at a very interesting time in Franco-American history, one that strictly speaking was said by onlookers to have ended in the 1960s. I am a child of the 1980s and I did not hear the term Franco-American until I was well into my thirties (my family never used the term). So, what was the cultural story? How did we go from fighting off assimilation to not even knowing who we are? Quite frankly, I will leave that to the historians. There are a myriad of factors that landed us where we are today. I'll start by listing the different types of Franco-Americans, as I see it:

1) People who have a French name but who are totally detached from their heritage
2) People who are disillusioned with their culture and want nothing to do with it
3) People who have kept some traditions, up to and including the French language
4) People who are curious about their heritage and looking to re-connect (sometimes called a reborn Franco).

Everything is complex in the Franco world, right? That said, even with millions of people who could be participating in the culture or learning language we are still very much invisible, and our language is in rather rapid decline.

Doom and Gloom

It is without question that the French-Canadian immigrants that came to the United States had a difficult time adjusting to their new home. Bullying from other immigrant groups, bullying from the Yankees (New Englanders of Protestant stock), Ku Klux Klan chapters marching throughout Maine, eugenics projects in Vermont, the list goes on. Some of those attacks live on into the 21st century in the form of little jokes or of families who take on different names or have their names mispronounced. That is a lot of traumas for a group to endure. The scars from that trauma have left us playing not to lose, rather than playing to win.

You might be asking yourself, what does that mean exactly? First and foremost, we talk about the past... a lot. When you talk about the same trauma over and over again, it is interesting at first, but at a certain point you have to let it go. We will never be able to defeat the British in 1759 or win in another street brawl with the Irish immigrants at the mill. It is important to remember where you came from, but the energy in the community should not be solely focused on reliving old trauma. It should instead be redirected towards things we can actually change. On the present, and eventually the future.

Secondly, many groups I encounter in New England are desperately trying to hang on to something. Sometimes, this can be a good thing. There are most definitely things we need to fight to hold onto. Just holding on, though, will only get you so far. If you are not growing, you are dying. Continuously focusing on what we have lost is not healthy and it creates a fear of further loss, which in turn leads to inaction. Look, history is important, but I also believe in this heritage and culture as a living entity that can extend its life into the future. The best way to honor the sacrifice of our ancestors who endured that trauma firsthand is to grow.

How to Grow

Before being able to grow, we need to face the reality that the past is not coming back. That is sad on some level, but it also presents an opportunity. Bringing all the different types of French-Canadians that I listed above together (besides those who want nothing to do with the culture) would be a start. We are all coming from different experiences and even backgrounds in the French-Canadian world. It will not be a recreated Petit Canada, and that is OK. Cultures grow and change over time. Afterall, poutine is barely 60 years old, but it is hard to remember Québec without it. The wonderful thing about New England is that there are already wonderful groups in place to do some of the work I am going to discuss below. All we need to do is come together and ignore those silly state borders the American Colonists created.

Where to Begin?

It is easy to play Monday morning quarterback and point fingers at what happened. It is a much different thing to work to fix it. But how? It starts with creating a sense of pride in the younger generation of Franco-Americans and fostering a strong relationship with the culture and heritage in their lives. That is clearly the way; it is how other ethnic groups find meaning and renew themselves. Why can't we?

Some contemporary examples of this are Irish-Americans and Italian-Americans. These are two of the other larger immigrant groups in New England and for whatever reason there is a larger sense of pride amongst them. Obviously, there was trauma amongst those two groups as well, yet shamrocks and pizza dominate New England. When I hear people in these groups speak of their immigrant story it is mostly about how hard they worked to get where they are. The rivalry between the English and French, and English being the dominant language in the States, probably plays a role in our lack of pride, but why not steal a page out of a successful playbook? This will all take a lot of work. Keep in mind Montréal was not built over night, it is always under construction. Here is an outline for a Franco Playbook that could work in New England. Granted these ideas are my own and come from observing our culture over the last decade.

Franco-Playbook: Re-establish Pride/Interest

There are parts of New England where French-Canadian/Acadian culture is very visible, mostly in northern and eastern Maine. In order to bring visibility back, a slight re-boot of Franco-Americanness is needed. It all starts with creating a new "brand" identity. For too long others have defined what the "French" are. We have some great assets at our fingertips to make this happen.

Fleur-de-lys

The Québec style fleur-de-lys is a very recognizable, clear, clean image. As they do in Québec, the fleur-de-lys should be incorporated into anything having to do with French-Canadians. Not just any version of it either, it must be the version displayed on the Québec flag. When people in New England see the fleur-de-lys they need to think Franco and not the Boy Scouts or the New Orleans Saints.

History in a New Way

Our history IS North American history. Shinning a light on our victories as well as our struggles can help reframe our story. As stated earlier, we tend to focus on the doom and gloom of our story in a significant way. It has not been all bad, though. After all, we are still here. History is written by the victors; I consider our existence and success a victory. We can use our proficiency in English as a method of teaching the new generations our version of the story. And, we do not have to rely on schools to do this.

It can start at as basic a level as having more in-depth and easy-to-find resources on New France and Acadie. Our story is only barely mentioned in the United States, usually when the "French and Indian" War is mentioned, but there is so much more to it than that. We need to expand on what happened before George Washington started that war. This can build into our crossing of the border and what life was like in the *Petits Canadas.* Then, of course, state that the story ends in the 1960's. Kidding, of course! From the 1940's to the present, highlighting famous folks of Franco-American descent and celebrating their success is a way to show that our story goes on. It is exactly what the other "ethnic" groups in the United States do, why aren't we doing the same?

Poutine

That brings us to food. Poutine is Québecois and we are their long-lost cousins. What better food to celebrate in New England than poutine? Over the last decade the number of restaurants offering poutine in New England has grown exponentially. It is important for the geographical origins of poutine to be very well known throughout New England. This serves two purposes it 1) helps Québec make their rightful claim to poutine in the Anglophone world and 2) provides a point of pride for Franco-Americans to celebrate. In 20 to 30 years' time, this dish will be firmly entrenched in New England and associated with the descendants of the land it comes from. The easiest way to help push the process along is to have food festivals and/or smaller events celebrating this food and its related culture.

In 2015, I developed the idea for New Hampshire PoutineFest and launched the event with the Franco-American Centre of New Hampshire. At first no one thought it would work, but in its six years of existence we have never had a ticket left to sell. The wonderful thing about events like this is they are embraced by the dominant culture in the area. People love to be supportive of big fun ideas. It allows us to extend outside of our Franco-American bubble and show everyone that being around Franco-American culture is fun!

Events also can raise a good amount of money. Money from major events can be used to grow the culture, teach the language, in short really help give us the push we need to support French learners and build up resources. To expand on the poutine success, an even larger event is needed outside our festival in New Hampshire. It is amazing to have a couple thousand people super-excited about poutine, but what about ten times that many? It could happen. The key is for folks all over New England to hear the word poutine and think French and for Franco-Americans to hear poutine and feel extremely proud.

Working with Québec and the Québecois

I used Irish and Italian-Americans as examples to emulate earlier on. Could you imagine if they could drive to Dublin or Rome in a single afternoon? They might never leave! A trip to their ancestral homeland involves booking a major trip; for Franco-Americans it is a simple car ride. We have underutilized our proximity to our motherland. Most Franco-Americans are now part of the dominant culture in the US. We have not been raised to look north for anything, let alone to the home of one of Boston's archrivals – the Montréal Canadiens. Yes, that is right, hockey has a bit of an impact. Amongst tough New England sports fans, you cannot show any empathy to Boston's rivals. Liking the Canadiens is the same as liking the New York Yankees. While Yankees fans get a ribbing from Boston fans, it is slightly different with Montréal.

The culture and language are routinely mocked as inferior. That is a problem. This one is not going away, but it will be important for Franco-Americans to brush back the sorts of attacks that can be heard from Michael Felger (he is from Wisconsin by the way) on 98.5 FM in Boston. The Québecois are not a group that you can mock using ridiculous stereotypes, just like any other ethnic group. Side note, Boston loves the idea of the Expos returning to Montréal. Strange. Besides defending against the anti-Canadian bias, building relationships with folks in Québec will also play a major role. There is also something to keep in mind when trying to establish contact with the Québécois. One thing that seems to come up periodically is that Franco-Americans are largely unknown in Québec. There are small pockets of Québécois who know of us and a large amount who do not. After a few years of social media interaction with the Québécois they fall into two generally defined teams.

> Équipe no 1 (E1): We view Franco-Americans as assimilated and dead.

> Équipe no 2 (E2): We are interested in our cousins in the United States, and we are happy they are interested in us.

I am a big fan of Équipe no 2. I do not dislike Équipe no 1; I understand their viewpoint. I have tried to engage with them, and it has not gone so well. Maybe they'll come around, but we are not there yet. Building relationships with Équipe no 2 at this stage does not necessarily mean solely communicating in French. We are fortunate to have many bilingual people in La Belle Province, as well as in the U.S. The age of social media has made this type of communication easier than ever before. The goal of these relationships is to create cross-border collaboration on events and/or cultural exchanges.

Visiting Montréal is an easy way to introduce Franco-Americans to their Franco roots. Montréal is similar to major United States cities in terms of its melting pot feel. There are many different cultures and languages spoken in Montréal, but with a heavy, heavy dose of French. It is enough for an American kid to take notice. Québec City is essentially the French-Canadian version of Plymouth Rock. It is where it all started and very much a Francophone city. It is the logical next step for cultural exchanges or/trips to explore where our story began.

What comes next?

I realize this playbook may be a lot of wishful thinking. However, it is trying something new as opposed to the technique of simply holding on for dear life, an unofficial policy in place since the 1960s. If we want this culture and heritage to survive, we have to take action. It will not happen overnight; it is something that has to be continuously nurtured and worked on. What is very clear to me is we are extremely lucky to have many of the pieces already in place. It is simply all about getting people excited about where they come from; the local communities will rally around that. I hope my children read this someday and see their old man was right. Time will tell!

14. Finding Franco-America: Language, community, and the Richelieu Clubs of New England
Elizabeth Blood

I was 42 years old when I found out that I was Franco-American. I always knew my paternal grandmother, Mimi, had been born in Québec, that her first language was French. That my father, born in the United States, had grown up spending summers at the family farm in Saint-Félix-de-Valois. I had learned some basic French vocabulary from my father as a child, and we had visited French-speaking cousins in Montréal on vacations when I was young. My father used to tap the maple trees in our suburban New York backyard to show me how they make maple syrup, and we made a *bûche de Noël* cake from scratch every Christmas eve. We went to our neighbors' house for a dinner party after midnight mass each year. As a teen, I learned to make *tourtière* from a recipe my Mimi had published in her church's fundraiser cookbook. But I was a suburban American kid with an Irish-American mother and an Anglo last name. I never felt that I belonged to any ethnic group and had never even heard the term "Franco-American" used to describe people of French-Canadian descent, until I started doing research on the French-speaking community in Salem, Massachusetts and discovered the Richelieu Club of Salem in 2008.

Initially, I joined this local French-speaking group as a kind of gown-to-town outreach for my job as a French professor at Salem State University, but what I discovered there was a community rooted in Franco-American traditions and filled with people who had stories to tell about growing up Franco-American. The more I heard their stories, the more I explored my own family connections to Québec, and the more I grew to see myself as Franco-American.

Shifting the Focus from France to French North America

Today, as a professor of French, my academic research centers on French North America, specifically looking at the cultural history of

Francophone Québec and Franco-Americans in the Northeastern United States with the goal of making those cultures better understood and more widely recognized by researchers, students, and the general public. But I did not become a French professor because of my French-Canadian ancestral heritage. Far from it. When I was young, I saw French as a foreign language and was captivated by the idea of learning to speak it and traveling in Europe. In fact, I was equally enthralled with Italian language and culture, which became my third language in college, even though I have no ancestral ties to Italy. My motivation came from wanting to travel and have adventures in Europe, not from my own family connection to the place. What I did not realize then was that my journey as an academic would take me full circle back to my childhood experiences, learning French words and experiencing Franco-American culture.

Although I had learned a few words in French from my father and grandmother as a young child, I did not really start speaking the language until high school. Again, in my mind, my interest in studying French had nothing to do with my French-Canadian ancestry, and the courses I took did not encourage me to make that connection. All throughout high school and college in the 1980's and even through my graduate studies for my master's and Ph.D. in the 1990's, my French courses only taught me about the history, culture, and language of metropolitan France. My high school French class traveled to France, my semester abroad in college was in France, and the Chateaubriand fellowship I was awarded for doctoral research sent me to Paris to study 18th-century French theater, which was my area of specialization up until I discovered my passion for Québec and Franco-American Studies.

In 2001, I learned about an opportunity to travel to Québec with a group of professors to learn more about Québécois history, culture, and literature. This travel seminar, sponsored by the American Association of Teachers of French and the Québec government, funded a small group of us to spend one week in Québec City and one week in Montreal, visiting historic sites and museums, listening to lectures from local experts, and learning more about the rich history and culture of Québec. This experience inspired me to learn more about Québécois literature and culture, and I would later coordinate an annual summer program to bring my undergraduate students of French to study at the Université Laval. As coordinator of this program for my university, I would accompany my group of students to Québec to help them settle into the program there at Laval's *École de Langues Vivantes*. After they were settled, I would extend my stay to further expand my knowledge of the province. For a decade, I read, learned, explored, and taught myself everything about Québec that I never learned in all my years of studying French. Ironically, even though I had French-speaking relatives in Montréal, I still understood this experience as one where I was learning about yet another foreign culture. But that would eventually change, for soon after that seminar in Québec, I started to research Franco-America and found that this was, in fact, part of my identity.

When I arrived at Salem State in the fall of 2003, I was told by many people that Salem had a large French-speaking community. I was excited to meet this group of people and discover more about them. Unfortunately, they were initially hard to find. The Point Neighborhood, which had been the "Little Canada" of Salem, was a predominantly Spanish-speaking neighborhood by the early 21st century when I arrived there; the local churches offered masses only in English and Spanish, to my knowledge; and the public monuments, museums, and heritage sites seemed to focus only on the city's Anglo-American history, with its Puritans and witch hunts, sea captains and its famous Anglo-American author Nathaniel Hawthorne. Nonetheless, in tandem with my studies on Québec, I began to research the French community in Salem.

I stumbled across a French-language newspaper called the *Courrier de Salem*. Published in the city in the early 20th century, it chronicled the lives of the region's French-Canadian immigrants and their U.S.-born children, called Franco-Americans. Intrigued by several articles where Franco-American community leaders described Salem as "*la ville que nous avons adoptée*" (the city that we adopted), I pulled together a conference presentation about the metaphor of adoption as a way to think about immigration and identity in the Franco-American community. It was, after all, the people who adopted the city and not vice versa, giving the French-Canadian community agency as caretakers of their new home.

I presented my research on this topic at the 2008 conference of the American Council for Québec Studies. During the question-and-answer part of the presentation, I was asked about the Franco-

American community in Salem today, and I explained how I had been unable to contact this community. One professor attending the conference suggested that I contact the local Richelieu Club. I had not ever heard of such a club, but she assured me that this Franco-American club was active in Salem. Finally, through a friend at Salem State who knew of the club because she was on the board of the Plummer Youth Promise (one of the local charities the Salem Richelieu Club supports), I was able to make contact with them and attended my first meeting.

The Richelieu Clubs of New England

The first Richelieu Clubs were formed as French-speaking social clubs in Ontario, Canada in the 1940s, modeled on Anglophone groups like the Rotary Clubs, but with the explicit goal of creating a sense of solidarity among French speakers outside of Québec, while promoting mutual aid and community service. The club was named in honor of Cardinal Richelieu, not because of his role in 17th-century French politics, but in memory of the Maison Richelieu, a home for orphans and children in need established in New France in 1637 by the Duchess of Aiguillon (Cardinal Richelieu's niece) thanks to private funding from the Cardinal himself. This establishment, still operating in Québec today, would later be renamed the *Hôtel-Dieu de Québec* and is recognized as the first hospital established in Canada. The mission of the Richelieu Society founded in the 1940s was to continue the spirit of the *Maison Richelieu* by supporting charities that help children in need in local communities wherever a club is established.

In the 1950s, the Richelieu Society became Richelieu International, as clubs were formed in Franco-American communities in the United States and later in Francophone countries in Europe and Africa. The first United States club was established in Manchester, New Hampshire in 1955. That club sponsored several other clubs in New England, including the Richelieu Club of Salem, formed in 1965 thanks to Monsignor Arthur O. Mercier. Mercier, then pastor of St. Joseph's church, a parish that served the Franco-American community of Salem, saw the need for his parishioners to keep the French language and culture alive in the community, as more and more Franco-Americans were assimilating into American culture and moving out of the "Little Canada" neighborhood that had nurtured the tight-knit French-speaking community from the late 19th century through the mid-20th century. He invited a guest speaker to talk about the Richelieu clubs and nominated local business leader George Aubertin to establish the club and become its first president.

The first meeting of the Salem club was held at the Hawthorne Hotel on January 16, 1965. Originally, membership was only open to men, and included many of the city's most prominent Franco-American businesspeople and professionals. A sister organization, the all-female Club Richelieu Nord de Boston, was formed in 1984. Although the Salem club opened its membership to women in the 1990s, both clubs still exist and continue to meet in Salem today, with one annual dinner bringing together the members of both clubs. In 2012, the Richelieu Clubs of New England split from Richelieu International (still based in Ontario) to form their own regional group called *Richelieu États-Unis*. This regional organization unites clubs located in New England cities with a strong Franco-American heritage. In addition to the two clubs in Salem, today there are clubs in Lowell and New Bedford, Massachusetts, Nashua and Manchester, New Hampshire, and Woonsocket, Rhode Island. Each spring, the organization sponsors a Concours Oratoire (French oratorical contest) for area high school students of French, with each club selecting a top student from schools in their area (sponsored by their French teacher) and a regional contest where the top students from each club compete for the regional title and cash prize.

The mission of the Club Richelieu de Salem has remained faithful to that of the original club's founders: to promote the continued use of the French language—through its monthly French-speaking dinners and community events like the *Concours Oratoire*—and to support charities that help children in need. The Salem Richelieu Club collects funds and donates annually to the Plummer Youth Promise and the Boys and Girls Club of Salem, among other organizations.

When I joined the Salem Richelieu Club in 2008, the club was still mostly made up of Franco-Americans who had been born and raised in French-speaking households in Salem or surrounding towns. There were only about twenty-five or so active members who attended the French-speaking dinners at the Hawthorne Hotel each month, and the vast majority were men over the age of 60, but they were a lively group! They spoke French with the characteristic Franco-American accent that sounded very similar to the *Québécois* accent I had grown to love. They loved to tell jokes, to sing songs from the Richelieu song book of French and French-Canadian folk songs, to drink wine, and to tell stories about growing up Franco-American in Salem and the glory days of the club in the 1970s when there were hundreds of active members.

As I mentioned at the start of this essay, I originally got involved with the Richelieu Club because I thought it would be good for me as a professor at the local university to have contacts with the French-speaking community in the area and because I was interested in researching the history of Franco-Americans in Salem, but after each meeting I attended, I started to feel more connected to the group on a personal level. Returning home after an evening of speaking French with the club members, I often felt as if I had just spent the evening with my French-speaking great aunts and uncles and cousins, and I started to reclaim—or maybe to construct—my own identity as a Franco-American. I came to realize that, even though I was not raised in a French-speaking household, and I never experienced life in a "Little Canada," I was still Franco-American. Being a part of this community allowed me to see that I was also part of the culture. Little by little, I became more involved with the club, helping to organize its annual *Concours Oratoire* for area high school students of French, becoming a member of the board, even serving as Vice President for a couple of years. In recent years, the membership of the club has changed. The Salem club has made an effort to recruit French speakers of all different backgrounds to attend our dinner meetings and join our membership. There are still many members of Franco-American ancestry, and a number who are Anglophone Franco-Americans who are just learning French as a second language or who are reviving a childhood language long unused, but there are also people who join our meetings who are from or have lived in Switzerland, Belgium, France, Burkina Faso, the Côte d'Ivoire, the Congo, Haiti, Tunisia, Lebanon, and other parts of the French-speaking world. There are also some members who just learned French as a second language and want to continue to practice speaking.

The Salem Richelieu Club, an organization founded to help Franco-Americans preserve their language and their culture, has persisted in the city I now call home. It has remained true to its mission. It is transforming itself to open up to other French-speaking cultures in order to continue the mission of perpetuating the use of French language in the United States in the future.

Advancing Awareness of French Language and Culture in North America

Thanks to the personal and intellectual experiences that brought me from France to Québec and back to Franco-America, my academic work in the past twenty years has centered on the promotion of French language and Francophone cultures in North America. As a teacher of French, I make sure that my students learn about the rich cultural heritage of Francophone cultures around the world, with a particular focus on French North America. I dispel the myth that Québécois French is not "real French" by inviting students to explore regionalisms and local expressions, to think about accents and different registers of language (for example, how you speak to your friends versus how you might write a college essay), and to consider the role of politics in the spread and development of languages. I teach them about the history of Québec and share stories I learned from Richelieu Club members about the "Little Canada" that used to exist in the Point Neighborhood just a few blocks from the Salem State campus. We also explore other Francophone cultures in North America, like Louisiana and Haiti. Many of my students at Salem State have studied French in Québec through the summer program I helped to organize, which has created a new generation of people interested in Francophone North Americans.

I promote this idea of teaching about French North America to other French teachers and professors through conference presentations and the creation of college-level textbooks. I have offered numerous workshops on Québécois and Franco-American culture, language, and literature at regional and national French teacher conferences, and my two textbook projects both promote better understanding of French North America. My first project, an intermediate French textbook published by Pearson Education in 2004 under the title *Intrigue: langue, culture et mystère dans le monde*

Francophone, uses a mystery story to explore a different Francophone culture in each chapter, opening with a chapter on Louisiana and closing with a chapter on Québec. Though now out of print, this textbook went through three editions and was widely adopted in colleges across the country. My second textbook project is an introduction to Québec Studies written for students of French as a second language. This book, co-authored with J. Vincent Morrissette and published by Georgetown University Press in 2015, is entitled *Je me souviens: langue, culture, et littérature du Québec Francophone*. It uses an interdisciplinary approach to introduce students of French to the rich cultural heritage of this region. While there are many materials in French about Québec, most are written at a level that is too difficult for language learners. This textbook allows professors of French to include a class more easily on Québec in their undergraduate French program curricula.

My scholarly work has also focused on promoting awareness of Québec and Franco-America and has bent towards public history projects more than literary research in recent years. My colleague at Salem State, Dr. Elizabeth Duclos-Orsello, and I completed an oral history project in Salem that includes recorded and transcribed interviews with over a dozen Franco-Americans who grew up in Salem, many of whom were members of the Richelieu Club. The information gathered in these interviews, now available to the public in the Salem State University Archives, has led to public talks, guided and self-guided walking tours of Franco-American Salem, a website about Franco-Americans in Salem, and community events to highlight the role of Franco-Americans in the history and cultural life of the city. The response to these events on a local level has been amazing, with many people coming forward to share more stories and reminisce about the lives of their grandparents and great-grandparents who grew up speaking French in Salem.

My latest work has been to create the French-Canadian Heritage Collection, a repository of English translations of histories of French-Canadian and Franco-American communities that were originally published in French. Many Franco-Americans—and there are roughly 10 million of us in the U.S.—no longer speak French. This collection of English translations of public domain histories makes information about our ancestors and their contributions to life in North America accessible to non-French speakers. While I believe that preserving the use of the French language in North America is important for supporting the continued evolution of French-Canadian and Franco-American communities, one can be Franco-American without being a fluent speaker of French.

This collection of histories of Franco-American communities in Massachusetts teaches us about the lives and contributions of French Canadians and their children in important Franco-American centers, like Salem, Southbridge, Worcester, and Fall River. The translations are free downloads from the university's digital commons and may be of interest to people exploring their genealogical roots in those cities or to people researching Franco-American life in the United States.

All of these projects (teaching, translations, textbooks, research, community events) seek to advance awareness of French North American cultures, not just among academics but more importantly in our local communities and across the country to other places Franco-Americans have adopted as their new homes. Technology has played an important role in connecting descendants of French-Canadian immigrants, from easy access to online materials to interactive online Facebook groups, podcasts, blogs, and hashtags. Now more than ever, Franco-Americans like me who grew up feeling disconnected from their ethnic heritage, are able to connect with others to share experiences and learn from each other. This, I believe, will be the key to reviving and sustaining French Canadian traditions and Franco-American communities in the years to come.

Conclusion

Through my experiences with the Richelieu Club, in teaching, researching, and translating, and more recently by participating in French Canadian and Franco-American groups online, I have come to realize that connecting with others and the feeling of belonging to a community is key to developing a strong cultural identity, even if it is a community that you have to search for and find, rather than one you are born into or one that recruits you in. You can find your community and adopt it, just as our French-Canadian ancestors adopted their new communities in the United States a century ago. It is time for Franco-Americans to make the invisible visible and the disconnected connected. It is time to seek out and embrace old traditions while inventing new ways of belonging to Franco-America. Franco-Americans who have lost the connection to their ethnic heritage can regain it: through the study of French, through travel, by reading histories or doing genealogical research, and by connecting with others, whether in person or online, in the French-Canadian diaspora now scattered across the United States. Together, we can ensure that the legacy of our ancestors is transmitted to future generations.

15. The Impact of Francophone culture on my life, and my thoughts and actions on advancing the cause of our culture in the United States
Melody Desjardins

"When we drive up again, we are going to visit my *mémère!*" I excitedly told my first-grade classmates. My upbeat statement was immediately met with confused stares. Some kids walked away from me. In fact, that was the usual reaction anytime I mentioned my *mémère*. Didn't they have a *mémère?* Doesn't everyone? This was not the first time my use of French terms caused puzzled reactions at school. I could not believe it when a classmate asked me what "bureau" meant. Obviously, the wooden cabinet with drawers that you put clothes into. *Bureau.* Of course, at six-years-old, I did not have that sophisticated of an answer. So, I kept trying to ram "bureau" into the vocabulary of other kids. I was using the correct word, not them! Not only was I the only kid in my class from a whole other state halfway across the country; I was also the only kid spouting off about *mémères, bureaus,* and the latest family road trip to the motherland of New Hampshire.

To the residents of southern Iowa, my home state was a strange and distant land. Cultures clashed from my first year of school in Iowa up until the day I graduated. But I never replaced my French terms. They were normal words in my life-- why would I change them? It was not until I was twelve years old when I first heard my mom describe us as being "Franco-American." I knew we were of some kind of French heritage, but I never knew there was a term to describe the French heritage of New England. Although I was disconnected from the larger parts of my heritage, such as speaking French or knowing the Franco-American story from Québec to the mills of New Hampshire, I was determined to find the answers.

I am advancing the Franco-American cause in the United States with my blog, *Moderne Francos.* Inspired by the past, I write about creating new traditions to garner more interest in Franco-American culture for the future. With my articles, I take on a creative and lighthearted approach to promote our story across generations to connect our personal experiences. From the perspective of an outsider who used "weird" words, I was never directly shamed for my cultural background because nobody around me had ever heard of a Franco-American anyway. Added to the fact that my family never expressed any shame, even in my *Mémère* and *Pépère*'s heyday. Being American was important to them, but they never hid their Franco-American heritage.

In honor of my *mémère*, I decided to use her maiden's name, Desjardins, to create my pen name. My *pépère* was born as Jean-Joseph and changed his name to John when he joined the Air Force. Although he passed away shortly after I was born, I value his dedication to our community as a source of inspiration. Being Franco-American made me stand out and appreciate my background that was unique to my surroundings. With this personal experience, I am working to bring more awareness of the Franco-American story in the United States and expand this reach into Québec. I am in my late 20s, so I am often asked by those older than me how to get the younger crowd of Franco-Americans involved in the community. How can we get them to create content or tell their story at all? In answering that question, the good news is we all have access to social media nowadays. We can pick up our smartphones, talk into the camera, and we have a video that can be shared instantly. The bad news is that the younger crowd doesn't seem to be interested in their Franco-American background. If they even know about it at all. Although I did not grow up in New England, where the Franco-American presence is at least acknowledged or seen by the public in some way, my knowledge of my background was hanging on by a thread. I had always wondered, if I had grown up in my home state of New Hampshire, would I have been more aware of being Franco-American? Maybe, but since living in the state again, I have discovered that there is a lot of younger people out here who potentially fall under a few categories.

- They know about their Franco-American background, but they do not care about it.
- They identify with another part of their background, such as Irish or Italian.
- They do not know about their Franco-American background.
- They know about their Franco-American background, but do not know anything about it or are unaware of what to acknowledge.

Personally, I have been under category number one in the past. Although I knew about my heritage, I also grew up around an Americanized view about "hyphenated" nationalities. The attitude I experienced was that if you were born in America or immigrated to America, you were only to call yourself an American.

> "In the first place, we should insist that if the immigrant who comes here in good faith becomes an American and assimilates himself to us, he shall be treated on an exact equality with everyone else, for it is an outrage to discriminate against any such man because of creed, or birthplace, or origin. But this is predicated upon the person's becoming in every facet an American, and nothing but an American...There can be no divided allegiance here. Any man who says he is an American, but something else also, is not an American at all. We have room for but one flag, the American flag...We have room for but one language here, and that is the English language... and we have room for but one sole loyalty and that is a loyalty to the American people."

— Theodore Roosevelt, 26th President of the United States

I understand the deeper meaning of what Roosevelt meant, that we cannot have a unified country if everyone remains in their own corner dividing themselves into multiple categories to describe their nationality. If someone were to ask me what my nationality is, I would answer, "I am American." However, if they asked me what my heritage, culture, or background is, I would answer "Franco-American."

This hyper Americanized view may be trying to be general to better form a nationality among its citizens, but it should also be okay to describe yourself first as a Franco-American, or any other "hyphenated" nationality. We can have our individual flags, like the Franco-American flag, and acknowledge who we are within the nation. But this Americanization has caused our presence to become very quiet, as Franco-Americans down the line decided that they were only Americans and that was the end of their story. If you do describe yourself as a hyphenated American, you open yourself to criticism by those who strictly go by American and would completely align with that part of Roosevelt's quote.

There was a time when I would only describe myself as an American. My family always had a sense of pride in our heritage, but it seemed more like a thing of the past. It was interesting to acknowledge in a conversation but going beyond that by digging deeper into what Franco-American culture meant was not necessary. In addition to limited knowledge of our background, I also grew up in an area where most people did not care about their heritage at all. Everyone was strictly an American, which is okay if that is your preferred label. But if you were to say to someone that you were "German-American," they would "correct" you by saying that you are not from Germany, so you are not in any way German. Only if you were discussing where your ancestors came from was it relevant to mention your family's background.

The first time I learned of the term "Franco-American," was while working on a simple family tree project in seventh grade. Finding out that my family tree extended back to Québec and not France was news to me. Learning that most people in Québec spoke French was another concept I was not taught until my social studies class briefly covered it. During this class, there was never any mention of the one million French-Canadians of the early 20th century who left Québec to have the possibility of a better life in the United States.

During this time, I tried to research online about Franco-Americans, but the information was so limited. Most of the time, I was reading similar things and finding only a few paragraphs about the history and culture. This led me to believe that we were not an important group, or that we did not contribute anything to the United States because we were barely mentioned anywhere in my hours of searching. Because of that limited information and no sense of a community, it was much easier for me to fully take on the descriptor of being only American. I was the only one in my class who used "Franco-Americanisms" in conversation, and I was always "corrected" into using the English terms. I continued using my French words, thinking that was all I had of my background.

Over the years, I would go through spurts of inspiration where I would try to find more of the Franco-American story, but I still could not find anything besides old, abandoned blogs repeating the same information. There is no culture for us, I would think as I gave up time and time again. So, what changed from just a few years ago to now, where I have found myself thrust in the middle of an active Franco-American community? New media. In 2019, my inspiration drove me back into yet another journey of discovery about my role in the Franco-American story. And I finally found the community I had been looking for. Through one interaction, I was led into a whole group of other people working on their own projects to promote the language, history, and culture of Franco-Americans. I never would have thought that there were a substantial number of people who cared as much as I did about our story and place in the United States, specifically New England. If it were not for new media, I never would have found the community that I was so desperately searching for in the past. And using the tools we have such as our smartphones, cameras, blogs, or even social media in general, we can not only talk about who we are, but we can share it with anyone interested in listening. Of course, there is a lot more to sharing content than just posting it online and leaving it at that. Knowledge of marketing, even basic marketing skills, can help in making our work more noticeable outside of our Franco-American bubble. I found this community because I was actively searching for it. So how can we make ourselves known by others who are not looking for this information? Such as the younger crowd of Millennials and Generation Z? Or those who have never even heard of the Franco-American story?

We can start by finding out what these groups generally enjoy; it could be art, music, literature, history, fashion, beauty, and anything else along those lines. Take an idea and then bring it back to being Franco-American. For example, I have written about music and fashion on *Moderne Francos*. My posts about these topics were about the stories of Franco-Americans that are described in their lyrical work that became music and finding a connection to the art form that is traditional cultural dress that is found all around the world. Something that the Franco-American community has been lacking for so long has been a celebration of the arts and creativity.

Academia is absolutely crucial for any group whether it is for a cultural heritage, a language, or a country. However, it is also important to balance that out with the arts because not everyone is academically minded, myself included. I come from a family of both academics and creative souls, so I realize the importance that both types of people bring to the work that is being done to preserve anything historic or cultural. But they must be balanced. If one greatly overpowers the other, your message is only going to attract people who are either academics with research papers or a budding artist who wants to dedicate their creative energy to the culture with their writing, visual art, or music.

Every culture benefits from embracing the arts because this medium can reach much further outside of the cultural bubble. Everyone can easily enjoy writing, music, clothing, and more through the creative lens. Academia can be challenging for people outside of our community to jump into because it can be intimidating. Whereas something creative can lead them in. Going back to the younger generations of Franco-Americans and becoming more visible outside of our community, here is a path that I suggest we follow.

If we do not create our own artistic space, nobody else is going to do it for us. One of those art forms is writing. We can reach so many people through blogging, fiction and non-fiction stories, poetry, musical lyrics, screenplays, or even reporting a news story in a creative way. Blogging can entail telling our stories through personal experiences, the latest happenings of our community, historical accounts, and more. If you are a natural storyteller or appreciate thorough research, creating a blog will help in self-expression and discovery.

When I created *Moderne Francos*, I did not think many people would be interested in reading it. I created it out of wanting to collect my thoughts and share ideas with anyone who was willing to listen to a younger voice. I did not know much of anything about being Franco-American at the time, and it is something that I am still learning about now, but the blog has immensely helped in my self-discovery. So, keep in mind that you do not have to be an expert on any subject to share your thoughts and add another voice to the community.

You could take just about any blogging genre and make it about Franco-American culture, or bring it back to Québécois, French-Canadian, or Acadian culture. Blogging genres are endless, but the main ones include food, fashion, travel, language, culture, politics, music, lifestyle, arts and crafts, sports, finance, parenting, business, entertainment, and even personal issues. Think about how you could take any of these genres and create a blog that would bring it back to our community.

The same goes for writing fiction or non-fiction stories with taking a subject and finding a way to encapsulate the Franco-American story through it. There is an immense need in fiction to create more representation for Québécois, French-Canadian, Acadian, and

Franco-American stories. This includes creating characters with endless possibilities of storylines within many popular fiction genres such as fantasy, historical fiction, science fiction, adventure, romance, dystopian, crime and suspenseful thrillers, mystery, young adult, and more. There may be fiction stories about Canada or the United States, but how many are about Québec or the connection to the United States through Franco-Americans? It is a niche that would greatly benefit from writers fleshing out these stories waiting to unfold.

For the non-fiction genre, of course there is room for more history and biographies about Franco-Americans, but we can expand into something more lighthearted like travel books, cookbooks, or arts and crafts books. We could share more of our culture through these more casual means of teaching someone without them even realizing it. Sharing travel stories or guides to the best sights in Québec or New England can reach more people than strictly sharing academia. The same goes for the hands-on approach in teaching people how to cook classic meals found in our culture. Or creating an art project or craft around a celebration or holiday in Québec and New England, like Saint Jean-Baptiste Day. What kind of art project could you create and display? When you can experience something right in front of you like traveling, cooking, or creating arts and crafts, it fosters a better connection for most people that goes beyond academia research and genealogy work.

Putting on a more creative lens in the writing arena, poetry and songwriting can provide thought-provoking content by presenting the Franco-American story through interesting wordplay. Whether it is fun, humorous, or serious, these storytelling techniques can inspire the exploration of different perspectives or retell a story in a new way. The poem, "Evangeline: A Tale of Acadie" written by Henry Wadsworth Longfellow in 1847, is one example of using poetry to share the story of two people caught up in the Acadian expulsion. Although neither Evangeline nor her fiancé, Gabriel, actually existed, the tragic history of this upheaval can be further illustrated through these characters. For Acadians, it is acknowledgment of this tragedy while also creating a story that they can relate to within their family ancestry. It is an engaging way to tell the history and get us to understand the trials and tribulations of not only the characters, but for the people who were there at the time.

In *Je ne suis pas Evangeline*, or "I am not Evangeline," a play by Carolyn Cook, this story nods to the original poem by telling the story of a young woman leaving Maine. While she packs up her life, she reminisces about the Acadian and Franco-American women that became a source of strength, admiration, and inspiration for her. Retelling history through a character's story is an excellent way to connect with Franco-American characters. It also helps in contributing to the larger story of our language and culture in New England, as well as throughout the United States. We are still here, so why not show it through media that the public is bound to be more interested in than strictly academia and genealogy?

Having a way to share our work is just as important. Early on with *Moderne Francos*, I tried to find social media groups focused on French-Canadian and Franco-American culture to share my blog posts with more audiences. But many of these groups were strictly for genealogy and did not allow any self-promotion or sharing of any other content about our culture and story. This is perfectly okay, as any group can set their own rules, but this resistance to any other relevant content is yet another reason our culture has been burning out. Another outlet that is not as artistic but could allow promoting content and offer some form of creativity is creating a Franco-American "news media" through a blog, podcast, or online videos.

As seen through The French-Canadian Legacy Podcast's 2021 GeoTour collaboration with the Museum of Work and Culture and Québec Government Office in Boston, there are dozens of towns throughout New England with a rich Franco-American cultural history, as well as throughout the United States. The local news media does not always get our story correct, such as mispronouncing French names or not doing the research necessary to have an effective news report. Manchester, New Hampshire has been referred to by the local news media as "The Most Irish City in America" when there has also been a heavy French-Canadian and Franco-American presence in its history. So why not tell our own stories in this way by becoming our own reporters? With live streaming services through Facebook and YouTube, you could report live or stream a pre-recorded report for the community to enjoy or create discussion around a certain topic. By reporting for ourselves, the local media could become interested in the Franco-American story and air our reports. You never know the possibilities until you try, so it is worth taking a shot. The *Moderne Francos* blog has caught the attention of Franco-American organizations when I previously thought that they would not be interested in a growing blog. But to my surprise, my doubts were proven wrong.

There is a great amount of interest out there, it is just difficult to find unless you know where to look. The more we put ourselves out there by way of new media, the more we will garner public attention as a distinct cultural group and spark interest among more people. For those of us in the 20-something age range, this is the best time to start getting involved. But the vast age difference is a factor that can stop most young people from participating, as those of us already involved in the Franco-American community throughout New England are aware that the more common community participants are typically in their 60s.

It is challenging to get involved when you are surrounded by people who are from an entirely different generation than you. Not that it only creates negative experiences by any means, but people within the same generation can connect much easier to each other being around the same age. Plus, most of us in the younger generation have mostly lost the French language. We grew up speaking a few words or phrases, but that is as far as it ever got. We were never taught how to speak French, just how to express a few things with it.

We are around others who can relate so much to our own individual Franco-American experiences, which creates a stronger feeling of belonging and connection. Many of us are determined to learn French and pass it on, as well as the other aspects of the Franco-American culture. I hear so often from the older generations that they have struggled to get younger people interested to become involved down the line. I believe what has been partly missing has been a few young people to simply start getting involved despite the loss of interest among our age range. Sometimes it takes a few people to jump in to pique the interest of others with a similar life experience. But those of us involved now will encourage more people our age to see what we are all about and possibly join in. Bringing a certain demographic into a community sometimes takes a few members of that demographic to be the first to get involved and share their work. It is an exciting time to be a Franco-American in the blooming renaissance that we are currently creating. We can take the culture and turn it in a new direction towards rebirth with fresh, new ideas and perspectives. We are moving away from the feeling of hopelessness that has purveyed over our culture for several years. As a group, we have been knocked down at times throughout our history in the United States, specifically in New England, but there is no reason to make this the focus of who we are today. We can face the past for what it was and embrace the future for what we can make of it. Dwelling on the past will never make necessary change going forward but finding hope and positivity in our culture's resilience will pave the way for the degree of confidence that we desperately need to ensure the survival of our language and culture. Although I state this as someone who has never had backlash for being Franco-American, it is because I never had those experiences that I have developed a strong, unwavering confidence.

When my childhood classmates and peers found my lack of a strictly English vocabulary strange, I never stopped speaking those French words because I was taught that there was value in my Franco-Americanisms. This goes back to my Franco-American side of the family who never experienced any hostility for their language and culture in Nashua, New Hampshire. They openly spoke French without issue and only used English when necessary. My *mémère* and *pépère* believed speaking French was important and crucial in being proud of who they were. If those of us help to rebuild the confidence in our culture for others who had less fortunate experiences, we can have a generation of Franco-Americans who speak French and value our culture. We can choose hope and inspiration to prove how resilient we are by making the greatest reappearance into the mainstream on our newfound mission in becoming the loud presence that is long overdue.

16. From France to Franco-America: Foregrounding Personal and Community Connections in the Heart of French Studies
Katharine N. Harrington

My love of French began with a seventh-grade textbook that featured a sweeping photo of the Mont St. Michel on the cover. I would stare at this photo during class and daydream about the romantic life I imagined one might live on the coast of France. Thanks to the enthusiasm from my always colorful and entertaining middle school French teacher, Madame Levesque, I loved the challenge of learning a new language from my very first exposure to it. After school, a friend and I would turn to the last chapter of the textbook and record ourselves trying to read the most difficult passages we could find, as we attempted to pronounce French words we had not yet encountered in our class. There was considerable giggling recorded on those early cassette tapes as we struggled to make the exotic syllables roll off our tongues.

For my seventh-grade self, the study of French seduced me with images of another world across the ocean, dotted with medieval villages and boasting impressive monuments. As I expanded my French vocabulary and knowledge of grammatical structures, I envisioned the glamourous life I would one day lead as a fluent French speaker. I studied French throughout high school and college, however, applying to college, I was convinced that I would not major in French. I pictured myself going to law school, so I pursued a major in Government. Deep down, though, the aspect of college that I was most excited about was the opportunity to study abroad in France. I chose my undergraduate institution, St. Lawrence University, based on their reputable Year in France program. I ultimately fulfilled my longstanding dream in 1991-1992 when I spent a year studying in Rouen, France where I lived with a host family and traveled across Europe during our university breaks. In the end, with my year of advanced French courses taken abroad, I was able to complete a double-major in Government and French.

After college, I traveled to South America for a year to learn Spanish. When I returned to the United States, I worked in a multilingual law firm for several years. While I enjoyed the work, I soon determined that law school was not the path for me. It occurred to me that the United States had plenty of attorneys, but too few Americans spoke another language. It dawned on me that my passion all along was the French language. It took me awhile to realize that my love of French would lead me to a fulfilling career.

What followed this revelation was the long road of graduate school. I pursued a master's and then a doctoral degree in French Studies during which time I spent another two years living in France where I taught English at a university in Lyon and continued my doctoral research. Looking back on my graduate programs, I realize that they were almost entirely focused on the literature of France beginning with *Le Serment de Strasbourg* up through twenty-first century French authors. I completed coursework on the history of the French language, canonical French literature through the centuries and thematic courses including *La vie intérieure, La figure de l'étranger*, The Francophone World, all of which were literature based. Curiously, I never had the opportunity to take a course on Québec and none of my thematic classes included writers or content from French North America. In fact, the study of Québec and North American French was absent from both my undergraduate and graduate French programs, but with an already overwhelming amount to read and to learn, this void might not have been apparent to me at the time.

Throughout middle and high school, I had only the faintest knowledge about French on my own continent. Originally from Beverly, Massachusetts, I grew up in the shadow of a former shoe machinery factory that, at its height, employed 9,000 workers, including many French-Canadians. I had classmates with French surnames such as Gagnon, Beaulieu and Tremblay, and our town had its own Franco-American Club. However, this notion of "French" had no connection to the subject I studied in school.

I attended college in upstate New York close to the Canadian border. While there, I went on several daytrips to Ottawa and Montreal as part of extracurricular opportunities, but the study of Québec, its literature, language policies, and separatist movements were not integrated into my French college curriculum at all.

Students in my French program spent a year in France but might not have ever crossed the border into Canada.

In her study of first-year French textbooks in the United States, Carol A. Chapelle investigates the presence of Canadian and Québec content, and how it changed over the course of five decades, from the 1960s through 2010. Her analysis notes the frequency with which the most popular textbooks include content about French Canada, both in the context of language learning exercises as well as in more focused cultural notes. Chapelle discusses the implications of this "hidden curriculum" in textbooks, which may "implicitly communicate to students the limited value of Canada as a site of interest as they study French" (416). While a previous study by Salien had cited a lack of knowledge about Canada by textbook authors or students' preference for learning about France as explanations for this limited content, Chapelle set out to provide a more politically based explanation. She hypothesizes that changes in Québec society over this time, as well as growing initiatives to promote the French language in North America by the Québec government would result in more Canadian content. Her study finds that this is true to a certain extent, though the incidence of coverage of Québec and Canadian French topics, particularly in the late 20th century remained abysmally low. In the 1980s and 1990s, when I was a student of French, the average number of mentions of Québec language, identity, and culture was only around two per textbook.

Beyond first year textbooks, it is also interesting to examine the course offerings of colleges who offer degrees in French. A cursory glance at a few dozen French programs shows that specialized courses in Québec or North American French are rarely offered. Even in New England, where our neighbor to the north, Québec, is the number one trading partner and where French-Canadian heritage is significant, French programs generally still focus on France. Notably, at many institutions, any Francophone course content is more likely to be focused on Africa and the Caribbean, rather than the French-speaking nation right next door.

A Cultural Awakening to French in Maine

By the time I had completed my doctoral degree, I had spent three years of my life living in France. I had studied French from middle school on through my graduate studies, and yet I was wholly unprepared for my first professional experience as a newly minted Ph.D. Upon graduation, I accepted my first university teaching position at the University of Maine at Fort Kent (UMFK). Like many New Englanders, I had only ever been to the coast of Maine and had never stepped foot in Aroostook County. I could see on the map that Fort Kent was located in the northernmost point in the northeast on the Canadian border, and the job description described the area as a bilingual, bicultural community. This region is sometimes referred to as "the other Maine," and rightfully so. It boasts a quietly distinct culture, one that is rarely seen by New Englanders "downstate" and beyond. The rolling hills and small towns of the St. John Valley maintain a flavor all their own and exist untouched by the mass tourism seen on Maine's famous coast.

It was there, in northern Maine that I was first introduced to the Franco-American experience. I had gone as far as I possibly could with my French studies and yet upon my arrival, I found myself embarrassed by my ignorance of the French speakers that exist in my native New England. The town of Fort Kent was originally settled in 1825 by Acadian refugees who had escaped deportation during *Le grand dérangement* by traveling overland to the St. John River Valley. The MLA Language Map, based on the 2010 census, shows that twice as many Fort Kent residents claimed French as their home language than English: 63.24% vs. 36.76% ("Fort Kent"). In Fort Kent, nearly all of my coworkers and neighbors proudly self-identified as French or Acadian and welcomed me, the new French professor, enthusiastically. When introducing themselves to me in French, people would often apologize for the fact that they spoke "Valley French" and not "Parisian" French. Their sense of linguistic inferiority seemed ironic to me since I was the outsider. During those first days and weeks, I experienced strong feelings of self-doubt as I struggled to understand the French spoken around me. While I had never considered myself a "Parisian French" speaker, I felt disingenuous arriving in a bilingual community, as the new French PhD, yet the locally spoken language initially remained just out of reach to my unaccustomed ears.

Yet, with time, I learned that understanding Valley French was just a question of exposure. I soon became familiarized with this new (to me) accent, and I learned many local expressions. And while

I never adopted the Valley accent, I learned to slightly change registers depending on my interlocutor. One of the courses I was slated to teach my first semester at UMFK was a French for Heritage Speakers course. The concept of French heritage speakers was completely novel to me, and I was unsure of how to approach this class. Fortunately, I found wonderful mentors, including a part-time faculty member who had previously served as the administrator of a local French immersion program as well as the director of the UMFK Acadian Archives. Both of these wonderful colleagues provided me with guidance, resources, and pedagogical ideas for this new cultural landscape in which I was teaching. I eventually taught this course several times and found it to be extremely rewarding. These students maintained a very personal connection to French and relished the opportunity to further their knowledge of the language they had grown up speaking.

It was also through my colleagues and mentors that I was connected with French and Franco-American groups and events around the state of Maine. I attended Franco-American conferences, became involved with the Madawaska-based community group *Le Club français*, served on several French related committees in the University of Maine system, and hosted several French cultural events on campus. These events included an annual French film festival, a very popular wine tasting, and weekly conversation groups. It was so heartening to see that whenever I organized a French event on campus, I always could count on dozens on community members to attend as well. While I taught a range of classes, including some on canonical French literature, my work at UMFK required so much more of me than just teaching the content I had specialized in during graduate school. My contributions as a faculty member in a bilingual, bicultural community, inevitably extended beyond the walls of the classroom. As the sole full-time French faculty member at UMFK, I saw my role, not just as an educator of college students, but also as a community organizer and advocate for the local language. My community outreach work was just as rewarding as working with the young adults in my classes. During my six years teaching in Fort Kent, I met an amazing community of Franco-Americans who are proud of their language and culture and are committed to its continued visibility through advocacy and cultural celebration.

Finding French in New Hampshire

My experience living in northern Maine forever transformed my approach to the teaching of French. Living in a bilingual community on the Canadian border it was impossible to ignore the linguistic and cultural context in which I was teaching. I found that connecting the study of the French language to the community around us opened up amazing and meaningful connections for students. While I still see the value of teaching the canonical literature of France, my focus has shifted in favor of the rich cultural heritage of my own continent.

When I moved to New Hampshire in 2010, given the state's proximity to Québec and similarly prominent French-Canadian heritage, I expected to find the same kind of Franco-American pride that I had found in Maine. Surprisingly, French in New Hampshire is much less visible. It exists, but you have to work harder to find it. French and French-Canadian remain the largest ancestry group in the state of New Hampshire with 25 percent of the state population claiming it, according to the 2000 census. Today, French is tied with Spanish for the most commonly spoken language in New Hampshire after English with nearly 27,000 speakers statewide ("Most Spoken Languages"). Historically, several Granite State communities boasted large numbers of French-Canadian immigrants including the towns of Nashua, Suncook, Somersworth, Laconia, Claremont, as well as Berlin and Colebrook in the northernmost county of Coös. Some of these communities have neighborhoods that still bear the legacy of the French populations they once hosted, such as French Hill in both Nashua and Laconia and the Petit Canada of the West Side of Manchester. While many of these communities have vastly changed over the past few generations, the French connection in New Hampshire is still alive if you know where to look.

In addition to a strong French-Canadian heritage, New Hampshire shares a border with Québec. Trade with Canada is crucial for our state. According to the government of Canada, Canada is the United States' number one export market, and New Hampshire alone sells $1.1 billion in goods and services to Canada ("State Trade"). On a local level, my university is located a mere 100 miles from the border at the base of the White Mountains. Our picturesque region is a strong draw for French-Canadian tourists who come to hike our many peaks. In 2017, a half million Canadian visitors spent $92 million in New Hampshire ("State Trade"). Their presence is critical for our local economy and yet, upon arriving here, I saw no evidence of businesses and communities recognizing this connection.

As the sole full-time French professor at the only university in the northern half of our state, I see it as my role to expose my students to the history and culture of Québec and Canada. My classes are likely the only place where they learn about the presence of the French speakers who frequent our downtowns, stores and hiking trails or why many students boast French surnames. For these reasons, I regularly teach advanced courses in Québec Culture and Literature as well as the Diversity of Francophone Communities in the United States. However, I also want students to learn about the North American French experience starting at the beginner level. Most of the students who take my beginner language classes will take just two semesters to fulfill a requirement. I ask myself, what do I want them to learn? What will they remember from their French classes ten or twenty years from now? Learning about café culture in Paris or faraway châteaux in France is lovely, but it is not necessarily relevant to my students' lives. Rooted in the geographic and cultural context where we are, I have found that students are inherently curious about Québec and the French speakers closest to us.

In my classes, I foreground North American French as much as possible. I cringe when I hear American French speakers who proclaim upon traveling to Montreal: "I could not understand a word of Québécois French!" In my view, if this is true, it is the fault of French teachers. Students need to be exposed to different variations and accents of French, and most importantly, the variation they will be most likely to come across. Here in central New Hampshire, many of my students can use their conversational French with French-Canadian visitors they encounter at their part-time jobs in the service and hospitality industries. For many students at my public university, study abroad in Europe is out of financial reach for them. However, exposing students to the international experience that awaits them just over the border can be equally transformative.

Additionally, over the years, I have sought out projects for my students that offer them opportunities to use French for an authentic purpose that goes beyond the walls of the classroom. In our region, there are endless opportunities to provide French language services to businesses and tourism providers who regularly welcome French-Canadian visitors. My students, in a number of different classes, have translated restaurant menus, brochures, websites, rack cards and conducted interviews of French-Canadian visitors. This applied use of French is challenging for undergraduate students, but they are proud to see the results of their work on display in the greater community in the French language products they create.

These student projects led to a larger idea when I met several like-minded individuals around the state, who also value our state's connection with Québec. With a core group of community partners, I co-founded the *Bienvenue au New Hampshire* project where we encourage businesses and communities to be "French friendly" through workshops and by providing French language materials. I have conducted several workshops over the years for the Appalachian Mountain Club, the White Mountain National Forest, and for chambers of commerce in the northern half of our state. We share information on the importance and economic impact of French-Canadian visitors in our region and compare data with neighboring states to show that New Hampshire has room for improvement. Participants are offered materials and resources, and workshops conclude with a brief French conversation lesson targeted to specific industries. One of our goals has been to simply give people the confidence and encouragement to put themselves out there and speak a few phrases in French when they encounter a French-Canadian visitor. While not a groundbreaking idea, we have found that a simple greeting in French goes a long way in creating connections with our neighbors to the north. It does take some encouragement though to nudge some Americans to venture out of their linguistic comfort zone.

Yet, despite the demand for French speakers in our region, the trends in French education here in New Hampshire are worrisome. During my tenure as President of the New Hampshire chapter of the American Association of Teachers of French, I have seen numerous French K-16 program reductions or closings. French teacher positions regularly become available, but many go unfilled. There is an evident lack of candidates for these jobs and many postings are less desirable part-time positions. When a French teacher position goes unfilled, some schools eliminate French altogether and only offer Spanish. In a state with such an important French heritage, located on a border with Québec, eliminating the option for students to learn French seems unthinkable, and yet, it is reality.

Coordinating and recruiting for a French major at a small regional comprehensive public university has proved equally challenging. Many of our students are first generation college students. They and their parents are seeking the best return on investment for their degree. Unfortunately, degrees in the languages and the humanities are increasingly perceived as impractical. The number of humanities degrees conferred has seen a steady decline in the past decade ("bachelor's"). Students who choose to major in a language such as French often attend liberal arts colleges and not small public institutions. We have recently seen several program closures in college French majors in the state, which will of course compound the issue of teacher shortages at the K-12 level. I worry that these trends will cause French to become an elitist language, one to which only students of select schools will have access.

In my view, the future of the French language in New Hampshire depends on several factors. These include the infusion of new French speakers in the state as well as the creation of meaningful connections with our French-Canadian neighbors to make evident the relevance and importance of the French language. There are increasing numbers of newly arrived French speakers in our state. Data from the New Hampshire Refugee Resettlement program shows that between 2011 and 2019 1,373 African refugees were resettled in several communities around the state ("Refugee"). Most of these refugees originate from the Democratic Republic of Congo, Burundi, and Rwanda, all countries where the official language is French. There is also a significant Haitian population, and even a Haitian Baptist church in the state's largest city, which offers services in French. It is not enough, however, to recognize that these Francophones exist. In order to allow them to maintain their language proficiency and to pass it along to their children, it is essential that French programs be available for these families. The French Heritage Language Program in states such as New York, Florida, and Maine is a wonderful model. The FHLP promotes French as an international language and an essential life skill to nurture. Bilingual high school students are now also able to pursue the Seal of Biliteracy. This wonderful program recognizes students who have attained proficiency in two or more languages by the end of high school. My hope is that the Seal will provide further incentive for high schools to continue to offer multiple languages through the AP level in order to build on students' linguistic and cultural backgrounds.

Northern New England states have the unique advantage of being located on an international border with a French-speaking Canadian province. Given our state's shared history and heritage with Québec, it is only natural that we foster strong cross-border connections. Yet, from an educational standpoint, this connection could be vastly improved. While it is true that Spanish is a vital language in the United States, here in the northeast, French is equally important, if not more so. It is my dream that the state of New Hampshire embraces its location and heritage and makes the commitment to offer the opportunity for all children to learn French. One could establish educational exchanges starting at the elementary school level where children could gain intimate knowledge about the foreign country right next door through personal connections and cultural programming. Linguistic and cultural understanding could be nurtured at an early age if students and families had the opportunity to come together and create long-lasting friendships with French-Canadians who live just over the border. With high-quality educational and cultural programs in place, northern New England could become like other bilingual, bicultural border regions in the world. A commitment to French education for all, here in the northeast, would offer our children unique advantages, life skills, and global connections while honoring our heritage and building bridges with our neighbors.

17. "It is all coming back!": When a community revived its lost French, it inspired many others to do the same
Ben Levine and Julia Schulz

The documentary film *Réveil - Waking Up French* has touched thousands of lives since it was first shown in 2002. From living rooms to classrooms, church basements to the Sorbonne, across New England and Louisiana, this film has sparked a renaissance among people of French heritage and an eagerness to share their personal stories and in so doing reclaim their Franco-American identity, language, and culture. *Réveil - Waking Up French* is a film made for and by all members of the Franco-American community who participated in a process of awakening that evolved over two years at Railroad Square Cinema in Waterville, Maine. The context for this awakening was the "Franco-American Film Festival," and the story we tell here is how the presentation of a series of films from Québec (in French-Canadian French), combined with a method for community participation that had been dormant for 45 years, helped this community revive its French identity and become a model for many others.

At the core of *Réveil* are the scenes shot at Railroad Square Cinema. Films made in Québec brought audience members into contact with language and heritage that had largely disappeared in their lives due to outside pressure. Hearing the language again, seeing the lives of their ancestors, evoked a yearning in both old and young to reconnect with their heritage. We used a process of video feedback in which we recorded and edited the discussions and frequently showed them back to the audience to reinforce and amplify the elements of the culture and their deepest feelings about it. This method had originally been developed by Ben Levine and the Peoples Video Theater on the streets of New York City in the 1970s but had not been in use since.

The main themes raised in that video feedback process, such as migration, discrimination against French-Canadians, loss of language and culture, the role of the Catholic Church, and personal self-doubt and shame, prompted Ben, a filmmaker, to build a documentary by seeking confirmation from Franco-Americans in other communities of New England, who bear witness to those experiences, doubts, and questions. What developed was the retelling of the emotional history of a people and the awakening of a community of Franco-Americans to each other, their collective history, and the choices they wanted to make for themselves.

The idea for the Film Festival arose in June of 1999 with help from community arts advocates Bruce Hazard and Lissa Widoff, who linked us into a collaboration with Waterville's Railroad Square Cinema and funding from the Maine Community Foundation's "The Art of Building Community" initiative supported by the Lila Wallace Reader's Digest Fund. Bob Chenard, of Waterville, joined the team as a member of Mid-Maine Arts Partners. Nelson Madore was Waterville's Mayor, and Penobscot Bay Language School served as fiscal sponsor. The late Françoise Wera, a Québec filmmaker, was our film consultant.

Over a two-year period (1999-2001) we showed films from Québec that had become hard to find in the United States or even in Québec. The films would stimulate memory and discussion about cultural themes related to identity. Over time, in these discussions, the audience began to see the existential threat facing their way of life. As one participant said: "I am 12th generation from France, through Québec, and it is sad to think the French language would end with me." A technique of dialog facilitation—a fusion of interview and counseling—was often employed when difficult to express feelings or ideas required more encouragement. A truly "Franco" cultural atmosphere was recreated with informal conversation in the lobby before each showing and related "soirées" we hosted, with refreshments, live music, meals, and special guests from Québec. Diverse examples of cultural emergence resulted, bringing French language back into public life again in this once French-speaking rust belt, former mill town in Central Maine.

This Festival was not your typical night out at the movies (for one thing it took place at 9:00 am on Saturday mornings). To give the reader a more immersive understanding of the atmosphere the festival created we will begin with a description of a scene that captures the essence of the Festival—a scene that subsequently appeared in the documentary *Réveil*:

In this scene, the camera pans a group of people in the cinema lobby/art gallery. Young and old are happily listening to a song sung in French about freedom by a folk singer from Québec. We see the laughing, smiling faces in the group. They are clearly enjoying what was at that time a rare opportunity—a French language event in public. Then the camera pauses on a woman seated off to one side. Her chin is resting pensively on her hand as she stares at the singer. She seems wistful, lost. Lost in thought, perhaps lost in life.

This is the first time that we see Sylvane Bulger Pontin, who later will become one of the leaders of a French language revival in Waterville. Had she been present at previous Festival film showings? We were not sure. With the singer repeating a French refrain: "*Liberté... Liberté.*", this 55-year-old woman had been brought face to face with the identity crisis that was defining her and her community's life: whether they would be able to regain the ability to be and speak French. The song's lyrics, the group passionately singing together, and hearing her Canadian French language spoken in public for the first time since she was a child had again woken up her desire to be French. But she had tried before without success. And yet she would soon be co-creating events which helped numerous people get their language back, such as fabulous soirées and a speaker's group now in its 18th year. How Sylvane went from feeling defeated at having failed to reacquire her childhood language to a language revival leader is best understood by looking closely at some examples of the films we showed and how the whole atmosphere of the event was shaped to recreate a safe place where anyone could explore their own feelings and learn from others what it meant to be, and how to be, Franco-American.

One of the first films we showed was *Les Tisserands du Pouvoir* (Claude Fournier, 1988). It is an historic reenactment drama made for Québec television. An early scene shows a 19th-century Québec farm family loading a horse-drawn wagon and tearfully leaving their rustic homestead for good. The scene powerfully portrays a family being torn unwillingly from its roots and way of life. The film goes on to portray the subsequent ghetto living and difficult working conditions and social relations in New England's textile mills where nearly one million Québecers were destined to live and work at the turn of the 20th century. Historically, it is unlikely that any

Québecers traveled to work in the New England mills in a horse-drawn wagon. Those who came from the Beauce region to Waterville, Maine walked for almost two weeks over a rugged trail that came to be called The Old Canada Road and is now Maine Route 201. From Sherbrooke and many other places in Québec, passage was paid by textile company recruiters on the Grand Trunk Railroad to major New England mill towns including Woonsocket, Rhode Island and Lowell, Massachusetts. But the scene does have an emotional accuracy: immigration—even temporarily—was a traumatic experience for the whole family. This scene was powerful for the Franco audience at the Festival because it portrayed the tearing apart of the fabric of the life and identity of their parents and grandparents. It was a familiar family memory, but not one they had ever witnessed so publicly before. To many it felt like a healing experience.

A surprising and much more positive corresponding experience was hearing "their" North American French used in a mass media product in public perhaps for the first time. Many people were motivated to speak and often recounted similar genealogies: "...My father came down and worked in the mills and so did all of his brothers." "We spoke only French in our family until we went to the convent school with half-day in French and half-day in English." Discussions about whose French is the "good" one, meaning "correct" French, would commence. Perley LaChance told a story familiar to everyone: he had been admonished, mostly by French teachers, that Franco-American French was not really French; it was a kind of jargon, something to be ashamed of. But during WWII serving in France, he was called to interpret for some villagers. He found he could communicate very well with the French people; there was nothing wrong with his French. We were learning about our audience: some had gotten past the stigma and sense of inferiority that had been put on the French-Canadian immigrants of a previous generation. They just had not told each other yet.

Les Dernières Fiançailles (Jean-Pierre Lefebvre, 1973) portrays in an intimate and closely observed style an elderly rural couple as they live out their last days tending gardens, inspecting the orchard, and taking care of each other in an almost wordless but emotionally charged film. Here was another film that presented people like the audience's grandparents as worthy of respect, holders of tradition, and caretakers of the sacred land. These characters in the film were the same farm people, closely tied to their land and each other as the festival audience knew their own ancestors to have been. In the feedback session people were enthusiastic: "Well, they were close, very close, and that reminded me of the French, where they were so close, and they helped each other." "This film shows the humility, and that was related to their Catholic faith and especially being French-Canadian." They were verbalizing their values and in turn reviving appreciation for their identity.

Participants brought their mothers. Local high school French teachers brought their students. Over the course of two seasons of the Franco-American Film Festival there was a growing awareness in the audience. We heard remarks, such as: "I know that woman: she's my neighbor, but I never knew she spoke French." "I was put down because I spoke English with an accent." Or: "I did not speak the right kind of French." We were seeing what forced assimilation looks and feels like. "I should have taught French to my kids!" Or: "I thought I was stupid because I did not learn French. I now see I was not alone—it was not just in my family." There are valid historical reasons parents stopped speaking French to their children, and the community stopped speaking it in public.

Another film *Madame La Bolduc* (Isabelle Monique Turcotte, 1992) recounts the life and times of one of the first singer-songwriters of Québec who gained immense popularity in the 1930s. The film portrays a joyful side of French-Canadian life, where families made their own entertainment in *"grandes fêtes"* that could last all night and the next one too. The amazing stamina for intense dance and music-making shown in the film was reflected from the audience who told stories of uncles who played the violin and aunts the accordion. These memories were fun for people to recount; it was still a part of themselves they were proud to claim as their own. Along with the kinds of comments already described they began to build a new appreciation for their identity. No longer a failed culture with a lost language suppressed and stigmatized as inferior by the English Protestant elites, this community, through the films, was opening a door to their memory of an emotional, strong, vital, French-speaking people, and they were voicing a desire for that to return.

After the first several months of filming the discussions, the soirées, and related events we made a short edit and showed it back before one of the feature films from Québec. The edit is called *Rire Ensemble*, and it is an emotional summary on video of what the audience had been saying and feeling (and a good example of how we used video feedback). At one point in the video, Cécile Vigue, an elderly Franco, captures with an authoritative eloquence a communal truth about the role of joy as a driver of hope for the community: *"Rire, c'est le meilleur remède!"*

Cecile's husband Alcée had been born in Québec and tells how he was working in the Maine forest when the border was closed for good in the 1930s. Like almost one million of his compatriots, he found himself trapped: if he returned to Québec he would starve, never being able to return to the United States. If he remained in Maine, he would be forever cut off from the rest of his family still in Québec and his land, religion, way of life, and language.

Readers may well be wondering: "How is it that there were so many serious, high-quality films being made in Québec? With an audience base of under ten million, who was producing these films and why?" The films and television series we were showing—many based on novels and all reflecting Québec realities—were supported by the Québec government. They were part of a movement that had its origin in a pamphlet written by five Québec artists in the early 1950s. Entitled *"Refus Global,"* loosely translated as "comprehensive refusal" or "resist totally," the essay made the argument that given the ongoing effort by the Canadian Government to assimilate Québec the elimination of French language and identity in Québec was inevitable unless Québecers mounted a campaign of total resistance. Taken up by a new political party with deep pocketsfrom hydro power and aluminum holdings, the Parti Québécois (PQ) mounted what came to be called the *"La Révolution Tranquille"* (1959-1970). With support from a French-speaking electorate newly awakened to its mission to do what the Church was failing to do—save Canadian French—the PQ won control of state governance and passed legislation that made French speaking predominant in education, the media, government, and business. A famous example, Law 101, forbade commercial signs in public in English only. The films we selected for the Festival had been part of the strategy of the PQ to build a new, modern activist Québécois identity based on a frank understanding of where they had come from, what they had suffered, and where they wanted to be in the world. And now the same films were supporting a Franco-American awakening in Maine. By encouraging secular education and professional training a newly educated populace rejected not only assimilation to English Canadian agendas, but to policies of the Catholic Church as well. And the decline of the church's power was rapid once the people were awakened to how it had served the English in suppressing Québec aspirations.

In 1980, only twenty years before our Festival, and soon after the most intense changes of the Quiet Revolution, the demise of the Catholic Church in Montreal would have been unthinkable. That was the year Julia was doing ethnographic field research in Acadian French communities in the St. John Valley and Ben was making a film called *Si Je comprends bien...* about why the PQ wanted to separate Québec from Canada. The film explores why Québec could be so ardent in protecting its French when from all indications Franco-Americans living just a few miles away across their shared border had stopped speaking their French. This polarization around identity in these two French related worlds, Québec and New England, keeps coming into focus for us. *Si Je comprends bien...*had been warmly received in a limited way in Québec in 1980, but Maine Francos were uncomfortable at being made so visible. They need not have worried as the film had limited distribution at the time and was not seen again until 18 years later. In the summer of 1998, Railroad Square Cinema asked Ben to show *Si Je comprends bien...*We fully expected an audience of a few people only to find a full house of highly appreciative Francos and others ready to see their own history and talk about it. Over those twenty years, Québec had tried twice and almost succeeded in separating from Canada. But it had made its point. You survive if you resist. And it had also shown there are many ways to resist. Now Maine Francos were ready to accelerate the process of inventing their own path but not before finding in themselves a darker vein of experience that required a confrontation with power in the community that was harder for the audience to face.

When the lights went up after the showing of *Mon Oncle Antoine* (Claude Jutra, 1971) there was an immediate negative reaction, "Why did you show this film? We did not like it." Prior to this it was easy for people to be spontaneous; we did not have to ask questions. They were happy to share memories and stories they had heard from their parents and what they had seen as well. They were re-establishing an identity that had been systematically negated by anti-immigrant movements, including an active campaign by the Ku Klux Klan with violence against French communities (*Les Petits Canadas*) across Maine and New England. *Mon Oncle Antoine* tells the story of economic deprivation in Québec through a struggling rural family in 1949. As with so many Québécois, the male head of house has had to leave home to work far away in the Maine woods cutting lumber for a large part of the year to earn enough money for the family to survive. It fell to the mother to run the family. The film is a dark portrait of the exploitation of the rural poor in which the church is complicit. What bothered our audience though was a scene in which a priest is seen privately drinking wine meant for communion. The film was provoking a silent code in this community that you should never criticize or show anything negative about the Catholic Church. The prevailing (and only partially true) myth had been that the church was the protector of the French against the dominant surrounding English Protestant majority; it was seen as the last and only bulwark against destruction of French Canada by the English. The church had come to control all aspects of Québécois life (and much of the Francos' lives as well). The discussion around Mon Oncle Antoine was challenging for us, forcing us to take a more active role as facilitators, bridging perspectives that had to respect delicate feelings about an institution still very central to the lives of our audience members and yet fraught with awareness of unspoken abuse of power. We had been brought to an edge: would the audience defer to power or look at all aspects of their collective history? *Bonheur d'occasion* (Claude Fournier, 1983) tells the story of a struggling Montreal urban working-class French family during WWII. The story centers on the women. The mother has perhaps ten children and is barely able to care for her brood. Her husband suffers the humiliations of being at the bottom of the economic system, frequently out of work yet fulfilling a church ordained command to keep having children even when the health and life of his wife are at stake. The oldest daughter on the other hand has some education and wants a different life from her mother. But absent generational models and before she can establish herself, she is seduced by a man from a higher class and becomes pregnant. The outbreak of world war suddenly offers new but tragic options for both the woman and the family, but not before one of the younger children, a sickly boy, dies from consumption. "*Respire par la bouche, par la bouche,*" mourns the mother at her child's deathbed as a trickle of blood slowly seeps from his mouth. It is a wrenching scene.

The audience response was at first difficult to interpret and required of us an even more active style of close listening and facilitation. Words and phrases were expressed in a halting manner. Finally, an older man says in a low voice: "It is about ...sex...But we can't talk about that." Then a woman begins to speak. The scene of the dying child especially affected her because it suddenly gave her insight about why her husband had acted so crazy and unsupportive when she had had a miscarriage. She connects the dots. She remembers that her husband's mother had told her that she had had five miscarriages. Our witness's husband had lived through all that turmoil and grief as a small child. Now from this film, and the discussion, she is starting to understand how traumatic that series of miscarriages had been for that family and for the young child who would eventually become her husband, a man so fearful of having and losing children that he could not support his wife when she actually did lose one.

The realization and sharing of this story was a powerful moment for our audience—a moment when they bonded firmly around the situation of women and how the church policy and its political correlation, known as "la revanche du berceau," had put them and their families at risk. The feedback was captured on video and became an important scene in *Réveil*. We found out that in Montreal in 1900 one child in four died within the first year of life. In the cinema, we were eliciting and experiencing together the emergence of a hidden part of the emotional history of a people. And part of that complex emotional package would be suppressed resentment at priests and others for enforcing this oppression on women for their own political purposes. Thus, the experience at any Festival session was a combination of filmmaking and viewing, applied anthropology, therapeutic intervention, and adult education approaches developed by Julia.

In the cinema, as people came to both embrace the French identity they felt they had lost and at the same time were wrestling with darker emotions, for some there was a path clearing, a sense they could act on what they felt: they could get their French back, but how? Many had tried with self-study and classes… and failed. Failed because they were ambivalent about it, having been told that their French was no good. As an active French teacher, Julia would ask after each show whether anyone would like to practice conversational French. When after several offers no one came forward, Julia began to realize it was not classes this audience needed or wanted. Finally, Linda Gérard der Simonian shyly approached Julia with her desire to speak her first language. Together they organized the first French language reacquisition group. About fifteen attended the first meeting, held in Linda's house. To her surprise Linda would later find herself pictured on the front page of the *Boston Globe* in an article describing her leadership in the movement to restore French language and culture in Central Maine. Her partner in the movement was none other than Sylvane Pontin.

Linda, Sylvane, and the other participants were confirming something Julia had learned in her research on language teaching about the "window" from age 0 to 4 for children to learn a language with native speaker ability. As we discovered more about the role of the developing brain in first language acquisition, we were encouraged to think of a child's brain developing a "map" for the first language. If this were true, and the physical structures existed in a child's brain for understanding and speaking that language, then those structures still remained in an adult's brain, even though the language seemed "lost" or hidden. Perhaps it was only sleeping and could be woken up again.

The French reacquisition group meetings were explorations of early childhood memories triggered by sharing songs and photos and stories told in whatever French words came to mind. Group members showed Julia that they did not need French instruction but rather a safe nonjudgmental space with an observer, a guide, who could confirm for them that they were speaking French she could understand even though she was not of their culture. It turns out that an outsider can play a useful role as a witness to the reawakening and recovery of a cherished though hidden language and identity. All of us were learning together about variants in French language and the history of its development from a particular source region of their ancestors in 17th century France. We used an etymological dictionary at times to see equivalent words and to verify that although there may be two or more ways to say something one way is not superior to the other—they are just different. And we explored "careful French": the idea that we can all speak in a natural way and by listening hard overcome any differences in pronunciation or usage. One by one, participants in the reacquisition group were beginning to get their first language back in the presence of their supportive and caring peers. Their motivation soon spread to the whole community. Among other actions, they transformed the city's annual Oktoberfest into a Franco-American Festival, convinced shops to carry music and cards in French, installed bilingual plaques at important historical locations in the city, and worked with city officials to create an economic development plan based on French language and culture.

The activities of the Festival and especially the French reacquisition group are examples of emergence. Following the emotional changes triggered by the films, the discussions and video feedback we see in many people—the expression of a confidence to try new things, sometimes small at first, are confirmed by others and become part of a movement. Some people, like Sylvane, become leaders. At one of the last Festival sessions in a scene included at the end of *Réveil*, high school students of Franco descent in the audience reflect on what they have just seen and heard. One starts out in halting French that he is "…ready for anything, I just want to get my language back!" He has to shift to English to finish the thought, and the audience understands very well the emergence he has just experienced and applauds enthusiastically.

But the story does not end there. In community showings of the finished film *Réveil-Waking Up French*, feedback sessions gave rise to a twenty-year journey for us—adapting the methods described above and applying them to reviving minority and endangered languages, including Passamaquoddy in Maine and several indigenous languages of Southern Mexico. There we developed the Community Self-Documentation approach training a team of young filmmakers and incorporating all the methods we had learned starting with the Franco-American Film Festival. Today that team is training other teams in ten communities in Oaxaca, Mexico. It is as if the Franco-American Film Festival lives on through the methods that are its legacy, helping other communities just setting out on their path for language and cultural revival.

18. French Language and Francophone Culture in New England and the French-Canadian Legacy Podcast and Blog
Jesse Martineau and Monique Cairns

It seems crazy that I am sitting in my temporary apartment in Québec City telling our story. I actually woke up very early this morning and walked from my place just inside the walls of Vieux-Québec, across the street from Kent Gate, and walked towards Basse-Ville. This is a walk I have made quite a few times, and this morning was a perfect spring day. This is not the first time I have made the walk down Petit Champlain in the spring, though I have done it more in the summer and winter. Today was, however, the very first time I have done it when I was the only person in sight. I had Terrasse Dufferin to myself and I walked down Petit Champlain all alone. I then stood in the middle of Place Royale looking up at Notre-Dame-des-Victoires, an amazing old church that I think carries a name given to it a bit prematurely. I saw the area in a completely different way than I ever had before. And it was awesome. The reason any of this is happening is a pretty crazy story. I think so, anyway.

My name is Jesse Martineau and my sister, Monique, and I are from Manchester, New Hampshire. My sister's name actually comes from the town my mom's family, the Provencher's, come from – Sainte-Monique, Québec. We grew up in a family that we would have called "French-Canadian." I know it is probably more common to hear "Franco-American" now, but that is something we never would have called ourselves growing up. In fact, my parents, Ben and Pauline (formerly Provencher), state they never heard the term until I started getting involved with the Franco-American Centre in Manchester. For them, Franco-American was canned spaghetti. Therefore, we never used that term. The Gatzoulis family that lived next door (Alex Gatzoulis has been my best friend since we were 4 years old) was Greek. The Luhovey's on the corner were Ukrainian, and the Murphy's down the street were Irish. We were French-Canadian.

Our family all comes from Québec. In fact, looking at our family tree, from the best I can tell, all 16 of our great-great-grandparents were born in Québec. I am not sure how common that is for Québécois today, but it seems unusual to me to have all 16 great-great-grandparents born in the same place. I believe the first of my direct ancestors to arrive in the United States was my great-great-grandfather Adolph Bénard, who came in 1885. Born in Montréal, he would eventually hold elected municipal office in Lowell, Massachusetts. Our nearest ancestor to Québec was our paternal grandfather, Richard Martineau. *Pépère* Richard Napoleon Martineau (neither of us would know his middle name was Napoleon until after he died in 2006) was born in Saint-Apollinaire, Québec in 1913 moved to New Hampshire in 1920. When our dad and our Uncle Joe took *Pépère* back to Saint-Apollinaire towards the end of his life, he did not remember much about the town. He did, however, have vivid memories of the strawberries on Île d'Orléans. In 1944, *Pépère* Martineau would land on Omaha Beach fighting for a country he was not born in. My other grandfather, Roland Provencher, served in the navy in World War II and family stories have been passed down of *Pépère* Provencher having himself quite the time as he served as an interpreter for the officers in France.

Though three of my four grandparents were born in Manchester, all four spoke French better than they spoke English. Both my parents actually spoke French in the house growing up. I have learned these would be surprises for quite a few people who are not from New England. However, for many years, French-Canadian immigrants in Manchester could live their entire lives in French. They had schools, churches, banks, stores, radio stations, newspapers...basically everything in French. You hear stories of people living their entire lives in Manchester without ever learning English, because they never had to. My dad tells a similar story about his maternal grandmother, who was born in Manchester, lived her entire life in Manchester, died in Manchester, but never spoke English. Though my dad thinks she probably could understand English, even if she always pretended not to. I also find it interesting that both of our parents grew up with a set of grandparents living in a separate apartment in the same building they lived in.

My parents both grew up in the same parish, Saint-Georges, and they attended the same elementary school, L'École Saint-Georges.

In what is a very fun story, when they were in second grade, they were First Communion partners. At L'École Saint-Georges they would go to school with half the day taught in French and half the day taught in English. This was not uncommon in New England. Many of the French parishes had schools attached to them where the day was taught half in French and half in English. What I find funny is that the only two subjects taught in French were French and religion. So, half the day was those two subjects, with the rest of the day in English for everything else. Since anything religion (meaning Catholic) related was always in French, my parents joke it was not until they were older that it even occurred to them that God might be able to understand English.

Like many families throughout New England, the Provencher side of the family all came to Manchester to work in the mills. We believe this initially started with my great-grandfather, Edmond Provencher (who was born in Sainte-Monique), though it is very possible Edmond's dad Timothe also worked in the mills. It is interesting that when he was in Québec, my great-grandfather would go by the name Urbain Edmond Provencher. However, when the family crossed the border, his first and middle names got flipped, and he became Edmond Urbain. It is this second name that appears on his grave today. I once spent the better part of an afternoon trying to find Edmond in the census of Manchester from a year in the early 1900's. I was pretty frustrated after a while, as I knew he had to be in Manchester, but I could not find him anywhere. It was not until I thought to check for alternate spellings that I was finally able to find him. He and his family appeared as "Provanchey," with the census taker evidently spelling the name as he heard it.

Pépère and *Mémère* Provencher, Roland and Irene (formerly Glaude), met each other in the mills. Waumbec Mill, specifically. *Mémère* was a smashpiecer. As I understand it, it was the job of the smashpiecer to take over when a ton of threads busted on the same machine all at once. They were taught specific knots to be able to get the machine back up and running as quickly as possible. *Pépère* worked his way up to the position of loom fixer, something of which he was incredibly proud. That was a very important job and possessing that title showed you had impressive skills. *Pépère* worked in the mills for around 40 years. When the mills moved south, *Pépère* was offered a job in the new location, but at that point he already had a family, and he did not want to relocate everyone.

Our mom, her older brother, our Uncle Paul, and many of their friends all worked in the mills as well. For a while, our mom worked full time at Chicopee Mill while she was going to high school. Mom would put in her day at school, then would walk across the bridge to Chicopee for the 3-11 shift, then walk back across the bridge and up Lowell Street back home, only to get up and do the same the following day. I had a couple of really fun times with my mom in museums that talk about the mill experience. The first was when we were touring the Millyard Museum here in Manchester. The museum has one of the exact type of looms she used to work on. My mom walked up to the machine and started explaining to me how it worked, which involved her actually popping out a couple of the bobbins. When I suggested I did not think she was supposed to do that with the exhibits (it was funny I was having this talk, as my mom has been a history teacher for nearly 40 years), she just noted that this was exactly how the machine worked and they could just be popped back in, which she then did.

The second fun museum experience with my mom came when we were touring Lowell National Park. This Park is an amazing place, and I highly recommend everyone check it out. Among the many exhibits they have is a working room of looms, so you get a small taste of what the noise in these buildings must have been like. At another exhibit, there is a floor that shows a number of the various jobs that had to be done in the mills. Mom went to seemingly every job identifying family and friends who performed all the various positions. The highlight of the day, though, came when we were taking the guided tour. This was led by a park ranger younger than I was, who was very enthusiastic about telling the story of the mills. One of the stops was in a room with a working mill, so that the ranger could explain all of the various parts and functions of the machine. At one point, this ranger forgot the name of a part of the machine, and my mom politely jumped in and provided the name. She explained the loom he was showing us was the same type of loom she had worked on for years. It was very awesome to see the rest of the tour participants' reactions. At the end of the tour, we stopped in the gift shop, and I purchased a shuttle that I could display in my apartment. We had a good laugh about how many shuttles *Pépère* would have taken home over the years had he known that one day he would be able to sell them for $20 each.

As I noted at the start of this chapter, my sis and I grew up knowing we were French-Canadians, even if we did not speak the language. We were both baptized at Saint-Georges (which is no longer a church and last I heard was being used by a local theater for storage), and French was frequently heard at family functions. We were very fortunate, as it was fairly common to have both sets of grandparents over the house for holidays. When the family would get together, my four grandparents and a couple of great aunts would normally sit together and speak to each other in French. So, while we did not speak it, we were familiar with how the language sounded. We also had a number of the other typical French-Canadian traditions. We always had pork pie at Thanksgiving and Christmas (I did not know it was called "tourtière" until I started doing my podcast) and we frequently went to school with gorton sandwiches in the lunch box. And for us, it was always gorton. We never called it, or spelled it, cretons. *Mémère* Provencher was a member of the Daughters of Isabella, so during the holidays she would be crazy busy making tons of pork pies. To this day, a Daughter of Isabella pork pie is my go-to pork pie.

Growing up, I always knew the French-Canadian/Catholic identity was very important to my grandparents. My mom's dad made sure everyone always spoke French in the house when my mom was growing up, and this very much included guests like my dad. They also had other common traditions such as when my great-grandfather would bless my grandfather each year on New Year's Day, and then my grandfather would go bless his family. My grandfather would also take my Uncle Paul to collect special water on Easter morning. I understand these were traditions many French-Canadians had. I have intentionally discussed language and religious traditions together in one bucket because, I think, to many French-Canadians the two areas of life were inseparable. You could not have one without the other. And if you lost one, you would necessarily lose the other.

I believe the first day it really hit me about how important the French identity was to my family was when I had a conversation with *Mémère* Marguerite Martineau (formerly Bénard) at the end of her life. She was dying of cancer and knew the end would be soon. She was super organized and made sure absolutely everything was lined up for when she passed. She had the funeral home picked out, she chose the readings for her funeral mass (along with who would be reading), she had the songs to be sung at her funeral selected, she had everything. I had just finished my sophomore year of high school and I was over her house when she asked me if I would be a pallbearer at her funeral. She then went on to explain to me that she was going to have almost the entire funeral mass said in English, so that my sister and I could understand it. However, it was important to her that the Our Father be said in French. And it was. In fact, all four of my grandparents had parts of their funerals in French, either songs or prayers or both. Something that still amuses me was that *Mémère* Martineau was buried with a deck of cards in the coffin. She loved playing cards, particularly cribbage. In what I think is very awesome, Monique (who was only 12 years old when *Mémère* died) was her last ever cribbage partner. They won. Of course. Monique inherited the cribbage genes from *Mémère* and my dad much more than I did. I love playing, but she is better at it.

I have often been asked why my sister and I did not speak French in the house growing up. I had the privilege of interviewing my parents on my podcast and was able to ask them. To my parents, it was an issue of simple convenience. Once they left their parents' houses and returned to Manchester years later (my mom from college in Boston and my dad from the military), it was simply easier for them to speak English. They could still understand French just fine if someone spoke it to them, but due to not using the language for a while, it was sometimes tough to remember all the French vocabulary. As a result, for reasons of convenience, they would just speak to each other in English. Therefore, that was also the language in the house when my sister and I grew up.

A lot of people on my podcast have also suggested that being a Franco-American in New England carried a stigma. To be a "frog" was to be low class. After all, you were either a poor mill worker yourself or the descendant of poor mill workers. Also, Franco-Americans were frequently told that the French they spoke was an inferior French. It was not the "real" French that was spoken in Paris. One teacher at Central High School, the oldest public high school in New Hampshire, which both of my parents attended, even went as far as to separate the French-Canadian students from the rest of her French class. She did not want these French-Canadian students corrupting the other students' efforts to learn "proper" French. It will come as no surprise to those who know my dad that he was not one to let this kind of thing slide and would often challenge those who considered French-Canadians to be speaking a lesser French. It was not inferior. It was different.

After my grandparents died, I pretty much lost the connection to my French-Canadian identity. I essentially never heard French being spoken anymore, and I hadn't joined any French organizations. It was never something I was ever embarrassed or ashamed of, it was not just something that played a major role for me. This all changed one day due to a discussion at the water cooler at work that transformed the entire trajectory of my life. My sister and I both work at Southern New Hampshire University, and one day I went on break with a coworker and friend, Dan Beaulieu. As we were getting water, we started talking about how the newspapers in Manchester were highlighting all the Irish events taking place in the city. Well, I just got on my soapbox and started ranting about how there were more people of French heritage than Irish in Manchester, but you would never know that from the media coverage. New England Cable News even promoted Manchester as the most Irish city in America! Most Irish! A city with significantly more French descendants than Irish.

I just continued to rant to Dan (I never even bothered to ask, but just assumed he was of French heritage based on his last name) about how everyone thinks the French-Canadians are dead. Or if we are not yet dead, we are dying and soon will be. That people think we are an ethnic group that existed only in the pages of history books. And even then, we were in way too few history books. I talked all about how we (meaning the French) needed to do a better job getting our story out there. We needed to make sure people knew we were still around and still practiced the traditions our grandparents did. To his credit, Dan patiently allowed me to complete my rant before politely telling me that I really needed to talk to his brother Tim. Meeting Tim Beaulieu changed everything for me. Tim is a brilliant person and is the creator of the hugely successful New Hampshire PoutineFest. Before too long, I was volunteering at the first ever PoutineFest, then the second. Soon, Tim had asked me to join him on the Board of Trustees of the Franco-American Centre (FAC) in Manchester. I am now very fortunate to consider Tim Beaulieu a friend.

The idea for the French-Canadian Legacy Podcast came about after my first year on the Board of Trustees of the FAC when I was trying to come up with ways I could better contribute to the mission. I do not have the genius for business Tim Beaulieu has. I certainly did not have the financial expertise that others on the board had. The one thing I came up with was that I had a pretty successful college radio show with my friend Lee Lubarsky at the George Washington University. I was hoping I could use this background as a way to promote the Franco-American (a term I was now comfortable using) story. I actually tried to convince a couple of others to do the podcast, with me hosting every third episode or so. While those I approached seemed to think the podcast could be successful, they did not have the time needed to invest in it. I would be on my own if I wanted to make this a reality.

I tried for about a year to get the podcast off the ground. I bought a microphone and a new computer. I read a bit about how the recording process worked. I spent a bunch of time listening to Sandra Goodwin's Maple Stars & Stripes French-Canadian Genealogy Podcast. It was also at this time that I discovered David Vermette's French North America blog. I read everything on the blog in 24 hours. I was hooked. I was motivated. In what was a big step for me, I reached out to Robert Perreault. Those who know me well can tell you I am a huge Robert Perreault fan. There is nobody I would rather hear speak. My friends and I joke about how I would pay to hear Robert Perreault read the phone book. Thus, it was hugely important to me to get his opinion on my idea for a podcast. When he responded to my email with support, and with a list of potential guests that I should reach out to, it was massive.

At this point, everyone I had spoken with seemed to think the podcast was a great idea. The only problem was that I have zero technical skills and could not figure out how to pull it off. After about one year of incredible frustration, I basically threw in the towel. In what has turned out to be incredibly fortunate for me, I convinced my good friend Mike Campbell to partner with me on this project. I actually met Mike a number of years ago through mutual friends, while watching professional wrestling. There was a group that would get together to watch pay-per-view wrestling events and Mike and I both knew someone who attended those viewing sessions. After a while, we became friends. At one point, we even discussed trying to start a wrestling podcast. Fortunately, I was able to get him to come along with me on the French-Canadian Legacy project.

Without Mike, the podcast never happens, and I am not in Québec writing this. My job for the podcast is pretty straightforward. I find the guests, I do the research, and I interview the guests. Mike does everything else. He does all the production and editing. He runs the social media and the web page. He handles the *Patreon* account and anything dealing with money. Mike is really good at what he does, and I am incredibly lucky. We were also lucky early on to work with Concord Community TV in Concord, NH. They showed us how to get a podcast off the ground, and all of our early shows were recorded in their podcast studio. We have since changed to recording in a studio space we created in Mike's basement in Hudson, New Hampshire, where Mike is an elected member of the school board.

When we started the podcast, we were not overly optimistic about the number of listeners we would get. We would both get some pretty interesting looks when we told people we were starting a podcast about Franco-American cultural identity. I cannot tell you the number of times someone laughed at me when I told them. We figured that we might get some relatives and a few members of the Franco-American Centre to tune in. We got the first hint that we may be onto something when, a few months after we started, a member of the FAC board posted that she was visiting an observatory in Québec City. She had told her tour guide she was from New Hampshire. The guide's immediate response was to ask if she knew the podcast. At the time, we had no idea we were getting any listeners at all north of the border, and it was a huge motivator to keep putting in the crazy hours Mike and I were both investing in the project. I am now very proud to say that we have listeners on six continents (we are still waiting on Antarctica) and hit 50,000 listens right around two years and 50 full episodes.

We definitely received a lot of both positive and negative feedback when we started. Much of the positive feedback was actually about the song we chose for the open and close of each episode. The song is called "French in America" by Josée Vachon. It is a terrific song and fits perfectly for what Mike and I are trying to do. The negative feedback was usually about either the name I chose for the show or the fact our show was not in French. I chose French-Canadian Legacy and not Franco-American Legacy because, as mentioned earlier, I never thought of myself as Franco-American growing up. As for the language, I made a video in French (translated for me by my friend Jean-Philippe L'Étoile of Dummondville, who I met because of the podcast) trying to explain why I was not able to do the show in French, though I really wish I could. It is the most watched YouTube video we have released.

Through the show, Mike and I have been able to meet some amazing people. We have spoken with authors, historians, politicians, poets, musicians, film directors, and many more. The schedule we use for the show is to release a full interview every other week, while releasing a much shorter program during the off-week. This off-week show features an update on the latest Franco-American news, a preview of the upcoming episode, and a bonus question with the guest, which frequently is just a fun question that has absolutely nothing to do with the subject of the interview itself. We have been very lucky to have the incredibly talented Melody Desjardins do the news segment for us. Melody is a terrific writer, with a super unique style that makes anything she writes a must-read. Her *Moderne Francos* blog is outstanding.

In addition to the podcast, Mike and I started a blog in which we asked people a very simple question: Why do you tell the Franco-American story? I have often thought about all of the amazing guests we have had on the show, guests who could dedicate their professional lives to just about any subject. Yet they choose to devote their incredible talents to the Franco-American story. I simply wanted to give them the opportunity to tell us why. The responses we have received on this blog have been fantastic.

The latest project Mike and I have worked on is the New England Franco-Route GeoTour. The heavy lifting on this project has been done by Mike, our good friend Mark Belluardo, and Anne Conway, Director of the Museum of Work & Culture in Woonsocket, Rhode Island. We also received very significant support from the Québec Government Office in Boston. This tour takes participants on a scavenger hunt at five different locations significant to the Franco-American story at each of five cities with a substantial Franco-American presence. The towns on the tour are Lewiston-Auburn and Biddeford, Maine, Manchester, NH, Lowell, Massachusetts, and Woonsocket, Rhode Island. It has been an absolute privilege to bring attention to these sites so important to our story.

I suppose I should probably end by talking about why I am writing this chapter from Québec City. I am here for six months simply to learn French. I am going to school full time at a language school for adults. It is obviously an enormous sacrifice of time and money, but it just does not sit well with me that I am the first in my family to not speak French. I also am well aware that there is so much of the culture that is just not open to me because I do not have the language. I obviously do not buy into the frequently stated idea that you cannot call yourself a Franco-American if you do not speak French. If I did, you would not be reading this. But I am also realistic and know that there is more out there that I cannot access unless I speak French. So, I am desperately trying to learn. I am really looking forward to returning to New Hampshire in half a year and speaking French with my parents for the first time. It would definitely make our frequent Sunday dinners more fun. Though, for now, I am going to have a bit of a different dinner and walk over to St-Hubert on Grande Allée.

I am having a really hard time articulating how much I appreciate being able to tell my family story, a story I am sure has a lot in common with other Franco-Americans of my generation in New England. I will now turn this over to my sister so she can tell you a bit about the relationship she had with our grandmother, as well as how she is passing along the Franco-American heritage to her son, my Godson, Ben Cairns. He is named after my dad, of course.

Thank you, Jesse, and I am glad that he gave the back-story of our family. I think the only addition (besides my fantastic card playing skills and my adorable son) that I bring to this is that I was extremely close with my *Mémère*, Irene Provencher. It was a relationship that shaped my upbringing and continues to impact who I am today. I strive every day to be the woman she was and have her patience and devotion to family that was unmatched. To begin, Jesse and I are two of Irene and Roland's nine grandchildren. My mother was close with her parents, and I do not remember having any other babysitters than them. At a young age, I can remember faking sick from school because I knew mom would bring me to *Mémère*'s for the day and I could not think of a more fun place to be. What was better than watching her "programs" (basically all the soap operas) with her before she went to work (she worked second shift when I was a child)? *Mémère* chaperoned field trips, never missed a dance recital, and came to any event I was involved with growing up.

Mémère was a second mom. She offered advice. She gave tough love when it was necessary (like the time I was so upset in high school that I did not make the homecoming court but had won two different senior superlatives that day – she said to me "what you do want kid, the world?!" This was her way of reminding me to be happy with what I had). She also provided another support system for me.

Upon retirement, *Mémère* hung out with many of her sisters and sisters-in-law. We often referred to this group as the *Ma Tantes*. They were feisty, fun, and truly loved having their grandchildren around. My cousin, Ashley White (whose *mémère*, my *mémère*'s sister-in-law, was one of the *Ma Tantes*), and I would always try to tag along with the *Ma Tantes* as they went bowling, out to lunch, or whatever other adventure was happening that day. Ashley, like myself, had a unique relationship with her *mémère* and it is that bond that still brings us together to this day.

I come from a line of strong females, and I think the backbone of both sides of my family were the women. *Mémère* had been through a great deal in her life, with the most traumatic probably being losing her father on her wedding day. Sadly, he died on the dance floor of a heart attack at her wedding. Even with this horrible event, she would have a positive spin. She used to tell me that she had never seen him so happy like he was out there on the dance floor at her wedding. Strong – truly a strong woman. This is a strength that I try to carry with me throughout life's journey.

Outside of strength, I learned from *Mémère* how important family really was and how it was important to celebrate each occasion together. *Mémère* loved holidays! I can always remember her laugh at our annual Christmas Yankee Swap (a tradition we did for the older grandchildren, aunts, uncles, and grandparents). She used to always get a kick of the craziest gifts. Family, to my *mémère*, did not necessarily mean blood. She knew my best friend, my brother's best friend, my cousin's best friend, and expected and hoped to see them at family parties. The amount of love and importance of family was made extremely clear when she was in the hospital dying. Her surviving brother and sisters came to her bedside. They remained with her until she passed. Though she was not speaking much, the love in that room was felt all around. It is why I really try to stay in touch with my aunts, uncles, and cousins. Family is and will forever be important.

Lastly, my brother mentioned my son and the fact that my husband, Kenneth, and I chose to name him after my father. Growing up with a name like Monique Martineau, it was pretty evident I was French-Canadian. I always loved that people knew that about me and that no one guessed my ethnic background because they knew it when they heard my name.

When I got married, I took my husband's last name, Cairns. I knew my children would not have the same experience because his name is of Scottish descent. We agreed that we would name my son something with more of a connection to my roots since his last name is Cairns. It was without question that we carried on the legacy and named our son Bernard. Not only does this tie my son to his *pépère*, my father, who is the best representative of both of those titles, but it connects him to my family's history. We are expecting our second child (a girl this time) and we have yet to agree on a name. I will say, I do push for a French name every chance I get, just to keep that legacy alive.

Like Jesse, being French-Canadian was and is just a part of who I am. I truly know nothing else. When I went to college, I roomed with five other young women, all of whom were Irish, and I was surprised that they had all never known anything about French-Canadians. It was then that I realized that there needs to be something done and I am so proud that my brother works so diligently to keep this culture alive and thriving. My charge is to ensure that my children know their roots and the legacy of the *mémères* and *pépères* stays alive forever. *Je me souviens*.

19. What it means to be Franco-American
Robert B. Perreault

Being Franco-American. Love it, hate it, ignore it, remain unaware of it. It depends upon each individual's era of birth, age, family history, upbringing, education, career, and life's experiences. It can mean strong identification with, and embracing of, Franco-American culture with or without the French language. It can also involve rejection or ignorance of one's Franco-American identity. Or everything between those extremes. Had someone asked me, as a child, what being Franco-American meant to me, I would have replied "nothing." I once tasted Franco-American Spaghetti. Once was enough. I saw no connection between it and my family, myself, and people like us. In fact, there *was* no connection. Although the French language and Franco-American culture had surrounded me since birth, I never heard the term *Franco-American* applied to us until my adolescence.

When Franco-American musician Lucie Therrien visits schools, she asks children to raise their hand as she names their ethnic origin. With each group, hands go up. But when she asks, "Who is Franco-American?" she sees no hands. She then asks, "Who calls their grandparents *pépère* and *mémère?*" Suddenly, several hands wave. Perhaps it is a question of terminology. Or maybe it is because, unlike other United States populations with roots elsewhere in North America—Mexican Americans and Louisiana Cajuns, both famous for their music and cuisine—New England Franco-Americans remain invisible even in French Canada and France. We are here, three million descendants of the nearly one million French Canadians of Québécois and/or Acadian heritage who migrated to the United States between 1840 and 1930. Yet we do not make noise, positive or negative, to attract attention. No wonder journalist Dyke Hendrickson entitled his book about us *Quiet Presence.*

Both my parents hailed from Franco-American communities. My father's side all spoke French but preferred English. They rarely discussed their ethnic identity and never participated in Franco-American organizations beyond their parish. But my mother, who had relatives actively involved in Franco-American journalism, fraternal insurance, and music, always called us *Canadiens*. That is the term French Canadians adopted to distinguish themselves from their English-Canadian conquerors, *les Anglais*. An elitist term in its early existence, *Franco-Américain* dates back to the 1890s, to distinguish U.S.-born children from their *Canadien* immigrant parents. However, average Franco-Americans continued calling themselves *Canadiens* for many decades, while in English, they used the designations French Canadians or French. Confusing terminology aside, being Franco-American means everything to me today, and has since my twenties. Earlier, it was a roller coaster of a growing process.

Born in 1951 in Manchester, New Hampshire, once a major New England industrial center with a Franco-American population sometimes reaching 50%, all I knew about my ethnic identity as a child was that a couple of other *Canadien* families and mine stood out in our neighborhood. I grew up in an ethnically mixed area on Manchester's East Side, where English dominated outside our home. That differed from Manchester's *Petit Canada* on the West Side. There, whenever we visited *mon oncle* Gérald Robert, my mother's brother, his neighbors' children spoke French with me. Kids in our neighborhood spoke English, as we had many Yankee and Irish-American families living nearby. There were more recent immigrants and/or their descendants from Sweden, Poland, Greece, and Hungary. Whenever grandparents visited, they spoke broken English with their grandchildren—including a few of the *Canadien* kids—who sometimes did not understand their respective family's ancestral language, whereas I spoke exclusively French with mine. Out of respect for my grandparents, my parents spoke French to me. I did not learn English till age four, when my mother began letting me out into our yard, where kids came over to play. I recall the Yankee lady next door correcting me for calling her pet "the dog black." I found "the black dog" confusing. Eventually, playing with kids and watching *The Mickey Mouse Club, Howdy Doody*, and TV Westerns taught me English.

Although French took precedence over English, from a cultural standpoint, my parents maintained a generic United States household in the domains of décor, furniture, and entertainment. The only exception was food, as my mother occasionally made chicken soup, *fricassée*, meatloaf, and other delights based on recipes handed down to her by my grandmother from past generations on her family's farm in Québec. Sometimes, my mother made *gortons* sandwiches—some call it *cretons*—a French-Canadian pork spread sold at Guillette's meat market.

For my Franco-American cultural upbringing other than food, my parents relied on my mother's relatives. My *grand-papa*, Adolphe Robert, president of l'Association Canado-Américaine (ACA) and editor of its publication, *Le Canado-Américain*, read me French-language children's books and taught me French and French-Canadian folk songs. He received and read *L'Action*, Manchester's French weekly newspaper, which my parents also received, along with *Le Canado-Américain*, though I never saw them read either publication, no more than I ever saw them read my *grand-papa*'s autobiography, *Souvenirs et portraits*, which won Québec's Prix Champlain. *Grand-papa* also had a short-wave radio to get stations from Montréal. My grandmother, Azélie, told me family stories and taught me several prayers in French long before I started school.

Mon oncle Gérald, who succeeded my *grand-papa* in both ACA positions and who was also a noted musician, orchestra director, and French radio host, brought me French-language records from his and my *grand-papa*'s business trips to French Canada. His wife, *ma tante* Rachel, who was active in both ACA and Fédération Féminine Franco-Américaine circles, fed me homemade *tourtière*—pork pie. When I became old enough to attend Christmas Midnight Mass, my uncle and aunt invited me to their *réveillon*, the after-Mass feast featuring traditional French-Canadian foods. Their home, furnished in the French Provincial style, and my grandparents' home, both displayed works by their Franco-American artist friends, including landscapes and family portraits by Lorenzo de Nevers and sculptures, including a bust of my *grand-papa* by Lucien Gosselin.

By the time I started school, I was fully bilingual, as required for entry into first grade at l'École Saint-Georges, one of eight in Manchester's Franco-American parochial school system, with its half-day of French and half-day of English. I studied there from 1957 to 1965. Besides *épellation*, *grammaire*, and *lecture*, the French half of our day included the *raison d'être* of Catholic education: *catéchisme*. The nuns taught prayers—most of which I already knew—by rote in a level of French that was above our heads.

Daily, our French nuns, usually immigrants from Québec, admonished us to *parler français*, because French was, theoretically, our native language. This meant proper, grammatically correct Canadian French. At the time, I had no idea that our language sounded different from France's spoken French. Depending on their family, a few of my classmates spoke excellent French, while most got by passably well. Others who struggled sometimes transferred to an anglophone parochial or—heaven forbid!—public school. We also had a few French-Canadian classmates from recently immigrated families who found English challenging.

One difference between some of my classmates and myself was that they often visited relatives in Québec. My parents considered our annual summer day at Rye Beach forty miles away as a major journey. My only trip to Québec as a child occurred at age twelve in 1963. My *grand-papa*, uncle, and aunt took me to the Robert family farm at Notre-Dame-de-Lourdes, near Joliette. *Grand-papa* and I walked the perimeter of the thirty-acre farm that the Canadian government had granted my third-great-grandfather, Pierre Robert, in 1818, for his service during the War of 1812-1815. As we walked, my *grand-papa* told me stories about the farm and our ancestors. The farm would eventually be sold in 1995 after 177 years and seven generations. Fortunately, I thought, my family made sure that my French was up to par for my Québec trip and for school. While my grades in English were slightly above average, I spent eight years of grammar school competing for first and/or second place in French with a classmate whose parents were French-Canadian immigrants.

However, looking back, I realize that a lot was missing. I do not recall ever hearing the nuns call us or themselves Franco-American, nor *Canadien*. In fifth grade, when we studied European explorers in the New World during English class, the nun lumped them together, never referring to Marquette, Joliet, La Salle, etc., as French like our ancestors. Why did we never learn about famous French, French Canadian, or Franco-American figures whom we could admire as our own? I also recall our seventh-grade French nun skipping *le passé simple*—the literary past—claiming she doubted we would need that verb tense, which only professional writers used. In retrospect, I think *she* found it too difficult, so why risk embarrassing herself in front of us? How I wish I had met her a decade later to tell her how I wrestled with that tense when I began writing for and eventually editing

Le Canado-Américain. Although I am grateful for having learned to read and write French, which I have used daily in my nearly fifty-year career, I wish that our parochial school curriculum had included Franco-American history, literature, and culture.

For many years, my grammar-school friends and I anticipated attending Bishop Bradley High School, a now-defunct all-male Catholic diocesan institution under the direction of the Christian Brothers. When, during a family gathering, I casually mentioned my desire to study there, *ma tante* Rachel blurted out snidely, *"Bradley, c'est pas Franco-Américain!"* It was the first time I heard that term, *Franco-Américain.* When my grandparents and other relatives agreed, my parents capitulated. I ended up at Assumption Prep in Worcester, Massachusetts. Founded by the Pères de l'Assomption from France in 1904, it once was part of Assumption College. Another uncle had studied there, so my *grand-papa* offered to pay my expenses if I passed the entrance exam. I did, and off I went.

French class at Assumption had little resemblance to that in grammar school—something else for which I wished my parochial school education had prepared me. On the first day of class, the professor asked us each our names in French with an accent I had heard somewhere but could not quite place. One by one, students replied in various ways. From my perspective, no one was a native speaker of French as I was. When my turn arrived, I proudly replied as I would have when I had acted in French plays, given French speeches or sung French songs during cultural events at l'École Saint-Georges. To my dismay, the professor squinted, turned up his nose, and twisted his mouth every which way while repeating what I'd said. He exaggerated every syllable to make my Canadian French accent—which I still was not aware of—sound like gibberish. Of course, everyone laughed. I was too shocked to react.

As an adult, I learned that some schools automatically placed Franco-Americans in lower-level French classes due to prejudice against Canadian French. Within weeks, that awful professor realized, by my written quizzes, that my French vocabulary, spelling, and grammar were far above the level in which the school had placed me. Consequently, he transferred me to the top-level French class where I belonged. There, I became friends with Patrick Fortemps, a Parisian-born immigrant who had studied at the Lycée Français de New York. From him, I learned that the French he and our professors spoke came directly from France. He also told me that I spoke a brand of French he had never heard and often did not understand. Because I did not know much about my own language and culture, all I could tell him was that I had grown up speaking French and that my grandparents had come from French Canada. An American who spoke French at home and whose grandparents came from French Canada? Patrick was mystified.

Although I succeeded in the writing portion of my new class, I had to spend extra time in the Language Lab, listening through earphones to tapes and repeating after the speaker, *to correct* my pronunciation. This caused me to wonder why, if I properly read and wrote French, did I need to change my accent? What would my family think if I came home speaking like a Parisian? As a Beatles' fan—they, who sang in American English, but retained their English accent when speaking—I asked myself why, if Americans do not have to change their accents to sound British, did we Franco-Americans need to change ours to sound like Frenchmen? What was wrong with our language? Why did American schools teach Parisian French but not British English?

During the second semester, I befriended a Franco-American senior who worked in the Language Lab. He told me that besides reel-to-reel tapes, there was a turntable. If I brought some Beatles' records from home, and if the Language Lab director were not around, he would play them just for me instead of those boring Parisian French tapes. I was eternally grateful to him. When my *grand-papa* died in May, I told my parents that, had he lived, I would have toughed it out another three years at Assumption, but now that he was gone, I wanted to come home to my family and friends. At Bishop Bradley High, a scheduling conflict prevented me from taking French in my sophomore year. In my junior and senior years, French classes were half filled with students from various Franco-American grammar schools. As long as we pronounced clearly and used proper grammar, our teachers did not insist that we speak with a Parisian accent.

Regarding ethnic prejudice, other than one not-so-Christian Brother who, in English class, used "stupid frog" to explain the word *redundant*, the trouble at Bradley revolved around Irish-American students. Some were cruel, and physical conflicts occasionally arose. More often, however, it involved harmless teasing. Many assumed

that if we were *French*—no one used the term Franco-American—
we lived on the West Side in *le Petit Canada.* "Hey, frog, did you
jump across the river to get here?" or "Did you bring your passport
when you crossed the river?" I had French and Irish friends, and we
teased each other. Some were from mixed marriages, students with
Franco-American names who could not speak French while others
with Irish-American names could. All depended on one's mother's
ethnicity, the famous *mother tongue.*

Throughout my high school years (1965-1969), I appreciated my
French fluency, not for its own sake but because it earned me an easy
"A." Being a teenager in the wild 1960s meant a fascination with rock
music and concerts, partying, and part-time work. Being Franco-
American meant little to me. In the fall of 1969, I entered Saint
Anselm College in Manchester as a sociology major because *my
generation* planned to change the world. One unexpected change in
my world influenced my thinking about my ethnic identity.

In August 1970, I attended the Strawberry Fields Rock Festival in
the Ontarian countryside with three friends. Knowing that I spoke
French, one of them asked me to help two girls he had found
wandering around in a panic. They were *Québécoises* hippies! Up to
then, anything connected with French belonged to my parents' and
grandparents' generations—outdated. It had never occurred to me
that there were hippies like my friends and me in Québec. Such a
revelation. One of the girls had ingested some bad LSD and needed
medical attention. We led them both to the festival's makeshift clinic,
where I interpreted for them. Afterwards, my friends, who had never
heard me speak French, praised me for having helped those girls. One
of them added, "You sounded so different in French, like another
Bob we never met before." That reminded me of my *grand-papa*'s
oft-repeated slogan—in French of course: "Speak one language, you
are one person. Speak two languages, and suddenly, *you are worth
two people.*" With this awakening fresh in my mind, I returned home
and to Saint Anselm. There, my French professor, Roger Blais, a
Franco-American from Manchester who had studied in Paris,
encouraged me to do likewise the following year, 1971-1972. So
again, off I went.

In Paris, to fit in, I did my best to imitate a Parisian accent. It felt
strange, because when I visited England, no one *corrected* my
American accent. On the contrary, our phonetics professor at l'École

de l'Alliance Française often told me to close my lips more when I spoke. She had no idea why an American spoke French with such a wide-open mouth. She never once asked me how or where I had learned to speak French, nor even suggested that I spoke Canadian French. Sometimes, other French people assumed I was *Canadien*. Again, so ignorant about our Franco-American culture, I could not explain myself. Who was I, this *Américain* who spoke fluent French, but with *un accent canadien*?

Occasionally, my fellow American students asked me for help with their French homework. When hitchhiking in Europe still remained safe, as one of only two males in a program of thirty-five students, coupled with my fluency in French, I often received invitations to accompany my female classmates, one at a time, to all four corners of France and beyond. Meanwhile, my roommate, Tom Venner, originally from Kalamazoo, Michigan, who had never studied French until he arrived in Paris, was amazed to meet an American who had grown up in a French-speaking household.

More reasons to be grateful for my upbringing.

Career-wise, I have devoted my entire working life toward promoting the French language, New England Franco-American culture, and the history of Manchester. In March 1973, with a B.A. in sociology and fluency in French, I became research assistant and oral-history interviewer for Tamara Hareven and Randolph Langenbach, to record the experiences of former textile workers of Manchester's famous Amoskeag Manufacturing Company, 40% of whom were French-Canadian immigrants and their Franco-American descendants. That project yielded several articles and two books by my employers, including *Amoskeag: Life and Work in an American Factory-City*.

Afterwards, I became librarian-archivist of the ACA. I also wrote and took photos for *Le Canado-Américain*, of which I eventually served as assistant editor, representing the third generation in my family to collaborate on that publication. While at the ACA, I studied for my M.A. in French with specialization in Franco-American Studies at Rhode Island College (1981). I consider my years at the ACA as my apprenticeship in the field of Franco-American culture to learn what they never taught at l'École Saint-Georges. Since 1988,

I have conducted conversational French sessions in the Native Speaker Program at Saint Anselm College. I also earned an M.F.A. in creative writing/fiction from Southern New Hampshire University (2008). Besides regular employment, I have freelanced as a bilingual writer, public speaker, documentary photographer, and historical tour guide of Manchester—including the Franco-American West Side.

Regarding the future of the French language and of Franco-American culture, as I often say, "With every new generation, we put a bit more American water in our French wine." But it is a long, slow process, unlike what Msgr. Thomas Hendricken, Bishop of Providence, predicted in 1884. He saw no need to replace the deceased pastor of a Franco-American parish with another Franco-American because in ten years, all parishioners would be speaking English. How surprised Bishop Hendricken might be to find pockets of Franco-Americans throughout New England who still speak French today, 138 years later. Granted, those pockets are smaller and there are fewer of them than there were in the bishop's era.

When I was a child in the 1950s and early 1960s, people spoke French on the street, in stores, restaurants, churches, schools, societies, sporting events, recreational areas, and more. Nowadays, other than in nursing homes, and perhaps some churches and a few "Canadian cuisine" restaurants such as Chez Vachon in Manchester, one must listen carefully to hear French in public spaces. Nonetheless, organize a *Soirée Canadienne* with traditional music, contradancing, food, and drinks, and watch several hundred Francophones party with their famous *joie de vivre*. True, most will be senior citizens. Will someone replace them in X number of years? A thorny question arises: do identity and culture depend on language? *Survivance française* is an age-old ideology requiring fluency in French, faithful practice of Roman Catholicism, and observance of our ethnic traditions in order to call oneself a loyal French Canadian or Franco-American. Its proponents would argue that without language, identity and culture mean nothing. Yet how many Jewish Americans take pride in their heritage without the ability to speak Yiddish or Hebrew? And how many equally proud Irish Americans do not know a word of the Irish Gaelic language?

I have met hundreds of Franco-Americans who grew up in an exclusively anglophone environment or who have forgotten their

French mother tongue, but who are eager to do genealogical research, read historical and literary Franco-American works in English, and celebrate our culture. Some take French classes and/or are trying to recapture their childhood French by participating in conversational French groups such as Manchester's Franco-American Centre's *Prêt-à-parler* or similar programs elsewhere. Personally, I believe it is possible to identify with and enjoy ethnic culture without knowing one's ancestral language. However, knowledge of that language is the key to an entire world that enriches one's ethnicity to the fullest degree. Because my family handed me the gift of the French language and certain aspects of our culture, just as my wife Claudette Ouellette's family did with her, we passed those gifts on to our son, who is now doing so with our grandchildren.

In recent years, I have reconnected with a few grammar school classmates who tell me that, recalling how much I enjoyed the French half of our school day, they are not surprised that I have pursued a career that involves the French language. They also admit to wishing they had continued speaking French so that their children and grandchildren were bilingual as are mine. Were I to base the future on what I have observed in my thirty-four years of teaching conversational French, I would guess that there might always be a minority of Francophones who maintain their ancestral language, and Francophiles who practice certain cultural traditions. However, a return to life as it was when I was a child and before is unlikely.

In the late 1980s and 1990s, several of my Franco-American students came from extreme northern Maine, where some Acadian families continued to speak French. There were also a few students born in the United States to recently immigrated Québécois parents. We occasionally had Québécois students who came to play hockey, and after graduation, decided to settle in this country. Granted, these students are rare, plus there is no guarantee that they are passing on to their children the language and culture in which they themselves grew up.

I have had Franco-American students who do well in French, graduate, and continue to speak it. Some even teach French. Others do well, but lacking someone with whom to practice French, they forget what they have learned. Still others arrive not even knowing how to pronounce their family name correctly, and a few resent my pronouncing it in French. A very few do not even realize that they are Franco-American! Some are fascinated with this discovery and wish to further explore their newfound identity, but most remain indifferent. There are other Franco-American students who speak no French but who study Spanish. Some become fluent, but most merely fulfill their language requirement and eventually forget Spanish.

Annually, our Modern Language Department has organized a series of activities during March, International Francophonie Month. Depending on the type of event, student participation varies from a half-dozen to perhaps fifteen or twenty attendees. Yet it amazes me when, for a single feast in mid-March, hundreds of students, whether Irish or not, celebrate Saint Patrick's Day. March is also the birth month of internationally famous Franco-American writer Jack Kerouac, who spoke exclusively French until age six. It pains me whenever my students from Lowell, Massachusetts, Kerouac's hometown, have never heard of him.

Call me a dreamer, but when I see that our glass now contains maybe 10% French wine, it still tastes pretty good because it is all we have.

20. The Question of a Franco-American Revival
David Vermette

In April 2021, historian Patrick Lacroix published a piece titled *Une révolution tranquille chez les Franco-Américains* in the venerable newspaper Le Droit, the only French language newspaper published in Ontario today. Writing for a Franco-Canadian audience, Lacroix's piece speaks to a "revival that is taking place today" ("le renouveau qui se produit à l'heure actuelle") as Franco-Americans in the United States Northeast seek to rediscover their ancestral identity : "Les communautés franco-américaines du nord-est vivent un nouvel engouement pour leur culture ancestrale…Maintenant, des jeunes franco-américains…s'affirment et souhaitent faire leur part pour la préservation de leur héritage." Lacroix presents evidence for a revival, noting a few among the modest but consistent outcropping of Franco-American related projects in recent years. We have seen Franco-American themed events (like New Hampshire's popular PoutineFest), YouTube channels, social media groups, blogs, books, works of theater and music, academic conferences, etc. popping up here and there like toadstools.

I can think of four podcasts about Franco-Americans, three of them pumping out a steady stream of content. The fourth is a newcomer that has already seen mainstream press coverage in its home base of Lewiston, Maine. None of these podcasts existed ten years ago and three of them did not exist five years ago. Most of these creative projects rise from the grassroots with minimal or no direct institutional support. These efforts also tend to cross-pollinate. There appears to be the beginnings of a vanguard, a small informal cadre of avocational activists who are starting to valorize the case for Franco-American revival. We can attribute some of this creative activity to the trend of the democratization of media. Any niche interest can spawn a podcast or two. But the current activity includes many younger (than me) people. In 2010, the demographic of committed Franco-Americans was decidedly over fifty. And knowledge of French was directly proportional to age. Not necessarily true anymore. I now see younger faces at Franco-American events and young Franco-American creatives are producing resonant work. Some of them are fluent in French. I have also received an animated response among younger people to my book *A Distinct Alien Race* and to my talks about it.

Meanwhile, some of the established institutions continue to exist and feed the renewal. Franco-American Programs at the University of Maine, Orono, the current incarnation of the 50-year-old Franco-American Centre, is building an impressive portal for Franco-American studies. It continues to publish the bilingual journal *Le Forum*. Beginning as the *FAROG Forum*, it is now one of the longest running publications in Franco-American history. Franco-American Programs also organizes an annual *Rassemblement* of Franco-American creatives that has become a rough modern equivalent of the *conventions générales des Canadiens-Français aux Etats-Unis* of the 19th century. The Rassemblement is where engaged New England Franco-Americans go to present and discuss their work, and to reflect on questions of identity.

The Museum of Work and Culture in Woonsocket, Rhode Island, the best facility of its kind in the region, continues to do its work of representing the classic Franco-American mill town story. The Museum also has an active speaker series. During the pandemic, both the Museum and Franco-American Programs produced regular 'live' online content in the form of presentations, discussions, and demonstrations. Taken together, these dozens of offerings testify to the scope of contemporary Franco-American creativity.

The Franco-American Center in Manchester, New Hampshire rose from the ashes of the Association Canado-Américaine, the latter an esteemed mutual benefit society of old. The Center offers French classes, French-language meetups, occasional speakers, and other events. Genealogical societies such as the American-Canadian Genealogical Society in Manchester and the American-French Genealogical Society in Woonsocket, and various mill museums and historical societies, continue to provide resources reconnecting Franco-Americans with their roots.

Not Revival, But Continuation

Despite these signs of life, I have listened to the talk of revival with benevolent skepticism. These conversations have been in the air for my entire adult life and yet little long-term emerged that could be called a revival. In retrospect, Franco-American aspirations toward cultural revival in the later 20th century reflected the struggle they faced to define themselves amid the continuing social changes of that period. The discourse around cultural revival over the past few decades indicates the degree to which Franco-Americans had become swept into the currents of the United States mainstream. For example, Gerard Brault's *The French-Canadian Heritage in New England*, published in the 1980s, contained a section called "Signs of a cultural revival in Franco-Américanie." In a sub-section on the causes of this alleged revival, Brault cited mainly events of the 1970s – a half-century ago – notably bilingual education programs under Title VII of the federal Elementary and Secondary Education Act of 1972 and the Ethnic Heritage Studies Program established by Congress that same year. Brault also cited the United States Bicentennial (1976) and the popular book and TV series Roots (1977) as events influencing what he, in the 1980s, perceived as a nascent Franco-American "cultural revival."

In 1999, Armand Chartier's *The Franco-Americans of New England: A History* appeared. Similar to Brault's work, Chartier has a chapter called "Ethnicity Rediscovered" with a section titled "A Cultural Awakening?" the author sifting in a measure of ambiguity with his question mark. And as did Brault, Chartier mentioned the Bicentennial and Roots as catalytic events in what he called an "ethnic wave" in the 1970s and 1980s. He made his putative Franco- American "awakening" a part of this national "wave." In the following decade, Ben Levine's influential film *Réveil: Waking Up French* bore the subtitle "the Repression and Renaissance of the French in New England." The promised "renaissance" links with the French language reacquisition efforts discussed in the film. The film's more optimistic vignettes tied the reacquisition of the language to the opening of the Franco-American community to the wider world, as when a woman from Woonsocket was moved to recover her French to communicate with an immigrant from Senegal.

But despite the talk of "revival," "awakening," and "renaissance," New England Franco-Americans have continued much as they have for decades. As Brault and Chartier implied, trends in United States society rather than events from within the Franco-American culture were driving the looked-for revival. What late 20th century observers saw as a cultural revival were attempts by Franco-Americans to respond to the problem of modernity as the traditional signposts of the identity, such as language and religion, became increasingly absent.

La survivance est morte

The French-Canadian tradition that was brought to the Petits Canadas of New England, and that birthed a regional culture, rested on three pillars: the French language, the Catholic religion, and the customs and mores of rural Québec. Well into the 20th century, these were the sine qua non of French-Canadian identity and its ideology of cultural survival (la survivance). It is safe to affirm that virtually no one, on either side of the border, practices this culture the way our great-grandparents did. For its part, Québec has become one of the most aggressively secular parts of North America, heresy to Ultramontane elites of the 19th century. While south of the border, Franco-Americans have largely lost their ability to speak French, another kind of heresy per the partisans of survivance.

While both Québécois and Franco-Americans today have distinct discontinuities with the old French-Canadian tradition, both sides of the border claim some continuity with the past. Today's committed Québécois would perhaps choose to see themselves as continuous with the Patriotes of 1837-38, if not with the Papal Zouaves, while today's Franco-Americans claim an historical continuity with the French-speaking industrial workers of a New England past. Nonetheless, the different responses to the problem of modernity on the two sides of the border created discontinuities with tradition.

On the United States side of the border, the problem of accommodating oneself to, or separating oneself from, the French-Canadian tradition began to appear in earnest in the mid-20th century as the Francophone enclaves in the industrial towns of the Northeast declined. Franco-Americans were exposed increasingly to homogenizing forces such as military service and participation in higher education.

Franco-Americans, between the 1960s and today, participated in two other trends of United States society: 1) the tendency of white-identified formerly "ethnic" communities to speak English, and 2) the decline in adherence to traditional religion. There may have been a path to a Franco-American modernity that preserved the French language but, by and large, this road became cut off as the Francophone enclaves declined. On the northern side of the border, Québec's Quiet Revolution was its response to the problem of modernity. In the 1960s and 1970s, this revolution reinvented the French-Canadians of Québec as Québécois. This new nationality would adopt a forward-looking stance; it began to conceive of itself as a potentially innovative society in a global context. This social revolution and its aftermath detached Québec society (understood as a nation, and no longer as an ethnicity) from its attachments to the religion and the rural mores that defined the French-Canadian tradition. What remained was the French language, and it became the main, if not the only, signifier of identity.

For the Franco-Americans of New England, there was no Quiet Revolution. There was no conscious break with the past. In the generations between the mid-20th century and today, there has been a gradual, rather than a revolutionary, transformation of the traditional Franco-American culture. Absent the customary signposts of identity, such as language and religion, why should anyone care about being Franco-American? I have no answer to the question. I merely observe that there are many Americans who continue to claim Franco-American, French-Canadian, or Acadian identity absent the traditional signifiers. We can mull the question as to why people who no longer rest on the traditional pillars of an identity continue to claim it, but the empirical fact is that many do.

To absorb this fact, we must constate that, contrary to survivance ideology, Franco-American culture is what we are doing now and not a thing of the past to be conserved. The preservationist attitudes of the past no longer apply because the objective conditions to which they were a response no longer hold. The older conceptions of identity were prescriptive: "You must speak French." "You must be Catholic." "You must marry a French-Canadian Catholic." The 21st century approach is descriptive. Membership in the Franco-American group does not depend on linguistic or religious litmus tests but on self-description, on self-identification.

Not as a Culture but as Individuals

In confronting the problem of modernity, Franco-Americans built their bridges from the past to the future not as a community, as a public matter, but as individuals. The bridge from the culture of preservation to one of self-identification was crossed by each of us as emerging individuals, or perhaps as families, but not as a culture. Why? Because the culture of preservation itself would brook no alteration to the package delivered from the past to the present. Further, institutions built by earlier generations to serve survivance ideology declined and with them went a source of solidarity. And then many people moved away from the Francophone enclaves. Physical proximity was lost and with it, actual community where people knew one another, went to school together, had local extended family, and formed clubs and interest groups, thus reinforcing language and customs.

The modern Franco-American experience is informed by the many adjustments persons and families made to work around the lack of a public, shared Franco-American modernity. The workarounds mediated conflict, as traditional boundaries of language, religion, class, education, gender, sexuality, etc. fell away around the Franco-American, who now became another white- identified individual in mainstream, United States society. We worked-around class differences we encountered in the environments we found ourselves in at Brandeis or at Swarthmore; we worked around identification with religion or non-religion; we worked around gendered expectations; we worked around the question of language, i.e. questions of who's a "real" Franco-American, based on the ability to speak French, and the type and fluency of that French; these questions include the guilt feelings of those who "lost" their language, even if they never had it to lose, even if that decision was made before they were born by parents or grandparents. For some, the older identity signifiers – Catholicism, the French language, and the folk culture – remained. Or some of these remained, even in bits and pieces, but not others.

Generational Trauma

The erosion of community and the language loss reminds us that there is likely to be a high incidence of cross-generational trauma in New England Franco-American families. If this trauma exists it is not only unprocessed; it is completely unrecognized. It remains unacknowledged within the traumatized families as well as by the dominant culture. That anything traumatic occurred in the mill towns, and in the poverty that made these places seem like an improvement on a previous existence, is unregistered not only in history books but in our psyches.

The entire Franco-American tale: the second-class status of the Canadien in 19th century Lower Canada; the rural poverty that drove the flight from Québec; the culture shock; a continuing, grinding urban poverty in a land of plenty; the segregation in enclaves; the attitudes of derision and suspicion our ancestors faced in the U.S.; the organized aggression that came towards them occasionally and intermittently between 1840 and 1930; the erosion of the language and the feelings of loss and defeat that were left behind; this narrative arc appears nowhere except in specialist histories. The invisibility did little to mitigate the consequences of trauma for subsequent generations. It now behooves us, the post-survivance generations, to acknowledge our story and the consequences of it. And we do this not as a grievance against anyone, nor out of a desire to be perceived as victims, but because reconciliation with the past begins with the truth.

An Obstacle to Cross-Border Understanding

One difficulty for our cousins north of the border is that "Franco-American" is no longer a linguistic identity. It is based on shared history, shared experience, and connections of family and community. This difficulty has given rise to an obstacle engaged Franco-Americans face today: an attitude among some Québécois who object to this chapter you are reading, or to my book, or to some podcasts relating to Franco-Americans, because they are in English. The Manchester-based French-Canadian Legacy Podcast felt the need to issue a statement on video in French because they had received messages branding as illegitimate or inauthentic a podcast that discussed the French-Canadian legacy in English.

There are competing sensitivities on the two sides of the border. Obviously, when Québécois people who fear the loss of French in Québec hear people with names like their own, sometimes anglicized, speaking English, it is triggering. It is their worst fears come true! And on their side, Franco-Americans are sensitive to the issue of language loss. There is shame and feelings of failure attached to the language itself. We understand the irony of our very existence as English-speakers who still identify as Franco-Americans.

I suggest that we take our fingers out of each other's wounds and find a way to work together. If promoting and preserving French as a minority language in North America is one's concern, then Franco-Americans, even those who do not speak French, are a natural ally. But we would need to reacquaint the descendants in New England with the value of their connection to the language. And that dialogue would need to begin in English because the small percentage of people who are bilingual do not need to engage in it. The descendants who now speak only English might. Like it or not, to insist on "French only!" on this side of the border in 2021 is not only impractical. It would silence us and effectively halt our efforts, thus depriving North American Francophonie of a potential ally numbering in the millions.

Franco-Americans, Race, and the National Conversation

Current discourse about Franco-American revival also occurs within the context of national conversations about race and about identity. In the current climate, any white-identified group that seeks to explore its identity runs the risk of having its conversations conflated with "white identity" movements that are nothing but overt racism and white supremacism. The discussions of race and racialization in my book were about interrogating and dismantling whiteness, while offering a different side of the history of North America. My exploration of the ambiguities around the racial identity of Franco- Americans in the 19th and 20th centuries was intended to shed light on how race, ethnicity, class, religion, and language intersect. My book explored the status of Franco-Americans in the context of the view that North America has had a stratified racial-ethnic caste system. Some say that our people were colonized after the British Conquest of Canada. But even if that is inaccurate, they were nonetheless proletarianized and subjected to cultural assimilation as a matter of public policy. And this happened to them as a white-identified people, within both the British Empire (and its Canadian proxies) and the United States. These are matters I deem worth exploring as part of a national conversation on race. However, we should also be clear that the Franco-American experience is not commensurate with the experiences of people of color in North America.

I also resist subsuming the experience of French-Canadian and Acadian immigrants in the United States into the stock "Ellis Island" narratives of European immigrants. And I remain dubious about dissolving French-Canadian/Acadian descendants in New England into a more ambiguous "French heritage" group that would conflate them with 17th century Huguenot refugees, or middle-class 19th century immigrants from France. Each of these stories is unique. Let us also be honest about the bigotries that were present in this community and expose them wherever they still exist today (the Vichy Regime's representative received a hearty welcome in Woonsocket and a few other places in Franco New England in the 1940s). We should not be in denial about where and when our values differ from those of our ancestors.

It is Not White Nationalism

Continuing criticisms of Québec's attempts to shore up the French language, and the debates around how it applies its principle of secularism (laïcité), muddy the waters even further. There is an ominous tendency to conflate Québec's ongoing assertiveness as a "nation within Canada" with white nationalism. Case in point, the recent tempest in a Twitter teapot involving a law professor at University of Ottawa; and a May 2021 piece in The Washington Post by J.J. McCullough making a preposterous, button-pushing comparison between Québec and Mississippi, while using terms like "xenophobic ethno-state." This conflation of the modern iteration of traditional *Québec patriotisme* with today's white nationalism is a serious mistake. It is based on a misunderstanding of history and of the dynamics of power in North America.

French is a minority language spoken throughout the Americas by people of many colors and races, and many different backgrounds. Although the majority of Québec's Francophones are racialized as white, they are also part of a North American Francophonie that is diverse. Commentators like McCullough see the Québécois through a parochial, folkloric lens, as merely the descendants of the habitants, rather than as a lynchpin in the Americas of a global Francophonie. Besides, historically the French-Canadian people were more likely to be the targets of nativists and white supremacists than their allies.

French-Canadians and Franco-Americans fell afoul of the avowed white Anglo-Saxon Protestant nationalists of bygone eras including the Ku Klux Klan, their Canadian allies in the Orange Order, and Eugenics partisans. They were deemed not quite racially pure enough for white Anglo-Saxon supremacists of the 20th century in part because they believed that French-Canadians were the product of extensive intermarriage between French settlers and indigenous peoples.

Eugenics proponents in the United States used these beliefs to justify marking some French-Canadian family lines as "degenerate." Some Franco-Americans, mostly women, were targeted for sterilization in State hospitals. In 2021, the Vermont Legislature apologized for its active involvement in these procedures, mentioning the French-Canadian descent people of the state among the targeted groups. French-Canadians were also one of the most proletarianized populations in North America. The French colonial society was decapitated after the 1763 treaty confirming the British Conquest. The decision-makers and policy-implementers of French colonialism returned to Europe. British imperial functionaries replaced those of an authoritarian French regime. The descendants of the French-speaking farmers, laborers, tradespeople, artisans, women, and children who remained in the new British Province of Québec were a made-to-order set of hands for Empire builders, be they British imperialists or United States industrialists. For two centuries our ancestors were the "hewers of wood and drawers of water," the people, wrote Lord Durham, "with no literature and no history;" they were useful for their labor which was "the only good use they can be put to," per the Massachusetts Bureau of Labor Statistics in 1881. In the long-term, the most salient fact about the historic French-Canadian population is that it was instrumentalized as cheap labor for the British Empire and the United States.

Make no mistake, until quite recently Anglo-Protestants have been the top caste in North America. Non-Anglo, non-Protestant whites were in a privileged position vis-à-vis people of color; but they were in a less privileged position with respect to Anglo-Protestants. Such distinctions matter far less today than they once might have. But after 1763, the French-Canadian never ranked particularly high in anyone's caste system on either side of the border. Ongoing Québec bashing in the press is a 21st century expression of Anglo supremacism, the view that North America's Anglophones represent enlightenment, while the Francophones are backward and benighted. In my research, I read charges that the French-Canadians were "ignorant," "bigoted," and undemocratic in the pages of the New York Times dating back to the 1880s-90s. These calumnies find their precise contemporary counterpart in McCullough's op-ed in The Washington Post.

United States readers imbibe such views uncritically because they confirm their own vague stereotypes about some French-speaking people somewhere. For the Mid Atlantic readers of *The Washington Post*, Québec is an unknown quantity to which Canadian pundits can assign any value they like. Their jaundiced messages, and their dynamic with the United States press, have been remarkably consistent since the 19th century.

Revival or Continuation?

Having explored the growth of Franco-American creativity, and some of the obstacles and difficulties involved, let us answer the question: is there a Franco-American revival? The unsatisfying answer is that it is still too early to tell. What I, and observers like Lacroix, can confirm is that the pot is slowly coming to a boil in and around the Franco-Americans of New England. While I have heard talk of revival many times before, and remain cautious, the recent spate of activity is undeniable. But current laborers in the Franco-American field do not appear to be reviving something from the past. They are defining anew what it is to be Franco-American. For now, it is urgent that Franco-Americans and Québécois clarify their shared history, and especially its relationship to French and British colonialism, and to the colonial successor states in the United States and Canada. This is both difficult to do and necessary in order to avoid catastrophic historical misunderstandings.

We have a great deal of work ahead of us.

21. My Story as a Franco-American
Anthony DesRois

As a Franco-American, my identity has been a place of both refuge and insecurity for me. My journey with my culture has been as complex as the history of the French American story itself. To truly understand how my culture plays a part in my life today, it is important to go back to the start. Although I credit my grandmother with being the matriarch of all things French in my life, my first memory of the French language would have to be seeing my mother's lips in a puckered round shape as she attempted to help me pronounce the French pronoun "ou." The memory occurred during a trip we were taking on the train from upstate New York to Florida, a destination nearly all Québecois find themselves at during some point in their lives. As I comb over the memory, my mother wanted to make sure I knew how to say a few things aside from counting in French and the mandatory salutations to my grandparents. That happens to be one of the fondest memories I have of my mother. My grandmother and the LaLiberte family arrived "to the states" from Levis, Québec to New Hampshire while her grandfather was working on the railroad. My grandmother was born out of wedlock. Her father was a soldier in World War II. For a die-hard Catholic family, that was unacceptable. As a result of the shame, my grandmother was sent to live at a monastery until her aunt and uncle brought her to their farm in Westbrook, Maine. In Westbrook, French was the only language used in her community. In my grandmother's later years, her mother asked that she come live with her and attend school. At school, my grandmother was introduced to the English language.

I can vividly recall my grandmother telling me stories about how she was picked on in school for not knowing how to speak English and how she eventually developed a feeling of shame for being French Canadian—a story I have now heard many times amongst that generation. I learned of my grandmother's school struggles in my childhood in response to my complaints about school children picking on me for the clothes that my grandmother picked out for me. It was her way of letting me know that it could be worse; I could be getting bullied and not understand what the bullies were saying. My grandmother grew to embrace many American customs that were later passed on to her daughters. However, some things could not be washed away with commercialism. My grandmother still passed on midnight mass, *réveillon*, French recipes and lullabies that I sang to my two children.

My mother eventually revolted against many of those French ideas and customs while growing up in the seventies. However, my mother would often tell me stories about visits to see *Pépère* and *Mémère* in Québec or at their summer house in New Hampshire and her trips to Westbrook. My mother and aunt spent their summers working on the family farm in Westbrook where they encountered the opposite problem of my grandmother—not being fluent enough in French. Over time, both my aunt and my mother became fluent in the French language and learned an appreciation for their roots while earning a bit of money for next year's school clothes. My grandmother and grandfather eventually settled in Port Salerno, Florida. It was, and still is, a commercial fishing community. My grandmother's family-built boats in Québec. Therefore, my grandfather, a jack of all trades and man of the sea, found Port Salerno as the perfect place to call home. Unfortunately, like other commercial fishing towns, life came with economic struggles. With those realities, my family went through hard times. Eventually, like my mother, I too became a product of growing up in that type of environment and the toll it took on my family. It is now easy to see how the American way of life washed away much of our customs; especially as my mother and grandmother's visits up north became more distant over the years. From my understanding, there was a disagreement between my family up north and my grandmother regarding my mom's American upbringing which led to the separation of our Florida family from my family up north permanently. This goes to show that once that connection to Québec is lost, the loss of the French language can quickly follow.

In my adolescence, my brother and I were removed from the care of my mother and grandmother and eventually separated. During this time, I questioned everything about myself and what it meant to "be." In response to that recurring self-reflection, I learned that I was indeed different from others. I had something unique about myself that made me special. In turn, my "identity" held me together in my adolescence. I could be taken away from my family, relocated, placed at a new school, separated from my brother, but no one could take my culture. Identifying with my culture was the rock that kept me grounded. This is not to say that I understood what identifying with my culture meant in its entirety. During those years, I was unclear of the difference between French and French Canadian because my grandmother did not differentiate between the two. In school, whenever I heard French history, I immediately became interested. I engulfed myself in French history and media. I became overly proud of my culture and when looking back, in myself too. I fell in love with sports like hockey and soccer (football). When choosing sports teams, I always chose teams with French or French-Canadian players. I watched the French football (soccer) league and the French National team, which later became valuable when I became a sportswriter for *Get French Football News*. By this point, French was a blanket term for my interest in my culture.

It was not until my adult years of hearing jokes that "the French are losers," the many times I had to defend being "French," or having a frog put on my work desk as a prank by my former supervisor who made sure I knew without him, a former soldier, France would be speaking German. I never understood why "Frenchness" was up for question amongst others. Any time cultures were brought up, I would proudly say French/French-Canadian and be met with requests to prove my "Frenchness" by saying something in French or a flat-out dismissal. I cannot recall witnessing an Italian or Irish American being met with the same request even when their families were several generations removed. I found discussing historical inaccuracies or responding to these types of reactions as pointless, but it did not change the fact that it caused countless arguments with others to the point that I had to re-examine my own history to make sure I was solid in my own reasoning. Digging into my own family's history was not only liberating, but it gave me a different level of appreciation for my family's journey and the struggles that we had to endure to even exist here in America. After speaking with my aunt and grandmother before she passed away, it became even more important to me to highlight the Franco-American story because through my own journey to find our stories and history, it was apparent that they were lost. For context, this was in 2010. Though not long-ago, it was before the push we see today to save the Franco-

American identity, the social media explosion and before the release of awesome Franco-American literature like *A Distinct Alien Race.* The absence of representation on Facebook at the time was the driving force that pushed me to start the Franco-American Facebook page in the first place. My thought was to connect the vast variants of Franco-American cultures and expressions under an umbrella with content that we could all relate to including the Cajuns, French Canadians, Québecois and Franco-Americans. Looking through the Facebook posts and engagement today, I am proud of the content and development of the page. I have learned more than I have shared which is always a gift in itself. When I travel, I have recommendations and connections through people I would have never known existed without the Franco-American Page.

The unexpected result of educating myself helped reshape my family. I found my brother in 2016 when he was sixteen. He had been adopted by an "American" family. He was only an infant when we were separated. During one of our first meetings, my brother expressed to me that he grew up with this inherent need to know his background and it was something that bothered him his entire life. Being old enough to remember our family at the time we were separated and through my additional studies, I was able to answer his questions and fill in the gaps. I did not speak fluent French when I left my grandmother, but I was very familiar with it. Enough so that I have been able to continue to expand my French without any formal schooling or training. I was able to create new memories to replace unpleasant ones by teaching my brother and my two sons the traditions and language my beloved grandmother taught me.

As an adult, my culture and language are a staple in my life and career. I currently write for *Get French Football News*—something I would have never done if I did not initially go look for the French League when I was younger (which was not easily followed in the United States at the time). With the French League's current popularity, I have been well ahead of the fan base simply by this previous knowledge and fanhood as a youth. Knowing enough French to hold a conversation has helped me in interviews and when listening to player's conversations. I have also used French when I worked as an account manager with our Québecois clients here in South Florida. Above and beyond any of that, I have developed lifelong relationships.

Previously, French was the cheat code for learning Creole when I met my mother-in-law. People were very surprised at how quickly I caught on to Creole. However, it felt familiar to me. Many of the words are the same, even though they are used differently. The verbs themselves are mostly all unconjugated French which was a huge plus for me. Learning the key differences was the biggest battle. After crossing that hurdle, I was able to communicate well enough with my beautiful mother-in-law who was then able to teach me more than anyone else on this planet, and in her own language too. Without that, I do not know if I would have ever connected so well and so close to her or to my wife's family.

My children, now almost teens, have lived a very Franco life. They both take French in school, and I do my best to teach them whatever I can in practical ways. They too open their gifts the night of Christmas Eve, eat "Kings Cake" on *Galette des rois*, hear stories of Jean and the *Loup-Garou* on Halloween and know how to cook the classics such as *tourtière, beignets* and *bourguignon*. Parenting in a Franco-American family is just as challenging as it is rewarding. My kids have the same reservations and desire to take the path of least resistance to an American lifestyle. However, giving them their own ownership of the culture has fostered within them a love for the language and traditions, so they usually only give one huff and puff before their French lesson.

With my children getting older, my hope is to continue with my mission of creating and connecting Franco-American content. Short term, I will continue sharing and applauding my fellow Francophone and Franco-Americans on social media, but I wish to do more than that. I want to create content so that people may truly be able to live a Franco-American lifestyle in French. Sometimes you just have to follow the format that works, and we can learn from other communities. We do not see Spanish-speaking families losing their language as quickly as the French. It is due to the lack of French content in the media and local meeting areas such as hangouts and places like synagogues and churches. If we can create localized communities with schools and places of social gatherings, then we can mimic some of the great enclaves around the country. Places where you are greeted with Bonjour at the register and by waiters.

The efforts I see from people on social media and larger projects like Tele-Louisiane, Jesse with the French-Canadian Legacy

Podcast, New Niveau/Sweet Crude and everyone involved with the AAFLFC project is more than inspiring. When we have diversified options in the media for the many palates of our Francophone consumers, I believe we too will be able to see a steady growth in the French language and Francophone communities. With projects like the ones previously mentioned, we can come to see Franco-American culture as all inclusive. Countless times I see a division amongst the community. With things as simple as the labels concerning what type of French they or we speak. Terms like Québecois, Cajun and New England French speak to very important dialects that should be cherished, but on a grand scale, when these terms for dialects are used to identify as their own language, it obstructs the advancement of true growth. These small differences should not be stumbling blocks. Rather, they should be differences we all appreciate for their unique expression of the French language. Beyond that, the differences are not as large as we make them out to be. When reading literature from Louisiana, even with my limited French, I rarely run into words or phrases I cannot understand.

In response to the debate of French vs French, I always say there is no such thing as being ethnically French. France's history is hundreds of tribes and travelers held together by language and culture...and with wine of course. I always laugh at the shock of people's reaction when they get their DNA results back with a laundry list of countries in our social media groups. I hope to one day do my own part and fill that void however I can. Right now, I am working on my next book project. It will come out in English but will be translated in French. It is a piece that speaks to the French history in a way that is tasteful and exciting. The story takes another look at one of our own "heroes" in a way that is a bit more Franco-American than it was originally told. The idea itself was sparked by my son's decision to pick another folk hero over this one. Me, being who I am, thought about it for days and realized that it was a story worth telling. It is projects and content like this one that will be the fuel to keep this movement going. I heard a woman once mention in a documentary that if we do not make an effort to speak French when it does not matter (i.e., when telling a joke, during random conversations with your family), then "it" will not work. Nevertheless, my personal goal is to speak French as my go-to-language so that I may also walk-the-walk. This is not to say that it is easy. I find myself making small attempts throughout the day, but eventually fall off the wagon and continue my conversation in English due to the difficulty in finding the words in French. However, it comes down to effort.

I am more hopeful now than I have ever been. Children in Louisiana are now becoming more fluent than their parents. I see the same possibility for my own sons. With our help, they can have access to the Francophone world I am speaking of, which is partially offered in my community here in Miami. My children play at a French-based soccer club; there is a thriving Haitian community that speaks French and Creole; French businesses and probably the most Québecois seasonal residents in the world. I do not see myself adding to a brick-and-mortar business that offers French, but I do one day hope to create a platform that offers a diverse array of French content for my local and non-local Francophone community. If French is not available in your child's school, there are exciting apps that offer access to French teachers like iTalki for as little as four dollars a lesson. I believe technology, local initiatives and media content in French are the tools to fuel a fundamental shift to reclaim Franco-American culture and a genuine interest in French in general.

How far that interest goes in expanding the French language in the United States is yet to be seen. Technology is creating opportunities to learn, speak and connect in French. However, I do not know if apps and social media are a feasible catalyst for the French America we are looking for. I believe it will take localized communities. COVID-19 has opened our eyes to the possibilities of working from home and living anywhere you want. Is the desire to live and function in a Franco-American fashion enough to uproot entire lives to move to a more French speaking area? I cannot answer that question, but I have seen plenty of videos of Franco-Americans and aspiring Francophones going to France and Québec to study so maybe moving to Louisiana or New England for a start-up community would not be too crazy after all. This is my ideal vision of French in America, but I know this is very far away. However, I am comfortable with the hands that we are in. With youth, there is energy, and with age comes wisdom. Luckily enough for us, we are in a time where both hands are in the pot. Now it is up to us to give effort and deliver. We will either take advantage of this window or let it fizzle out and sit down, waiting for the next generation to pick up the task where we left off.

22. Fundamental beliefs: Stand to deliver
Jean Mirvil

Stand up! Why not soar and discover new adventures, face the conflicts, and leave your stain in a world that is so englobed in issues that few have the last word. Today, after decades of turmoil we are not exempt from more environmental issues, political upheavals have reaped our minds, and we find questioning the legitimacy of our current standing. In a nutshell, we must question what is right or wrong. In that case, why are third political parties so few to reach their goals? One thing is for sure, in the mid of such mayhem, the need to communicate, to produce innovative ideas, and maintain motivated thoughts can no longer be accurate by taking a solo path linguistically.

In earlier years, when the emergent immigrants were struggling with their identity, they were made to fit a mold and join the majority in that designed mold. Such was determined by virtue of their financial status. You could pay to learn more, feel free to accumulate as much as possible what you so desire. However, as the world was shrinking and democratization was eminent, albeit its challenges led to many metropolises to address languages in various approaches in order to lead the way. This phenomenon led me to become a bilingual teacher in the New York City Public Schools. My dilemma was to channel opportunities for learners to communicate. Thereby tackling vicious issues about their background, financial, political experiences, racial, religious, gender, the overall social status which is still being questioned. Since I was fortunate never to fall in any trap where someone had to determine my desiderata, I brought to the classroom that open minded approach to teaching languages. My approach helped students to enjoy the freedom to learn, by drawing from their own resources as well as borrowing from other sources, which they will eventually sculpt to finally creating their own and enrich their communicative repertoire.

Let me argue that being skeptical had always has its place when approaching one's beliefs. Given the natural selection that one has inherited in life, albeit geographical setting or not, certain realities would become obvious for one to absorb, debate with, and finally adopt. This may not be so for all species, to each its own! Be sure to stand for what is conducive for everyone even though it is a concept that is different from your own reality.

In my classrooms, my student's experiences and realities are always welcome and have their place in the classrooms, specifically in a multicultural setting. I take great pleasure when I am in a setting, and people makes the effort to integrate me in an audience one would use the usual "Good Morning, Bonjour, Buenos Dias, and stop there. Let us be clear that they do not exclude those who should be called by *Mbolo, Bongiorno, Annyeong haseyo*. We language-minded people must reach out and highlight the *Et vous?* concept. Leave no one behind. No language is less than another if we truly affirm that people are people. I do not recommend in any audience to survey each identity in a gathering to stand correctly. How much time would we consume just to stand politically correct? Let us be real and stay open-minded in what we want others to know and feel. We are who we are. Our mission is to learn about each other to pacify our tumultuous warlike world. Let us not proclaim the wrong attitude.

My bilingual classes whether they are in Creole, French, or Spanish, demonstrated at the elementary and junior high school level that many Americans and new students that immigrated to the public school can be successful when they are under the tutelage of teachers who are "Dyanm." They take no-nonsense; they are determined in their mission to have *all* students to learn and to achieve to their highest potentials. These teachers stand for the rights of their children. They care about them, their language, and cultures. Moreover, they care about the future of this country, the United States. It is through this commitment that they have been able to walk into their school despite the changes from reforms, new curriculum, new leadership, they face the odds and stand to deliver meaningful instruction to their learners.

I recall, the creation of a book, *I can learn French*, designed to address gaps many Haitian students brought into the classrooms simply because such designed materials were needed to help student succeed. After completing the thirty-one chapters of challenging themes, the transition to standard French textbooks was effortless. The same group of students looking to be promoted, guess in certain language classes to adjust to the desired level. Sometimes it was necessary to feature language institutes, accelerated language immersion courses, and periodical sessions to reach the desire outcomes. Our students were never isolated to one referred program. We integrated challenging exchanges among various students and languages including Greek and Latin. In the end there were strong efforts to motivate, select, apply, and evaluate all skills to enhance our school culture. Also, specifically in my French class, we learned to develop a taste for French cuisine. My Friday lesson plans would feature math, while selling French *croissants*, *pain au chocolat*, creating our *premiere salade niçoise*, or *crêpes*. Often, we would transform our classroom like a restaurant or dining room to bring the real-world experience and blend in social etiquette norms as well. As a result, there were no barriers in transferring our acquired manners at *La Bonne Soupe* in the city, or at *Duc de Lorraine* in Montréal. For several years, annually our student groups had patronized *la belle ville de Québec*. *Je me souviens encore du petit coin Juliette et Chocolat à Saint Denis*.

Teachers who think big for the world set no limits.

I have learned to consider putting sparks in my language instruction. If I do not have the necessary ingredient, I work towards making it possible. That is how I structure my presence in front of the students. Certain strategies, models, of teaching may have already been discovered. However, too many times, we are the inventors of a technique that has already been discovered. Except that we had not been exposed to it nor did we connect it with any lecture we could have had back at the university level. The idea of being a seasoned educator sounds just right for the language teacher. It is not about time in the field. In this case, just as our favorite dishes need seasoning, think about it, being the person who will motivate learners and professionals in our school to do the right thing by children, I also knew to season my lessons and never let my class look the same, unappealing for the students through all our sessions. I searched for my themes and looked for elements that will accompany my lessons to bring the sparks needed. I dug from students what they may be able to retrieve from home to add zest to my lessons or to ornate our bulletin boards. I recalled my colleagues getting hooked to these attractive efforts and even felt at ease to ask me if I would allow them to sit in on a lesson that interested them simply from the captured attraction that they noted. Those *rencontres sympatiques* exhibited joy for my classes. It is like putting an accent or the last spice to a concoction. Overall, you know that you have invested quality time to your plan, you have always had your audience in mind, no one can take that away from you. You are on top of your world.

Nevertheless, you will meet obstacles from those who may think you are crazy. They do not wish to invest as much as you do. Your mission is your thinking. Do not expect everyone to wish to soar out of the ordinary. Your gifted mind will get you through not only in one foreign language but in multiple languages. I have always said that teaching language and culture is like being an ambassador. What is the role of an ambassador? A major part of his/her responsibilities is handling conflicts. So, be a language ambassador. Demonstrate your language ambassador abilities and teach it to the world. Unless you take a stand in what you are to do, you may contribute to those negative implications.

I have been a French foreign language teacher at both elementary and secondary school levels. I have also taught English as a Second Language both in the United States and abroad for some time. Most recently, I continue teaching language and explain about culture or trans-language concepts and identity whether I am visiting classes or speaking to teachers at any forum. When you are an ambassador, one is always an ambassador. It is the truth; I have never left the classrooms. Daily, after decades in the field, I continue to find opportunities to add my grain of salt to execute an issue related to linguistic and cultural teaching experiences. The bottom line is that there is no end to learning! Growing up and developing a bilingual mind helped to see life and its dualities. I have been blessed to be raised with a bilingual mind. When I learned English, which has become my third language, my critical thinking had flown exponentially. I am still fascinated to be among my peers who are quadrilingual. Just know that it is not about being confused when one is exposed to many languages, or one language is more valuable than the other. The bottom line is we must invest and get all the pieces in some order so that we do not asphyxiate others from the gift they have inherited.

Let us think about it, languages and those whose culture offer them new ways to connect to history and honor the generations that sacrificed so much to secure a better life for their descendants. There are those who are still blasting certain languages, people with their cultures. Some go as far as comparing one language against the other. Most recently I heard one group filtering the argument about a country that has two official languages. The leader was a person who was ignorant in speaking one of the two referred official languages. He demanded that the language he spoke, the dominant one be used. The autocratic approach to language as means of communication refutes the concept of language being used as a way to build bridges and willingness to strengthen ties. Taking such approach repudiates and encourages discordance. As language and culture ambassadors, we must stand as advocates for the just cause. We cannot contribute to humanity if we continue to destroy some groups by virtue of how they have inherited the language they speak to today. It is their history, their tribulations. Whether they are perceived to be good or bad by anyone's judgment, this is their contribution in the history of our world. What we do with the knowledge we have acquired of groups that have endured some of the evil doings that men have perpetuated worldwide, will eventually come back to us as a challenge that only history will tell.

Below, I would like to highlight how language tolerance changes a neighborhood. Beyond the vicissitudes that are sometimes traced from one's journey in this field, I acknowledge their existence. I lived through them firsthand, as I tried to remain afloat and do the right thing. Resiliency will take you far. The urge to combat the odds, at time, could not be done with just love and prayers. Simultaneously, you must be resolute and always think that it is about the impact that you were born to make, in support of those in need. This is how I landed on my two feet at a school that one would have characterized or deem to be very needy in an emergent New York City neighborhood. It became my very special place. Unbeknownst to me, I was going to enter a garden that would be willing to offer me the opportunity to grow and to spark the fruits of joy to educate, discover with others who were waiting for a motivator to regain their confidence, and move the instructional agenda forward.

This was when the idea to implement a dual language program started to germinate. I have had prior exposure to such valuable programs. Through various trainings and institutes, I have attended and acquired a lot of knowledge from various advocates of the most successful French programs in the city and in France, thanks to the French cultural services.

In implementing the dual language program, a major prerequisite was to apply a language survey. I give credit to the already existing procedure and the idea of initiating the home language surveys to schools that welcome many newcomers. Through those surveys, I was able to assemble enough students who had the same linguistic background. With a critical eye in analyzing these students' adaptations to the standard curriculum, I drew the conclusion that a specific program could boost the knowledge and interest for this group of learners, thereby opening the doors to the integration of their families, to help improve the school culture.

My first step was to call for a meeting with the parents of children that I had identified from the language survey. Little that I knew, it was like shaking a dormant population at this school location. I did not know then that there were so many parents from Mali, Senegal, and Ivory Coast who were developing a network among them to also attain their American dream. It was very apropos that I help them understand how to capitalize their children's French language background to help them meet their dreams.

This awakening has become the challenge for an entire neighborhood. Community leaders embraced our school effort to the point that we become the pet of many educational leaders who had been striving for raising the entire Highbridge, Bronx community. This effort could not have been possible had we not received the scaffolding and support of the French Service center. Our package was made up of on-going staff developers, and the implementation of activities that were extremely gifted in early childhood French immersion programs. Additionally, we were then equipped with an adequate French library to equate any balanced literacy classroom that was in vogue in schools and effectively worked for children. Moreover, an exchange teacher program between France and the States, found its implementation in the South Bronx for the first time. I recalled the brilliant teachers who became stakeholders as soon as they entered the program. They brought in all their skills and expertise to help us attain our program's goal.

As we moved on and kept accurate records on all our targeted students who stood to benefit from our dual French English program, our academic growth escalated exponentially. We were a school on the go. Our school climate had never been better. We were able to institute programs that were innovative in all the grades so that all students would be on board our train to success. In retrospect, we found out that teachers were not afraid of new challenged endeavors. Rather, they wanted to see the drive from their administrators that would culminate to raising their consciousness daily and ignite their hidden talents.

Not too many people would think that a passion in teaching languages, French, could turn around an entire school based educational program. Out of one there are many. This can be translated by how one language teacher sees himself in relation the gamut of the *WH* words in English:

- When: The way you set your time to research and implement what is important to teach in the language will bring you wonders.
- How: Maintaining an allure of being authentic is the characteristic to have for you will always be valued by what you represent.
- What: It is about teaching French to impact on those numerous French communities who have so much to contribute to the world. You are using French to tap on those contributions either to learn, teach and to exchange. You are contributing to make the world go around through your original lenses.
- Why: Just remember, if it is not you, who is it? Each one of us has a destiny. Too often we hide behind others who are seeking powers, but do not have the true investment to do what it takes to bring about change. It is not always about how much is being spent for collaboration to evolve. To achieve to success is why we do what we do. Stand for your contribution to make the world a just and better place with your given talent to teach.
- Who: For the love of the language and culture we teach, to quote the eminent French singer Charles Aznavour, "Who will take our weakness with caresses and the words of love covering with oblivion our days of madness? Who can best take on the language teaching at the end with all the challenges of a monolingual sentiment?" You and I are blessed with our multilingual minds.

While I have been impressed with approaches that I have seen implemented in countries like Guadeloupe and Gabon etc., with dual language realities among their patriots, I stand to condemn places that have not made a dent in modernity to meeting the needs of their countrymen to offer patrons new ways to connect to history and honor the generations that sacrificed so much to secure their freedoms. There exists many smoke-screened dispersing of documents held from many ministers of education's offices, like in Haiti. No apparent change has reached a reasonable part of the population, let alone to raise the bar in how languages must be taught in multicultural and multilingual communities. UNESCO and USAID have already invested in too many of these failed ministers 'plans.

In my humble contribution to spending the last few years running an establishment in Haiti, I met the challenges to implement academic instruction in a city located in the Northeast of the country. As someone who is not new to the implementation of language programs, I had my challenges to tackle the social linguistic awareness: My familiarity with Haiti in general, my own idiosyncrasies from a native who has lived afar, and my discoveries at first hand, bring about changes that will manifest into successful students, parents, and teachers' experiences.

I want to reiterate that the level of sensitivity in such an atmosphere was the key to any change that I made. How good was good enough in terms of what I knew? Who among all the articles and books I have read from a plethora of authors, have written to talk about the true voice of the peoples of Haiti? I spent sleepless nights debating about replicating the dual language teaching experience I was able to implement with my African descent French speakers. I also questioned what component of the program can enhance the work I am responsible to launch? How would my work be perceived with the current state of language instruction across Haiti? Would I be able to depend on the teachers to move this agenda forward? What funds are available to reach my goal? How would my work be evaluated?

To date, I am proud to say that my time in trying to address the odds that I encountered to run the school has not been vain. Although I can affirm that a dual language French could have been beneficial to a small group of early childhood students, what had turned out to be meaningful was implementing a transitional trilingual Creole, English with a strong French as a second language, model. I rate our success by the result of the national exams for grade 9 over the past two years.

Language instruction relates to sociolinguistics in many ways. Different social factors affect language teaching and language learning. The relationship between sociolinguistics and language teaching impacts on my work at Lekòl S & H. Some social factors such as situation, context, financial standing, and social setting have been identified in research. They showed their dominance in setting the tone for linguistic instructional adjustments. I had to explore and come to terms with them in order to move forward. These factors have influenced my linguistic community as well as the teaching approaches I chose. As a contemporary model for my learning community, we abide to it and made us accountable to the model. It still accommodates us in our pursuit of obvious levels we must reach in our performance level communicatively and academically. It permeates among those who are part and belong to various facets of the school culture.

My motivating factor has reached a point to get people to be interested in how we speak differently in varying social contexts, roles, and how we may also use specific functions of language to convey social meaning or present aspects of our identity. As I stated before, my agenda exemplifies a desire for all to comprehend real-life attitudes and social situations. We have worked towards creating a family eager to meet our mission despite all odds.

As the principal of this unique school, and a board member of a local organization that supports child and adult development, coming to the table with no set cookie cut mold but with a mind and spirit open to exchange with my community of learners, I have firsthand experience of the value of these kinds of dialogues, at times difficult, for certain, but necessary. That is what being an advocate for languages and cultures can teach and has taught me.

I traveled through expansive collection of artifacts and first-person oral histories, taking tours inside memorable sites on stories that changed the world. Teaching and learning language with sociolinguistics helps to distinguish who, where, whom, when and why. Therefore, associating our advocacy in a social context will bring life to those to be served, be it from a second or foreign language teaching and learning experience. Stand by that notion.

To date, when I reflect on my past experiences as a language teacher and supervisor, I often provide for all students in the language class and in any school setting with which I am associated. I am most grateful for having worked with extensive supportive teachers, colleagues and supervisors and some great friends that I made along the journey. Without these people, I would not have been able to transform the difficulty that I had in the beginning into a positive experience, worthy of sharing with people in the field. We must carry the legacy further for the sake of educating all students in our school and our nation. I am pleased to see the outcome of those endeavors discussed earlier. Concurrently, there has been new transformation of issues related to Teaching French in an online educational world. We must take charge and assure that indeed language learning is and enrichment and a positive experience.

Conclusion: Toward a Resurgence of French Language and Francophone Culture in the United States
Kathleen Stein-Smith

It has been an honor and privilege to have worked with such a wonderful group of authors in developing this book. Their stories, ranging from powerful personal narratives to fascinating academic and historical accounts, which we have read in the previous chapters, demonstrate the breadth and depth of the influence of French language and Francophone culture in our lives. Following the example of our inspirational chapter authors, I will begin by sharing my relationship and experience with French language and Francophone culture. While I am not aware of any French heritage in my personal background, I have always been conscious of the importance and strong appeal of French language and Francophone culture, encouraged by both my mother's firmly held belief that knowledge of French was an essential part of life wherever one may be, and by early encounters with French-Canadians during family trips to Québec and summers at the Jersey shore, as well as in my neighborhood.

These encounters were followed by study of French at school and in college, where I had the wonderful experience of earning both an Honours Bachelor of Arts and master's degree at a Francophone university in Québec and of living in *la capitale nationale* during the years immediately following the *révolution tranquille* and the enactment of the Official Languages Act. As a doctoral learner, I focused on multilingualism as a global competency, and as an educator, I have taught students about French language and Francophone culture for many years. French language and Francophone culture have always been a part of my life.

As a *Francophone de coeur*, if not *de sang*, and a language educator and advocate, I firmly believe in the importance of multilingualism in a globalized world and in the significance of multilingualism in the development of a global citizenship mindset and skills. Within this context, the role of French is indisputable – as a global language of culture, humanistic ideas and values, communication, and education, and as a means of working together with people from around the world to make our world a better place. In addition, French is not only a global language, but one of the languages that form an integral part of our United States history and cultural identity. However, French transcends its historical role, dating from the earliest years of European exploration of much of what is now the United States, and is a language of our present and of our future – spoken in over two million in the home in the United States (Ryan, 2010). French is the language not only of early Americans and of immigrants throughout our history, but also of an increasing number of the newest Americans of all ages (French Morning Staff, 2017).

For all these reasons, and many more, it is essential to protect and to promote the French language presence in the U.S. While it may be easy to think that the French language is so widely respected that there is no need to protect it, French programs everywhere face funding and other challenges, exacerbated by the COVID-19 global pandemic, and college programs have been especially hard hit (Johnson, 2019). The good news is that we can all support French and other languages in our educational institutions.

Also, while it may be easy to think that we as individuals have little influence, nothing can be farther from the truth. Languages live in our families and communities, and in the media, arts, and the public conversation, as well as in the workplace – we can certainly protect and promote French (or whatever our heritage or adopted language may be) by using it in our daily lives, everywhere we go, and – most importantly – with our children and young people, using French in our daily conversations and providing career pathways and opportunities requiring or enhanced by French for our young people. We can also protect and promote the French language presence in the United States by advocacy and engagement, and these are most effective when data-driven and supported by both motivation and a skill set that varies among individuals. In other words, we need to stay informed, so that we are ready to defend and promote French whenever the need arises, or an opportunity presents itself. We also need to be flexible and willing to get involved in language advocacy campaigns and initiatives.

Staying Informed – Readiness for Data-Driven Advocacy

French is an American language – but many in the United States remain relatively unaware of the significance of the French presence both in the world and in the United States. A knowledge of the facts is essential in persuading institutional decision-makers, elected officials, and sometimes even family and friends of the enduring value of French both in public settings and in informal conversations. Despite the prevailing narrative highlighting only our national legacy as a British colony, the United States includes areas that were colonies or were influenced by a variety of European nations, including France. France has had a major presence in the Americas – Canada, the United States, the Caribbean, and South America – since the earliest days of European exploration. In the United States, place names from Montpelier, Vermont, to New Orleans, Detroit, St. Louis, New Orleans, and Boise demonstrate the French presence. In North America, more than 33 million speak French (Nadeau, 2021). In the United States today, more than 10 million have claimed French heritage, more than 160,000 French nationals currently live in the United States, more than 80,000 Francophones live in New YorkCity, and over 33 million Francophones live in North America (French Morning Staff, 2017; French Americans, 2021; Sicot & Brunet, 2020). In terms of language learning, French is the second most studied language at both the K-12 and college and university level, with nearly 1.3 million learners at the K-12 level and nearly 176,000 learners in colleges and universities (American Councils, 2017; MLA, 2019). French language supporters can be found in government and business, and those who appreciate the appeal of French language, French and Francophone culture, and the ideas, ideals, and values of the Francophonie can be found throughout the United States.

French has been part of our history and cultural identity since the earliest years of European exploration, and it is certainly important that we remember this. However, the present is also important. It is wonderful in the sense that French language and Francophone culture are thriving – and in some cases, have enjoyed a renaissance, in many parts of the United States (Louisiana (2018). In Louisiana, the Council for the Development of French in Louisiana (CODOFIL) celebrated its 50th anniversary in 2018, and Louisiana joined the Francophonie in 2018. In New England, the Franco-American Centre of New Hampshire (FACNH), the French-Canadian Legacy Podcast and Blog, the New Hampshire Poutine Fest, and the recently-opened Alliance Française in Portland, Maine, are among the many indications of a resurgence in interest in French language and Francophone culture. The Bilingual Revolution has brought dual-language immersion programs to New York City public schools and beyond (Jaumont, 2017), and the American Association of Teachers of French (AATF) has long worked to support French language learning to our schools.

With the number of Francophones worldwide predicted to increase, reaching over 700 million in the coming years, the future of French as a global language is bright (OIF, 2014; OIF, 2018). In the United States, while over two million speak French in the home and over ten million Americans are of French heritage, and while local initiatives, especially in Louisiana, New England, and New York City are inspirational, the fact remains that the role of French in our American narrative is often understated, and that Franco-Americans have been described as "invisible" (Vermette, 2018). It is important for French language supporters in the United States to embrace the fact that French is often spoken – and has thrived – in multilingual environments around the world and can thrive even in our anglophone and increasingly multilingual North American and United States context. The challenge to the French language and Francophone culture in the United States is multi-faceted and complex, centering on both the learning and use of French.

In terms of learning, the primary challenge is the lack of opportunity for students to learn additional languages. This lack of opportunity includes not only the dramatic decline in the number of French language programs at the college and university level in recent years, but also the lesser-known decline in the already small percentage of public schools at the elementary and middle schools that offer foreign language programs (AMACAD, 2017). In addition, foreign language programs everywhere have been impacted by educational and funding challenges due to the COVID-19 pandemic. This challenge can be effectively addressed by support for French programs in all our educational institutions, especially of opportunities for continuous learning from the earliest grade level, and for opportunities for the development of pre-professional language and cultural skills.

In addition, beyond traditional school and academic programs, there are opportunities for learning in after-school, weekend, and summer programs, and learning can be with an immersion or traditional French as a foreign language approach and can be either in person or virtual/online. The most important factor is to make French language and cultural learning available to all interested learners. Importantly, learning opportunities tailored to meet the specific needs of heritage speakers, whether those with a long history in the United States who may have varying degrees of language skills and cultural knowledge as well as the children of the newest Americans, whose families speak French and would like to maintain their family language, need to be available. However, the question of French language learning is itself multi-faceted – while learning needs to be available to all in an accessible and affordable manner, French language and Francophone culture in the United States transcend language learning and includes language use in all aspects of traditional and popular culture, as well as in the media and in our society. In order to reflect the true scope of the French and Francophone presence, they both need to have a place in our daily lives.

Getting Involved – Advocacy, Leadership, and Social Movements

French is one of the most highly in demand languages in the United States workplace (ACTFL, 2019; NAE, 2017), and French is the second most widely studied language in the United States (American Councils, 2017), but French programs at all levels face funding and other challenges, all made worse by the impact of the COVID-19 pandemic. Even if we have the motivation and the facts to make a data-driven argument for French, many of us may think that we do not know how to advocate effectively in order to make a difference, or that we may not have the time. However, the skills involved in effective advocacy generally build on skills we already have, and can be built on or learned gradually, as the need arises. In a world of many issues, advocacy is essential and has been defined as in "persuading people who matter to care about your issue," making the case for languages to all language stakeholders – parents, educational decision-makers, society in general, and students themselves.

In order to achieve the goal, it is "about getting listened to, being at the table when decisions are made, being heard by people who make decisions," a clear road map for language advocates. Advocacy is also "about speaking and writing in compelling ways that make decision makers want to adopt your ideas" (Daly, 2011). Among concrete questions to consider are goals, methods, and partners.

Beyond a general goal of safeguarding and promoting the French language and Francophone culture space in the United States, it is important to support French language programs and French language educators, to make French learning affordable and accessible, and to support French language learning in all its aspects – from the earliest years through postsecondary education, learning for proficiency and pre-professional language skills, and learning environments for both mother-tongue and heritage speakers as well as for English-speaking Americans and others to learn French as a new or additional language. In terms of learning for proficiency, immersion and an early start to continuous learning are key. We also need to look beyond the traditional classroom and support after-school, weekend, summer, and online learning in our communities. Most importantly, we must work together to ensure opportunity – access and affordability – for all interested learners, with our public schools, online learning, and low-cost community-based programs the most effective ways to lower costs, and scholarships and grants necessary to provide funding as needed for potential learners and their families.

In addition to establishing goals, it is necessary to consider the skills and methods most likely to achieve those goals – skills including online and social media, as well as negotiation and lobbying, and theories including change management, social marketing, the psychology of persuasion, blue ocean strategy, and many more. The most important thing to remember that advocacy is a broad umbrella, with room for many voices, and not everyone needs to be an expert in every aspect of advocacy. While many advocates have limited time, every voice is needed, and we can all play an important role in advancing the cause. However, for those language supporters who want to do more, beyond developing advocacy skills, they can take on leadership roles. While leadership is a responsibility, it is also an opportunity for personal and professional growth. Leadership has been defined as is "a process whereby an individual influences a group of individuals to achieve a common goal" (Northouse, 2013). Often broader support is needed in making the case for language, requiring an understanding of negotiation, lobbying, and social movements, and leaders can certainly engage in political and social action, ranging from online petitions to running for political office. In the United States, the Joint National Committee for Languages, bringing together organizational partners from across the language enterprise, sponsors Language Advocacy Days and lobbies for languages at the national level, and the American Council on the Teaching of Foreign Language has initiated the Lead with Languages campaign. Social movements are not a new idea, and "throughout history, social movements— small groups that are loosely connected but united by a shared purpose—have created transformational change" (Satell & Popovic, 2017).

However, although a great deal can be achieved by individuals and individual groups, partnerships have a positive impact on advocacy initiatives. There are many different kinds of partnerships – they can be local, regional, national, and international; they can include organizations of a similar nature, or can bring together educators, businesses, government, and external partners. School districts can collaborate with local colleges and universities, as well as with local businesses and communities that use French. The AATF has state chapters and regional representatives throughout the country, along with numerous initiatives including National French Week, the National French Contest, and many more. The Alliance Française has more than 100 branches in the United States (AF, 2019). Organizations like the FACNH, CODOFIL, the French-Canadian Legacy Podcast and Blog, and the New Hampshire Poutine Fest, are just a few of the many organizations that work to protect and promote the French and Francophone space in the United States. Language enterprise partnerships can include educational associations, potential employers of young people with French language skills in business and government, and external partners. The French government, which had launched a worldwide campaign for French in 2018, based on learning, communicating, and creating in French (French Diplomacy, 2021), offers a wide variety of programs and initiatives of potential interest to French language supporters, and the Délégation générale du Québec (Québec Government Office) has offices in many United States cities.

Sustainable French Language
and Francophone Culture in the United States

Just as language learning success depends greatly on motivation, so does sustainable advocacy, and the preceding chapters have clearly demonstrated the significance of the French and Francophone presence in our United States history and cultural identity. In addition, the undeniable role of the French language in the expression of great ideas, and the motivation to safeguard and protect this language and culture which are our own is assured. However, the use of French in the United States has declined in recent years, due to legal, social, and economic pressures to assimilate by using English only that are a well-known aspect of United States history. It is time to act–to support French and Francophone education and initiatives, to make participation in French language and culture accessible and affordable for all, to develop needed advocacy skills, to assume leadership roles if appropriate, to seek out partners in advocacy, and to engage in political and social action as needed.

Advocacy is a broad umbrella, and we can all work to support French language and Francophone culture as individuals and through our professional associations. We can all bring our time, energy, and dedication, as well as our talents and resources to the process–every day, in conversations with family, friends, and local and institutional decision-makers; through professional engagement, research and writing, and speaking; and through political and social action, ranging from signing online petitions to running for public office. However, this is not a short-term initiative, and in order to be sustainable, advocacy needs to be based in our core values and beliefs. In order to achieve lasting success in ensuring that French language and Francophone culture have their rightful place in the United States, we need to believe both in the importance of French language and Francophone culture within the broader context of a multilingual world and our own increasingly multilingual society. While necessary, language learning is not an end in itself, but rather multilingualism is a tool to make a better world. A "bilingual revolution," bringing dual-language education to all interested students and the benefits of multilingualism to an entire society, is essential (Jaumont, 2017). "The future in America, and everywhere, is multilingual. And so is the present" (Montlaur, 2019).

For those who wish to learn, or to re-acquire, a lost heritage language, or to adopt a new additional language, it is important not only to develop a learning plan, but also to determine the role of your new language in your life and how you will use it–where it will "live" in your life (Leveen, 2021). These concepts offer a wonderful gateway for creative spirits and innovative leaders in appealing to present and future generations. However, while language and culture are closely related, and as important as multilingualism is, it is also important to remember that many in the United States (including many Americans of French heritage) have lost their heritage language due to the passage of time, and in order for the Francophone cultural space to be authentic, it needs to include those who do not speak the language. Just as advocacy is a broad umbrella, including all those who want to work to support French language and Francophone culture, so too must advocacy goals and initiatives for the United States Francophone space include non-French speakers.

Concluding Thoughts

French language and Francophone culture have always been important, and they have always been part of our United States history and cultural identity. However, they are more important than ever in a globalized and interconnected world where French plays a major role as a global language, and in an increasingly multilingual world where new arrivals from France and throughout the Francophone world have added their voices to the millions of Americans of French and Francophone heritage. We can all play a role in bringing about a resurgence of French in the United States, as individuals and through our professional associations, as advocates, leaders, and change agents. We can do this through learning and education, and it is essential that we support our French language educators and French programs at all levels, as well as programs beyond the school day in our communities–after-school and weekend programs, and summer programs, whether they be in person or online–and these learning opportunities need to be available and affordable for all. We need to support an early start to continued language learning, and immersion programs through our educators, our schools, and educational policy.

In addition to supporting our schools and our educators, we can also support the learning and use of French in our society–through supporting local businesses who offer services in French, through internships and experiential learning allowing students to use their language skills and to actually demonstrate the benefits of language knowledge in real-life situations, through creativity, through local community programs, and by supporting local media in French. However, the resurgence of French depends on a broad coalition of support, including those who speak French and those who may not, not yet. Many Americans of French heritage have been North America for hundreds of years, and some may have limited knowledge of French,or may not speak French at all. It is important for the French space to be inclusive–including all supporters, no matter what their language skills may be.

It is important for all of us who care about the French language, about the powerful ideas and core values it has expressed and articulated, about our role as global citizens in a multilingual world, and–most importantly–about the language of our families and of United States history and culture, to work together to build an evolving French presence in our country. We can best do this as individuals and by working together, leveraging existing resources and skills sets to make the case for French and for language learning and multilingualism generally. While resourcefulness, energy, and perseverance characterize successful campaigns, and the methods range from informal conversations to social media campaigns and political action, the defense and promotion of languages and language learning are most effectively framed by and grounded in advocacy, leadership, and social movements.

In order to bring about the resurgence of French in an increasingly multilingual United States, it is necessary that all who support French language and Francophone culture work together to provide the opportunity to learn French to all interested students from the earliest grade levels and to support immersion programs. Beyond the classroom, we need to promote the use of French in our society, from our homes and communities to our arts and media–and, importantly, in the workplace and business settings. This is a complex process, involving education and the development of both proficiency and pre-professional skills as well as the creation of career pathways through partnerships with business and government and the development of internships and authentic experiential learning.

Most importantly, we must be inclusive, working to meet the needs of all French language and Francophone culture supporters, developing initiatives, learning opportunities, and events that respond to a wide range of interests and language skills. It is especially important to always bear in mind the needs of both the anglophone French-language learner and the Francophone parent and family seeking to maintain a heritage language. Most importantly, language learning must be accessible and affordable for all interested students, offering traditional classes in schools and educational institutions, as well as after-school, weekend, and summer programs, both online and onsite.

The authors of the preceding chapters have clearly demonstrated the importance of French language and Francophone culture in the world, in the United States, in our past and present, and–most importantly–in our lives and in the lives of our children. It is up to us to honor our multilingual past and heritage and to step up to the challenge of advocacy– to protect and promote an integral part of our American cultural identity whose future has not yet been secured. It is equally important to prepare our present and future generations for their role as global citizens in a multilingual world, in which French plays a preeminent role. We can do this! Let us work together to support our educators and all our local French language and Francophone culture initiatives! *L'Union fait la force!*

References

AMERICAN ACADEMY OF ARTS & SCIENCES. 2017. America's Languages: Investing in Language Education for the 21st Century.

AMERICAN ACADEMY OF ARTS AND SCIENCES. 2021. "Bachelor's Degrees in the Humanities"

AMERICAN CONFERENCE ON THE TEACHING OF FOREIGN LANGUAGES. 2019. Making Languages Our Business: Addressing Foreign Language Demand among United States Employers.

AMERICAN COUNCILS FOR INTERNATIONAL EDUCATION. 2017. The National K-12 Foreign Language Enrollment Survey Report.

ANCELET, B. 1988. A perspective on teaching the "problem language" in Louisiana. The French Review, 61(3), 345- 356.

ANCELET, B. J. 2007. Negotiating the mainstream: The Creoles and Cajuns in Louisiana. The French Review, 80(6), 1235-1255.

ANCTIL, P. 1979. La Franco-américanie ou le Québec d'en bas. Cahiers de géographie du Québec, 23.58, 39-52. 2000. French Canadian Emigration to the United States, 1840-1930.

ANYA, U. & RANDOLPH, L. J. 2019. Diversifying language educators and learners. The Language Educator. 23-27. October/November 2019.

BÉLANGER, D. 2000. French Canadian Emigration to the United States, 1840-1930. Readings in Québec History. Marianopolis College.

BÉLANGER, D. 2002. L'abbé Lionel Groulx et la survivance franco-américaine. Francophonies d'Amerique (13), 91-105.

BELBASE, S. LUITEL, B, & TAYLOR, P. C. 2008. Autoethnography: A method of research and teaching for transformative education. Journal of Education and Research, 1(1), 86-95.

BLOOD, E. 2019. French-Canadian Heritage Collection. Salem State University Archives and Special Collections.

BLOOD, E. MORRISETTE, J.V. Je me souviens : histoire, culture et littérature du Québec Francophone. Georgetown University Press, 2015.

BLOOD, E. DUCLOS-ORSELLO, E. 2011. Franco-American Salem Oral History Collection, M.11. Salem State University Archives and Special Collections.

BLOOD, E. DUCLOS-ORSELLO, E. 2018. French-Canadian and Franco-American Heritage in Salem, Massachusetts. Salem State University Archives and Special Collections.

BLOOD, E. DUCLOS-ORSELLO, E. 2018. "La Pointe, site de patrimoine franco-américain à Salem, Massachusetts" Encyclopédie du patrimoine culturel de l'Amérique du nord.

BRASSEAUX, C. 2005. French, Cajun, Creole, Houma: A primer on Francophone Louisiana. Baton Rouge, LA: Louisiana State University Press.

BRAULT, G J. The French-Canadian Heritage in New England (Hanover, NH: University Press of New England, 1986), 171-84.

CANADA, GLOBAL AFFAIRS. "State Trade Fact Sheets – New Hampshire." GAC, Government of Canada, 21 Jan. 2020,

CAPUTO, J. D. 1997. Deconstruction in a nutshell. A conversation with Jacques Derrida. New York: Fordham University Press, 13-14.

CHAPELLE, C. A. "Five Decades of Canadian and Québec Content in French Textbooks in the United States" American Review of Canadian Studies, vol. 44 no. 4, 2014, pp. 415-432.

CHARAUDEAU, P. 2005. Réflexions sur l'identité culturelle. Un préalable nécessaire à l'enseignement d'une langue. Ecoles, langues et modes de pensée. Creteil : CRDP Académie de Creteil

CHARTIER, A. The Franco-Americans of New England: A History (Manchester, NH: ACA Assurance and Worcester: Institut Français, 2000), 327-389.

CHASSÉ, P. 1977. Les Arts et la littérature chez les Franco-Américains de la Nouvelle-Angleterre. Bedford, N.H./Fall River, Mas. National Assessment and Dissemination Center.

COMITÉ PERMANENT DE LA SURVIVANCE. 1945. La Vocation de la race française en Amérique du Nord. Québec: Ateliers de l'Action catholique.

CULTURAL SERVICE OF THE FRENCH EMBASSY IN US. 2019. French for Professional Purposes.

DAJKO, N. & WALTON, S. 2019. Indigenous Languages. Language in Louisiana: Community and Culture. Jackson, MS: University Press of Mississippi.

DALY, J.A. 2011. Advocacy: Championing Ideas and Influencing Others. New Haven: Yale.

DAVIS, J. 1992. African-American students and foreign language learning. Eric Digest.

DAVIS, J. J., & Markham, P. 1991. Student attitudes towards foreign language study at historically and predominantly Black institutions. Foreign Language Annals, 24, 227–237.

DIAWARA, M. 2008. Edouard Glissant's World mentality: An Introduction to One world in Relation. Documenta 14

DORSEY, A. & COLLIER R. 2018. Origins of Sociological Theory. Waltham Abbey, Engl.: ED-Tech Press.

DOTY, C. STEWART. 1997. "'Monsieur Maurras Est Ici': French Fascism in Franco-American New England," Journal of Contemporary History 32, no. 4 (1997): 527-38.

DURHAM, Earl of. 1839. Report on the Affairs of British North America. Toronto: Robert Stanton, 127.

FEDERATION DES ALLIANCES FRANÇAISES USA. 2019. About the Alliance française.

FRENCH MORNING. 2017. The French Population Has Officially Increased in North America. October 2, 2017

GAILLARD, A. 1997. Assimilation, insertion, intégration, adaptation : un état des connaissances. Hommes et Migrations (1209), 119-130.

GATINEAU, F. 1927. Historique des Conventions Générales des Canadiens-Français aux Etats-Unis 1865-1901. Woonsocket : L'Union Saint-Jean Baptiste d'Amérique.

GIGUÈRE, M. Ed. 1981. A Franco-American Overview, Vol. 3: New England (Part One). Cambridge, MA: National Assessment and Bilingual/Bicultural Education.

GLYNN, C. L. 2012. The role of ethnicity in the foreign language classroom: Perspectives on African American students' enrollment, experiences, and identity. Doctoral Dissertation, University of Minnesota.

GROULX, L. 1956. L'Appel de la race. Montréal : Fides.

HAMON, E. 1982. Les Canadiens-Français de la Nouvelle-Angleterre. Montréal/Manchester, N.H. : Éditions du 45e Parallèle Nord Inc.

HEGEL, G. W. F. 2019. The Phenomenology of Spirit. Cambridge: Cambridge University Press.

HÉMON, L. 1924. Maria Chapdelaine. Paris: Grasset.

HIGHAM, J. 1955. Strangers in the Land: Patterns of American Nativism, 1860-1925. New Brunswick: Rutgers University Press.

HOOKS, B. 1989. Choosing the margin as a space of radical openness. Framework: The Journal of Cinema and Media, (36), 15-23.

HOOKS, B. 1994. Teaching to Transgress: Education as the Practice of Freedom. New York, NY: Routledge.

HUBBARD, L. J. 2014. Foreign language study and the Black student. CLA Journal, 57(4), 300-304.

HUDSON, C. 2000. Les Protestants Francophones en Nouvelle-Angleterre, 1885-1910. Études d'histoire religieuse (66), 49-68.

JAUMONT, F. 2017. The Bilingual Revolution: The Future of Education Is in Two Languages. NY: TBR.

JOHNSON, S. 2019. Colleges Lose a 'Stunning' 651 Foreign-Language Programs in 3 Years.

KLINGER, T. A. 2003. Language labels and language use among Cajuns and Creoles in Louisiana. University of Pennsylvania Working Papers in Linguistics, 9(2), 77-90.

LACROIX, P. 2021. "Une révolution tranquille chez les Franco-Américains," Le Droit, April 25, 2021.

LANDRY, T-M. 1962. Mission catholique et française en Nouvelle-Angleterre. Québec: Éditions Ferland.

LASSITER, L.E. 1989. The relationship between race and attitudes of students toward foreign language study at selected universities. Doctoral Dissertation, The University of Mississippi. Proquest Dissertation Publishing.

LEMAIRE, H. 1966. Franco-American efforts on behalf of the French language in New England. In J. A. Fishman (Ed.), Language loyalty in the United States (pp. 253-279). The Hague, The Netherlands: Mouton & Co.

LEVEEN, S. 2021. America's Bilingual Century. Delray Beach, FL: America the Bilingual.

LIBRARY OF CONGRESS, Religion and the Founding of the American Republic. America as a Religious Refuge: The Seventeenth Century, Part 2

LINDNER, T. 2008. Attitudes toward Cajun French and International French in South Louisiana: A study of high school students. Doctoral Dissertation. Proquest.

LINDNER, T. 2013. Access to French education and attitudes toward international French and Cajun French among South Louisiana high school students. French Review, 86(3), 458-472.

LO BIANCO, J., & PEYTON, J. K. 2013. Vitality of heritage languages in the United States: The role of capacity, opportunity, and desire. Heritage Language Journal, 10(3), i-viii.

MCCULLOUGH, J. J. 2021. "Opinion: Québec wants to declare itself a 'nation.' Canada's politicians do not mind," The Washington Post, May 28, 2021.

MENDEZ, M. 2013. Autoethnography as research method: Advantages, limitations, and criticisms. Columbian Applied Linguistics Journal, 15(2), 279-287.

MINISTERE DES AFFAIRES ETRANGERES ET EUROPEENNES. 2021. International Strategy for the French Language and Multilingualism.

MLA Language Map Data Center. "Fort Kent (Town of), Maine."

MLA Language Map Data Center. "Most Spoken Languages in New Hampshire in 2010."

MODERN LANGUAGE ASSOCIATION (MLA). (2019). Enrollments in Languages Other Than English in United States Institutions of Higher Education.

MONTLAUR, B de. 2019. Do you speak my language? You should. New York Times, March 3, 2019.

MOORE, Z., & ENGLISH, M. 1997. Linguistic and cultural comparisons: Middle school African American students learning Arabic. In J. Phillips (Ed.), Collaborations: New goals, new realities (pp. 173–211). New York: Northeastern Conference Reports.

MOORE, Z., & English, M. 1998. Successful teaching strategies: Findings from a case study of middle school African Americans learning Arabic. Foreign Language Annals, 31, 347–357.

NADEAU, J-B. 2021. 33 millions de Francophones dans les Amériques

NATIONAL CENTER FOR EDUCATIONAL STATISTICS. 2021. Table 322.30. Bachelor's degrees conferred by postsecondary institutions: 2017-18 and 2018-19.

NEW AMERICAN ECONOMY. 2017. Not Lost in Translation: The Growing Importance of Foreign Language Skills in the United States Job Market.

NEW HAMPSHIRE DEPARTMENT OF HEALTH. "Refugee Resettlement Country of Origin FY 2013-2019." NewHampshire Department of Health and Human Services.

NIETO, S. 1992. Affirming Diversity: The Sociopolitical Context of Multicultural Education. White Plains, NY: Longman Publishing Group.

NORTHOUSE, P.G. 2013. Leadership: Theory and Practice 6th ed. Los Angeles: SAGE.

ORGANISATION INTERNATIONALE DE LA FRANCOPHONIE. Cadre stratégique de la Francophonie 2015-2022.

PBS. 2018. A Louisiana French Renaissance. Louisiana Public Broadcasting. March 15, 2018

PERREAULT, R.B., 2010. Franco-American Life and Culture in Manchester, New Hampshire: Vivre la Différence. Charleston, S.C.: The History Press

POLLOCK, D. 2018. Black students' experiences and motivation to pursue foreign language study at an HBCU: A holistic single case study. Doctoral Dissertation, Florida State University. ProQuest.

PRATT, C. 2012. Are African-American high school students less motivated to learning Spanish than other ethnic groups? Hispania 95(1), 116-134.

QUINTAL, C. 1990. Les Institutions Franco-Américaines : Pertes et Progrès [Franco-American institutions: Losses and progres]. In R. D. Louder (Ed.), Le Québec et les francophones de la Nouvelle-Angleterre. CEFAN Culture française d'Amérique. Les Presses de l'Université Laval.RAFN, S. 2013. Jacques Derrida: Of Hospitality. Voices on Asylum and Migration Visavis. February 2013.

REYNOLDS, C. 2021. "Trudeau calls for end to 'Québec bashing' after Ottawa professor says province run by 'white supremacist government'," National Post, March 22, 2021.

ROCHE, F. 1981. Les Francos de la Nouvelle-Angleterre. Anthologie Franco-Américaine, XIXe et XXe siècles. Le Creusot: Coédition LARC/Centre d'Accueil Culturel.

ROSS, Jane Flatau. Two Centuries of French Education in New York: The Role of Schools in Cultural Diplomacy. TBR Books, New York, 2020.

ROSS J., & JAUMONT, F. 2014. French heritage language communities in the United States. In T. Wiley, J. Peyton, D. Christian, S. C. Moore, & N. Liu (Eds.), Handbook of heritage and community languages in the United States: Research, educational practice, and policy. Oxford, UK: Routledge.

ROSS, J., & JAUMONT, F. 2013. French heritage language vitality in the United States. [Special Issue on Language Vitality in the U.S.] Heritage Journal Review, 10(3).

ROSS J., & JAUMONT, F. 2012. Building bilingual communities: New York's French bilingual revolution. In O. Garcia, Z. Zakharia, & B. Otcu (Eds.), Bilingual community education and multilingualism (pp 232-246). New York, NY: Multilingual Matters.

RYAN, C. 2010. Language Use in the United States: 2011. American Community Survey.

SALOMONE, R. 2021. The Rise of English: Global Politics and the Power of Language. Oxford University Press.

SANTERRE, R. 1981. Anthologie de la littérature franco-américaine de la Nouvelle-Angleterre, Tome 9. Manchester, N.H.: National Materials Development Center for French & Creole.

SATELL, G. and POPOVIC. S. 2017. How Protests Become Successful Social Movements. https://hbr.org/2017/01/how-protests-become-successful-social-movements

SERRES, M. 1993. Les Origines de la géométrie. Tiers livre des fondations. Paris : Flammarion.

SICO, J. & BRUNET, R. 2020. New York, la capitale méconnue de la Francophonie. March 20, 2020.

SUKIENNIK, G. "Senate passes resolution apologizing for role in eugenics," Bennington Banner, May 12, 2021.

U.S. CENSUS BUREAU. 2019. Table B16001: Language spoken at home by ability to speak English for the population 5 years and over, United States. American Community Survey 2019 1-year Estimates.

UUSC. 2022. U.S. Tribes Facing Climate Crisis Unite to Address Human Rights Violations uusc.org/initiatives/climate-justice/special-rapporteur-letter

VALDMAN, A. 2010. French in the USA. In Potowski K. (Ed.), Language diversity in the USA (pp. 110-127). Cambridge University Press

VERMETTE, D. 2016. Why are Franco- Americans So Invisible? French North America. March 2016.

VERMETTE, D. 2018. A Distinct Alien Race. The Untold story of Franco-Americans. Montréal: Baraka Books.

WATTERSON, K. 2011. The attitudes of African American students towards the study of foreign languages and cultures. Doctoral Dissertation, Louisiana State University.

WOODSON, C. G. 1990. The Mis-Education of the Negro. Trenton, NJ: Africa World Press.

WRIGHT, C. D. The Canadian French in New England, Massachusetts Bureau of Statistics of Labor, from the 13th Annual Report for 1881, Boston, 1882.

ZEPHYR, F. 2004. The Haitian Americans. Westport, CT: Greenwood Press.

ZUNZ, O. 1987. Genèse du pluralisme américain. Annales (42) 2, 429-444 Public Collections

Notes

1. As Patrick Charaudeau puts it, "the idea that culture is like an "essence", which sticks to the people, is born in the 18th century. To that extent, each nation was seen as characterized by its own "genius". More rational in France (it is the Enlightenment and the triumph of reason over barbarism), more irrational in Germany (it is the century of an anti-scientist philosophy and the triumph of romanticism)" (2005: my translation). For cultural difference is a master word borrowed from G. Wilhelm Friedrich Hegel's The Phenomenology of Spirit (Phänomenologie des Geistes, 1807). According to the Hegelian theory, every nation on the earth has its own national spirit that represents the ideal this nation is trying to reach.

2. HAMON, Edouard. 1982. Les Canadiens français de la Nouvelle-Angleterre, Montréal – Manchester, N.H: Editions du 45e Parallèle Nord Inc., p. 143: "These emigrants, we believe, are called of God to cooperate in the conversion of America, just as their ancestors were called to plant faith on the banks of the Saint Lawrence" (my translation), p. 146: "The march of colonization towards the United States has begun, nothing will stop it from now on" (my translation).

3. HUDON, Christine. 2000. Les protestants francophones en Nouvelle-Angleterre, 1885-1910. Études d'histoire religieuse. 66, 64-65: "The opposition of the Catholic authorities and their followers manifests itself in different ways. Protestant sources abound with examples of pressure and physical or psychological violence suffered by converts. Mothers anxious for the future and for the salvation of their apostate children burn lanterns for their return to the Catholic faith. Some are beaten, disinherited, or thrown into the streets by their parents. In the Little Canadas, neophytes are insulted, singled out, excluded from national organizations, such as the Saint-Jean-Baptiste societies. Some lose their homes, others their jobs. From the pulpit, priests call for a boycott of businesses belonging to Protestants. Prayer meetings are disrupted: eggs, stones, sticks are flowing at the pastors and their audience. Sometimes, spirits heat up so much that Protestants and Catholics come to blows. In the spring and summer of 1894, the police intervened on a number of occasions to suppress the riots, which rocked the "Canadians Coast" in Worcester. The following year, similar tumults stirred the town of Danielson, Connecticut. The police intervention resulted in the arrest of some demonstrators.

4. As Jacques Derrida puts it, "fighting for your own identity is not exclusive of another identity, is open to another identity. And this prevents totalitarianism, nationalism, egocentrism, and so on" (CAPUTO, John D. 1997. Deconstruction in a nutshell. A conversation with Jacques Derrida, New York: Fordham University Press, p. 13-14).

5. The author assumes his multiple identity without any complex: "Et désormais je sais que j'aurai deux patries/La France, et toi, Amérique" (SANTERRE, Richard. 1981. Anthologie de la littérature franco-americaine de la Nouvelle-Angleterre, Tome 9. Manchester, N.H.: National Materials Development Center for French & Creole).

6. Jane Ross and Fabrice Jaumont "French Heritage Language Vitality in the United States "New York University Heritage Language Journal, 10(3) Winter, 2013.

7. Heritage Language Students: Profiles and Possibilities Guadalupe Valdés Stanford University Heritage Speaker definition:

8. Jane F. Ross and Fabrice Jaumont: "French Heritage Language Communities in the United States".

9. Building bilingual communities: New York's French bilingual revolution Jane F. Ross Fabrice Jaumont Published in Garcia O., Zakharia Z., Bahar Otcu G. Bilingual Community Education for American Children: Beyond Heritage Languages in a Global City. Multilingual Matters: New York. 2012

10. Maya Angela, Smith Université of Washington French Heritage Language Learning: A Site of Multilingual Identity Formation, Cultural Exploration, and Creative Expression in New York City

11. OIF (Organisation Internationale de la Francophonie): francophonie.org/node/305

12. 70% of them will be under 29.

13. Lauren Ducrey: Social Impact Assessment, HEC, 2016

14. Fabrice Jaumont The Bilingual Revolution: The Future of Education is in Two Languages by Fabrice Jaumont (TBR Books, 2017)

15. 2018-2019 English Language Learners Demographic Report NYC Department of Education: infohub.nyced.org/docs/default-source/default-document-library/ell-demographic-report.pdf

16. US Census Bureau 2018, Languages spoken at home.

17. Carlos Echeverria-Estrada and Jeanne Batalova: Sub-Saharan African Immigrants in the United States, November 6, 2019, Online Journal of the Migration Policy Institute.

18. Culturally Responsive-Sustaining Education Framework nysed.gov/crs/framework

19. The International Network for Public High Schools is a consortium of schools which only welcome students who have been in the US for 4 years or less. As stated on their website, "at International High Schools, a badge of prestige replaces the "stigma" of immigrant status for students, families, and faculty. It is understood that near native fluency in English and proficiency in a second language are valuable resources.

20. Jane F. Ross Fabrice Jaumont: Building bilingual communities: New York's French bilingual revolution Published in Garcia O., Zakharia Z., Bahar Otcu G. Bilingual Community Education for American Children: Beyond Heritage Languages in a Global City. Multilingual Matters: New York. 2012

21. Louisiana Travel Association, louisianatravelassociation.org

22. Louisiana Office of Tourism, Department of Research

23. University of Louisiana at Lafayette Department of Management, management.louisiana.edu/programs/hospitality-management-major

24. Council for the Development of French in Louisiana and Louisiana Department of Education

25. CODOFIL French Friendly Oui: crt.state.la.us/cultural-development/codofil/programs/francoresponsable

26. Per the OUI! website: "Due to frequent changes in the service industry, this initiative requires constant updates. CODOFIL makes an effort to update this information regularly but cannot always assure its validity."

27. Joseph Dunn, Director of Public Relations & Marketing, Laura: Louisiana's Creole Heritage Site

28. David Cheramie, Executive Director, Bayou Vermilion District

29. Out of respect for the woman's privacy, I have changed both her first and last name, replacing them with other common Louisiana names that are equally as French.

30. The site includes some resources for Kouri-Vini (Louisiana Creole) as well. CODOFIL is also supporting a project by a partner organization to develop a separate site entirely devoted to Kouri-Vini.

31. Abeille means 'bee.' Bourdon means 'bumblebee.'

32. "You live your culture, or you kill your culture - there's no middle ground."

33. "We are the last generation! We are the last generation!"

34. An opinion piece entitled "Le Cajun mort-vivant" ("The living-dead Cajun") appeared in Le Journal de Montréal in October 2016.

35. "As soon as we're ready to close the coffin on the cadaver of French in Louisiana, well, the cadaver sits up and asks for a beer." I attribute the quote to both men because I have heard both of them say it and am not sure where it originated.

36. The term Black is meant to denote students of Afro-diasporic roots (e.g., Haitian, Afro-Canadian, Afro-Mexican, Nigerian, Senegalese). The term African American is used to denote students with Afro-diasporic roots with a lineage extending only from those born in the United States of America.

37. The term Black and African American will be used interchangeably throughout the rest of this chapter to reflect the labels used by the NCES & LBoR.

38. Fanzine: a zine is a small magazine created by amateurs, hand-made, copied in a small number, on a particular topic or for a specific audience.

39. francophoniedesameriques.com/zone-franco/la-francophonie-des-ameriques

40. Beaudoin-Bégin, Anne-Marie. "La langue affranchie – Se racommoder avec l'évolution linguisitique", Éditions Somme toute, 2017, p. 112.

41. Baggage, documentary by Paul Tom and Melissa Lefebvre, Picbois Production, 2018. vimeo.com/ondemand/baggagefilm

    A wonderful book of poetry linked to this project exists: Bagages, mon histoire. Poems were written by the same newcomers, learning French as a foreign language. Writing sessions were conducted by their teacher and the author Simon Boulerice. English translation has been published under "Carry-on, poetry by young immigrants".

42. William H. Keating journal titled Voyage in a Six-oared Skiff to the Falls of St. Anthony in 1817, published in 1860. See also Jay Gitlin, The Bourgeois Frontier: French Towns, French Traders, and American Expansion, (Yale University Press, 2010).

43. Charles Flandrau, The History of Minnesota and Tales of the Frontier, (E.W. Porter, St. Paul, Minnesota,1900), p.400. This quote is in an article titled An Advocate's Opinion on his Own Eloquence is Not Always Reliable, pp. 400-401.

44. Le Sueur first entered the Minnesota region in 1683, so it is believed this is when he named the river.

45. Christine Marie Petto, When France was King of Cartography: The Patronage and Production of Maps in Early Modern France, (Lanham Lexington Books, 2007).

46. William E. Lass, Minnesota: A History, Second Edition, (W. W. Norton & Company, 2000), pp. 77-79.

47. David Lavender, Winner Take All, The Trans-Canada Canoe Trail, (McGraw-Hill Book Company, 1977), pp. 200-201.

48. Information obtained from article titled The Fur Trade-Indian Country, Wisconsin, (published by the Milwaukee Public Museum, 2018).

49. William E. Lass, Minnesota: A History, Second Edition, (W. W. Norton & Company, 2000), pp. 70-83. For a more complete history of the War of 1812, see Walter R. Borneman, 1812, The War that Forged a Nation, (Harper Collins Publishers, New York, 2004).

50. Will Ferguson, Canadian History for Dummies, Second Edition, (John Wiley and Sons, Mississauga, Ontario, 2005), pp. 181-182, 184.

51. Mary Lethert Wingerd, North Country, the Making of Minnesota, Illustrations complied and annotated by Kirsten Delegard, (University of Minnesota Press, Minneapolis, 2010), p.124

52. Mark Labine, In the beginning, there was a Chapel, (published by the French-American Heritage Foundation, 2016).

53. William E. Lass, History of Minnesota, (W.W. Norton & Company, 2000), p. 66.

54. Mary Lethert Wingerd, North Country, the Making of Minnesota, Illustrations complied and annotated by Kirsten Delegard, (University of Minnesota Press, Minneapolis, 2010), p.125.

55. Jay Gitlin, The Bourgeois Frontier: French Towns, French Traders, and American Expansion, (Yale University Press, 2010).

56. Jean Lamarre, French-Canadians of Michigan, (Wayne State Community Press, 2003); See also Aidan D. McQuillan, "French-Canadian Communities in the Upper Midwest during the Nineteenth Century," Cahiers de Géographie du Québec, vol. 23, n° 58, 1979, pp. 53-72, and also John P. Dulong, French-Canadians in Michigan, (Michigan State University Press, 2001).

57. Ives Roby, The Franco-Americans of New England: Dreams and Realities, (Mcgill Queens University Press, May 16, 2005) pp. 11-12.

58. Andrew R.L Clayton. Richard Sisson, and Chris Zacher, The American Midwest: An Interpretive Encyclopedia, (Indiana University Press; 1st Edition, November 8, 2006) p.199.

59. Holy Family Church Files located in St. Cloud Visitor Office, St. Cloud.

60. Annabell Raiche, CSJ, and Ann Marie Biermaier, OSB, "They Came to Teach" the Story of Sisters who Taught in Parochial Schools and Their Contribution to Elementary Education in Minnesota, (North Star Press of St. Cloud, Inc. 1994).

61. "Illinois" is the modern spelling for the early French Catholic missionaries and explorers' name for the Illinois Native Americans.

62. Andrew R.L. Clayton and Richard Sisson, and Chris Zacher, The American Midwest: An Interpretive Encyclopedia, (Indiana University Press, 2007), p.199.

63. Echo de l'Quest, July 28, 1911.

64. Echo de l'Quest, October 19, 1893, February 1, 1895; Le Canadien, March 17, 1887 and September 13, 1888.

65. Sarah Rubenstein, The French-Canadians and French, found in June Drenning Holmquist, They Chose Minnesota, a Survey of The State's Ethnic Groups, (Minnesota Historical Society Press, 1981), p.49.

66. Sarah Rubenstein, The French-Canadians and French, found in June Drenning Holmquist, They Chose Minnesota, a Survey of The State's Ethnic Groups, (Minnesota Historical Society Press, 1981), p.49; and Henry Scholberg, The French Pioneers of Minnesota/Les Pioniers Francais du Minnesota, (Northstar, Eau Claire, Wisc.,1996).

67. Maximilienne Tetrault, Le Role de la Presse dans l'"Evolution du people Franco-Americain de la Nouvelle Angleterre, (Marseilles, France, 1935), pp. 35-37.

68. Sarah Rubenstein, The French-Canadians and the French. found in Holmquist, June Drenning, They Chose Minnesota, a Survey of The State's Ethnic Groups, (Minnesota Historical Society Press, 1981).

69. "Publications in Foreign Languages: French", Ayer & Son's American Newspaper Annual, (N. W. Ayer & Son, Philadelphia, 1907).

70. W.B. Hennessy, Past and Present St. Paul, Minnesota, being a relation of the progressive history of the capital city of Minnesota from the earliest historical times down to the present day, (S.J. Clarke Publishing Company, Chicago, Illinois, 1906).

71. Id.

72. Sarah Rubenstein, The French-Canadians and French, found in Holmquist, June Drenning, They Chose Minnesota, a Survey of The State's Ethnic Groups, (Minnesota Historical Society Press, 1981), p. 48.

73. Id. pp. 48

74. Id. pp. 48

75. Id. p. 48

About the Authors

Mélissa Baril is an ideater and problem solver. Her common thread: publishing. Her approach: transmission. The big idea: to connect people through cultural diversity. Moving to Detroit, she found out a new playground to promote French youth literature and culture in a community surrounded by Francophone roots. As a parent, she was struggling to find books and resources to nurture the language with her children. She figured out she was not the only one and created the Caribou à lunettes: a French youth library with creative workshops and activities with authors and illustrators, for native speakers and learners. She recently launched an online bookstore to support parents and teachers in the United States in their search for books in French, offering quality, diverse and inclusive stories. Because understanding and sharing cultures is the key for just movements.

Timothy Beaulieu is the founder of NH PoutineFest. He was named to the 2019 New Hampshire Union Leader 40 under Forty class for his work on the event. He received his B.S. from the University of New Hampshire and his M.B.A. from Plymouth State University. Tim currently lives in southern New Hampshire. He enjoys being very involved in the Franco community, working on small business projects, and spending with his family.

Dr. Elizabeth Blood is Professor of French in the World Languages and Cultures Department at Salem State University in Salem, Massachusetts. She earned her B.A. in Anthropology from Connecticut College, and her M.A. and Ph.D. in French and Romance Literatures from Boston College. She is co-author of *Je me souviens: histoire, culture et littérature*, a Québec culture reader for students of French (Georgetown University Press, 2015). She is also a French to English translator who has established a digital repository of free translations of Québécois and Franco-American texts. Her current research focus is on North American Francophonie, including Québec and Franco-America.

A native Louisiana Cajun, **Dr. David Cheramie** is the author of three books of French poetry and has published numerous articles about Louisiana French and culture in English and French, notably his regular features, *En français, s'il vous plaît* and *Plus ça change...*, in Acadiana Profile magazine. He has a doctorate in Francophone Studies from the University of Louisiana at Lafayette and is the former executive director the Council for the Development of French in Louisiana. He is the co-founder of the literary review, Feux Follets, to which he is a regular contributor. He is a Knight in France's Order of Arts and Letters and a member of Québec's Order of American Francophones. He is presently the Chief Executive Officer of the Bayou Vermilion District, which operates Vermilionville, a Living History Museum and Folklife Park in Lafayette, LA.

Melody Desjardins is a freelance writer and shares the Franco-American experience through personal stories and lighthearted topics on her blog, Moderne Francos. Through writing blog posts, Melody hopes to reach other Franco-Americans and discuss older topics with new perspectives. She is originally from Wilton, NH, and spent most of her formative years in Lake Sundown, IA. She currently resides in New Hampshire. You can check out her blog at modernefrancos.com.

Anthony Thomas DesRois - Feature Writer for Get French Football News, social media contributor for *Franco-Américains* pages, husband, and father, Anthony Thomas DesRois was raised in Florida in a Franco-American household with his grandmother until eventually moving in with his wife's family as a teen. His hobbies include writing, painting, reading, playing soccer, and spending time with his family.

Joseph Dunn's understanding of Louisiana's French and Creole languages, cultures, and heritage has afforded him the opportunity to work at the highest levels of the state's tourism and cultural industries for more than 25 years. He is currently the director of public relations and marketing at Laura: Louisiana's Creole Heritage Site. In addition to his work at Laura, Joseph regularly collaborates on projects that highlight the social, professional, and economic value of Louisiana French and Creole. Joseph Dunn is a Knight in the French National Order of Merit.

Dr. Georgie V. Ferguson is a member of the Pointe-Au-Chien Indian Tribe. She is a clinical psychologist and devoted parent who is proud to represent her Tribe as the first Tribal member to earn a Ph.D. Dr. Ferguson currently serves as the Pointe-Au-Chien Indian Tribe's Public Affairs/Communications Specialist and manages the Tribe's Twitter account. She also has a background in Mass Communication, that marries well with her training in Psychology, which she applies to her work for the Tribe as well as when advocating for ethical standards of practice in engaging with Indigenous populations by the community at large. In addition, she is involved in a variety of research projects focused on Indigenous Resilience.

Dr. Katharine Harrington is Professor of French at Plymouth State University where she has taught since 2010. She is the author of *Writing the Nomadic Experience in French and Francophone Literature* (Lexington Books, 2014). She is co-founder of the Bienvenue au New Hampshire initiative and currently serves as President of the American Council of Québec Studies and President of the New Hampshire chapter of the American Association of Teachers of French.

Marine Havel is an international leader recognized for building bridges between organizations and people. She believes that education can dramatically improve the social and economic outcomes of every child, change societies, and that access to a high- quality education is a right for all. In 2012, she launched a nonprofit organization in Philadelphia to implement a FLAM program (French as a Native language) in Philadelphia for French-speaking kids to be sure that no child will lose her/his/their language, and their cultural heritage, their identity as global citizens, their link to their family and to the Francophone community. She rapidly created new schools in Princeton, Allentown, PA, and she will open one soon in Hoboken, NJ. To support other FLAM associations, she created the Federation FLAM USA with other FLAM in the United States. When the pandemic started, we were ready to support all teachers and be sure that all students could continue to receive a French education! Since June 2020, our support goes to all FLAM in the world, with whom we are creating a Federation FLAM World, with the support of the French government.

Dr. Fabrice Jaumont is a scholar-practitioner, award-winning author, non-profit leader, and education advisor based in New York. He currently serves as Education Attaché for the Embassy of France to the United States, a Research Fellow at Fondation Maison des Sciences de l'Homme in Paris, and an adjunct professor both at New York University and Baruch College. He is President of the Center for the Advancement of Languages, Education, and Communities, a nonprofit publishing organization based in New York and Paris. He has published six books on bilingualism and education, philanthropy and higher education, including *The Bilingual Revolution: The Future of Education is in Two Languages*. Jaumont holds a Ph.D. in Comparative and International Education from New York University.

Dr. Marguerite P. Justus is a native of Lafayette, Louisiana, and an activist for the state's French-speaking minority. She took an interestin the language of her maternal grandparents at an early age and completed her doctorate in French Studies (with a specialization in Linguistics) at Louisiana State University in 2017. She is currently in charge of community programs for the Council for the Developmentof French in Louisiana and serves on the board of directors for Louisiana Folk Roots and the advisory board for the upcoming Saint- Luc French Immersion & Cultural Campus in Arnaudville,Louisiana.

Dr. Emmanuel K. Kayembe received his Ph.D. in French Language and Literature from the University of Cape Town. He was therecipient of the Golden Key International Honour Society Award for his outstanding achievement at the University of Cape Town in 2012. Former Research Fellow at American Council of Learned Societies (Carnegie Corporation, New York, 2012), he has served as a Senior Lecturer and a Teaching Assistant respectively at the University of Lubumbashi and at the University of Cape Town, before joining the University of Botswana, where he taught French Language,Literature and Culture from 2013 to 2017. He is currently working as an Instructor of French and Latin and a Research Associate for Franco-American Studies at University of Southern Maine Franco- American Collection, whose mission is to preserve and to promote culture and heritage of Maine's Franco-American population. Apart from having extensively published on Francophone literatures and cultures, he is the author of a book on the Francophone Congolese writer Pius Ngandu, Professor at Louisiana State University (Baton Rouge). He has contributed to several AUF funded-research projects on French and Francophone literatures and cultures. He is a member of the Association pour l'Étude des Littératures Africaines (Université de la Lorraine), the Modern Language Association, the Association Internationale d'Étude des Littératures et Cultures de l'Espace Francophone (McGill University), the Conseil International d'Études Francophones, the American Association of Teachers of French, and of the Centre de la francophonie des Amériques.

Dr. Etienne A. Kouakou is affiliated to Hostos Community College, where he has served as an instructor in the City University of New York's Language Immersion Program since January 2013. His primary area of interest is English as a Second Language. However, he is also interested in writing and rhetoric, and he currently teaches various freshman English composition courses at Queens College. Many years ago, he was a secondary school English as a Foreign Language teacher in his native Ivory Coast. When he moved to the United States in 1996, he became a middle and high school English teacher here in New York. He also spent a year teaching middle school English in Washington, DC in the 2009-2010 school year. Back in New York after this stint, he taught French in the French Heritage Program administered by the Cultural Services of the French Embassy. In his spare time, he enjoys reading, writing, and practicing Shotokan Karate, a Japanese martial art, which has been his passion for over forty years.

Mark Labine graduated from the University of Minnesota in 1977 and received a J.D. from Hamline University School of Law in 1980. He practiced Law and worked part time as an Administrative Law Judge, Arbitrator, Magistrate, Referee and Mediator until June 2005 when he appointed to be a full-time Judicial Referee for Hennepin County District Court. He retired in March 2020 and has served in temporary judicial assignments since his retirement. Mark has served on numerous non-profit boards and is currently the president of the French-American Heritage Foundation and past president of La Société Canadienne-Française du Minnesota. He is also on the board of directors for Dispute Resolution Center, Community Mediation Minnesota, the State Office of Collaboration and Dispute

Resolution, and the ADR Section for the Minnesota State Bar Association. Mark has taken a keen interest in his French-Canadian ancestry and genealogy. He has written a number of books on his family history and ancestors. His book, *Ancestral Pathways*, documents over 1700 of his ancestors, including many French ancestral lines that go back to France. He also is the chief author or compiler of three books published by the French-American Heritage Foundation, including *They Spoke French*, *In the beginning there was a Chapel*, and *Where the Waters Meet*.

Ben Levine is a documentary filmmaker, trained as a clinical psychologist. Aspects of his video feedback approach to filmmaking to deepen and recall emotional response and creative action to further the story, starting in 1971 at a camp for teens with disabilities, are illustrated in the 2020 Oscar-nominated film *Crip Camp*. **Julia Schulz**, trained in Cultural Anthropology and French, became a French Teacher, curriculum innovator, and co-founder of a nonprofit language school. Together they founded Speaking Place, a nonprofit with support from grants from the Administration for Native Americans, the National Science Foundation, the CDC, the Maine Community Foundation, and other donors. For more information about their current work, see speakingplace.org, especially "Key Concepts" in the Archives section.

Jesse Martineau, Esq. and **Monique Cairns**, like their parents, grew up in Manchester, New Hampshire. They can trace all branches of their family tree back to towns in Québec. Jesse and Monique are products of Manchester's Catholic school system. Jesse holds a B.A. in History from the George Washington University in Washington, DC and a Juris Doctor from Temple University in Philadelphia, Pennsylvania. He has served two terms as a State Representative in New Hampshire and hosts the French-Canadian Legacy Podcast. Monique has a B.A. in Social Science Secondary Education from Providence College in Providence, Rhode Island, and a Master of Science in Special Education from the University of Southern Maine in Portland. Monique owns and operates Northern Explosion, a dance studio in Sanford, Maine. Jesse is an Assistant County Attorney in Hillsborough County, New Hampshire, and Monique works for Southern New Hampshire University.

Jean Mirvil is a Haitian-American who has specialized in working with immigrant children and their families for nearly three decades as a teacher, administrator, and principal in the New York City Public School system. After studying French Literature and Linguistics at Queens College, N.Y, his studies extended at the Sorbonne in France, followed by three years of teaching English to high school students in Gabon, Africa. During his career, he has served as the Bilingual Coordinator and later, Assistant Superintendent for language and immigrant issues, in District 29 Queens. In District 29, he has been principal of elementary schools in Queens, Lead Principal, and Assistant Superintendent for Special Education and Language Learners in the Bronx. In 2009 he was inducted into the Order of Academic Palms, as a knight, an honor which was founded by Napoleon to honor educators. This award was bestowed to him for his success in achieving a model French-English dual-language program at P.S73, which he led until 2013 when he retired from the NYC Board of Education. As a linguist, he served as board member and President of the New York State Association for Bilingual Education and many others. He has been involved in initiatives to improve the educational system for bilingual students nationwide. He authored many teacher supporting articles.

Dr. Jerry L. Parker is an instructor, Undergraduate Program Coordinator, and Director of the Foreign Language Resource Center in the Department of World Languages and Cultures at Southeastern Louisiana University (Hammond, LA) and an adjunct assistant professor of Spanish at Morris Brown College (Atlanta, GA). His research centers on issues of curriculum, instruction, and leadership in foreign language education through the framework of critical multicultural education. He also specializes in Caribbean Studies and Louisiana Studies.

Since 1973, Manchester, N.H. native and lifelong resident **Robert B. Perreault** has worked in various capacities to promote Franco- American culture and Manchester's history. His works of nonfictionand fiction, in French, English or both languages, include seven books and more than 160 articles, essays, short stories published in the United States, Canada or France. His books include a novel, *L'Héritage* (1983); a post-card history entitled *Manchester* (2005); *Franco-American Life and Culture in Manchester, New Hampshire:*

Vivre la Différence (2010); and a collection featuring his original photos of Manchester from 1971 to 2005, entitled *Images of Modern America: Manchester* (2017). He is the recipient of the following: Historic Preservation Award from the Manchester Historic Association (1994); Prix Spécial du Jury for a short story, *Les mains du père et du fils*, sponsored by France / Louisiane / Franco-Américanie, Paris, France (2000); Franco-American of the Year, from Centre Franco- Américain, Manchester (2012).

Dr. Kathleen Stein-Smith, Chevalier dans l'Ordre des Palmes académiques, is a dedicated foreign language educator and advocate. She serves as Chair of the American Association of Teachers of French's Commission on Advocacy and as a member of the ATA Education and Pedagogy Committee and the Modern Language Association's Delegate Assembly. She is also active in foreign language education associations, including the Northeast Conference on the Teaching of Foreign Languages Advisory Council, Central States Conference on the Teaching of Foreign Languages Advisory Council, and as a Southern Conference On Language Teaching sponsor. She has presented at numerous professional conferences at the state, regional, and national level, is the author of five books and numerous articles about the foreign language deficit and the importance of multilingualism, has given a TEDx talk on the United States foreign language deficit, has been interviewed by press and radio, and maintains a blog, "Language Matters."

Scott Tilton is the co-founder and director of the Nous Foundation – a platform for exchange between Louisiana and the French- speaking world. This work was rooted in his growing up in New Orleans in a household that partially spoke French. Prior to Nous, he worked as a consultant at Ernst & Young France on projects for the European Union, the United Nations, and the French government. He graduated with a dual degree in Political & Social Thought and Foreign Affairs from the University of Virginia, as well as with a master's degree in International Relations from Sciences Po Paris. Along with his fellow cofounder Rudy Bazenet, Scott launched and spearheaded the initiative that saw Louisiana become the first United States state to join the International Organization of the Francophonie in 2018.

Born and raised in Senegal, **Agnès Tounkara**, studied Economics in France where she worked in the private sector before moving to the United States for family reasons. Ever since, her career path has been driven by her passion for French and Francophone cultures. At the Alliance Française of Boston, she led the Education Department; she then moved to New York and joined the French American School of New York where she oversaw the extracurricular activities, promoting the French language through many programs to students but also parents. As a Francophone parent raising children in the United States, Agnès was extremely excited to join the French Heritage Language Program in 2019 as a Program Officer. For the past 14 years, the French Heritage Language Program has been helping Francophone immigrants and young Americans with Francophone background to maintain their linguistic and cultural heritage. Today, the program is present in New York through six schools of Internationals Network for Public Schools, in the Bronx, Brooklyn and Manhattan. The program is also present in Massachusetts, Maine, and Florida.

David Vermette is the author of the book A Distinct Alien Race: The Untold Story of Franco-Americans (Montreal: Baraka Books, 2018). He is a researcher, writer, and editor. He has spoken at colleges, universities, and at genealogical and historical societies. Vermette was born and raised in Massachusetts.

About TBR Books

TBR Books is a program of the Center for the Advancement of Languages, Education, and Communities. We publish researchers and practitioners who seek to engage diverse communities on topics related to education, languages, cultural history, and social initiatives. We translate our books in a variety of languages to further expand our impact.

🎬 BOOKS IN FRENCH

Deux siècles d'enseignement français à New York : le rôle des écoles dans la diplomatie culturelle by Jane Flatau Ross

Sénégalais de l'étranger by Maya Smith

Le projet Colibri : créer à partir de "rien" by Vickie Frémont

Pareils mais différents : une exploration des différences entre les Américains et les Français au travail by Sabine Landolt and Agathe Laurent

Le don des langues : vers un changement de paradigme dans l'enseignement des langues aux USA by Fabrice Jaumont and Kathleen Stein-Smith

La Révolution bilingue : le futur de l'éducation s'écrit en deux langues by Fabrice Jaumont

🎬 BOOKS IN ENGLISH AND OTHER LANGUAGES

Peshtigo 1871 by Charles Mercier

The Word of the Month by Ben Lévy, Jim Sheppard and Andrew Arnon

Open Letters to Dual-Language Immersion Stakeholders. Part 1: Letters to Teachers by Valerie Sun.

One Good Question: How to Ask Challenging Questions that Lead You to Real Solutions by Rhonda Broussard

Bilingual Children: Families, Education, and Development by Ellen Bialystok

Can We Agree to Disagree? by Sabine Landolt and Agathe Laurent

Salsa Dancing in Gym Shoes by Tammy Oberg de la Garza and Alyson Leah Lavigne

Beyond Gibraltar; The Other Shore; Mamma in her Village by Maristella de Panizza Lorch

The Clarks of Willsborough Point by Darcey Hale

The English Patchwork by Pedro Tozzi and Giovanna de Lima

Two Centuries of French Education in New York: The Role of Schools in Cultural Diplomacy by Jane Flatau Ross

The Bilingual Revolution: The Future of Education is in Two Languages by Fabrice Jaumont

📖 BOOKS FOR CHILDREN (available in several languages)

Rainbows, Masks, and Ice Cream by Deana Sobel Lederman

Korean Super New Years with Grandma by Mary Chi-Whi Kim and Eunjoo Feaster

Math for All by Mark Hansen

Rose Alone by Sheila Decosse

Uncle Steve's Country Home; The Blue Dress; The Good, the Ugly, and the Great by Teboho Moja

Immunity Fun!; Respiratory Fun!; Digestive Fun! By Dounia Stewart-McMeel

Marimba by Christine Hélot, Patricia Velasco, Antun Kojton

Our books are available on our website and on all major online bookstores as paperback and e-book. Some of our books have been translated in over a dozen languages. For a listing of all books published by TBR Books, information on our series, or for our submission guidelines for authors, visit our website at:

www.tbr-books.org

About CALEC

The Center for the Advancement of Languages, Education, and Communities (CALEC) is a nonprofit organization focused on promoting multilingualism, empowering multilingual families, and fostering cross-cultural understanding. The Center's mission is in alignment with the United Nations' Sustainable Development Goals. Our mission is to establish language as a critical life skill, through developing and implementing bilingual education programs, promoting diversity, reducing inequality, and helping to provide quality education. Our programs seek to protect world cultural heritage and support teachers, authors, and families by providing the knowledge and resources to create vibrant multilingual communities.

The specific objectives and purpose of our organization are:

- To develop and implement education programs that promote multilingualism and cross-cultural understanding, and establish an inclusive and equitable quality education, including internship and leadership training. [SDG # 4, Quality Education]

- To publish and distribute resources, including research papers, books, and case studies that seek to empower and promote the social, economic, and political inclusion of all, with a focus on language education and cultural diversity, equity, and inclusion. [SDG # 10, Reduced Inequalities]

- To help build sustainable cities and communities and support teachers, authors, researchers, and families in the advancement of multilingualism and cross-cultural understanding through collaborative tools for linguistic communities. [SDG # 11, Sustainable Cities and Communities]

- To foster strong global partnerships and cooperation, and mobilize resources across borders, to participate in events and activities that promote language education through knowledge sharing and coaching, empowering parents, and teachers, and building multilingual societies. [SDG # 17, Partnerships for the Goals]

SOME GOOD REASONS TO SUPPORT US

Your donation helps:

- develop our publishing and translation activities so that more languages are represented.
- provide access to our online book platform to daycare centers, schools, and cultural centers in underserved areas.
- support local and sustainable action in favor of education and multilingualism.
- implement projects that advance dual-language education
- organize workshops for parents, conferences with large audiences, meet-the-author chats, and talks with experts in multilingualism.

DONATE ONLINE

For all your questions, contact our team by email at contact@calec.org or donate online on our website:

www.calec.org

Printed in the USA
CPSIA information can be obtained
at www.ICGtesting.com
LVHW041746080823
754338LV00008BA/645